THE
COLD WAR

OPPOSING VIEWPOINTS®

D0027205

Other Books in the American History Series:

The American Revolution
Immigration
Slavery

THE
COLD WAR

OPPOSING VIEWPOINTS®

David L. Bender, *Publisher*
Bruno Leone, *Executive Editor*

Teresa O'Neill, *Series Editor*
John C. Chalberg, Ph.D., professor of history,
    Normandale Community College, *Consulting
    Editor*

William Dudley, *Book Editor*

Cover Photos (left to right): AP/Wide World Photos, AP/Wide World Photos, Library of Congress, and Bettmann/Hulton.

The following copyrighted material has been included in this volume: **Chapter 1:** George F. Kennan, "The Sources of Soviet Conduct." Reprinted by permission of *Foreign Affairs*, Spring 1987; p. 51. Copyright 1987 by the Council on Foreign Relations, Inc. Excerpts from *The Cold War: A Study in U.S. Foreign Policy* by Walter Lippmann, © 1947 by Walter Lippmann; p. 62. Reprinted by permission of HarperCollins Publishers. **Chapter 3:** Excerpts from *Peace and War in the Modern Age*, Frank R. Barnett, William C. Mott, and John C. Neef, eds. New York: Doubleday, Anchor Books, © 1965 by the National Strategy Information Center. Reprinted with permission; p. 142. Excerpts from *Struggle Against History*, Neal D. Houghton, ed. New York: Washington Square Press, 1968, © 1968, Washington Square Press. Reprinted with permission of the publisher and Prof. Maurice L. Albertson; pp. 168 and 184. **Chapter 4:** Excerpts from *Kissinger's Grand Design* by G. Warren Nutter reprinted with the permission of The American Enterprise Institute for Public Policy Research, Washington, D.C.; p. 207. David Riesman, "The Danger of the Human Rights Campaign." Published by permission of Transaction, Inc. from Society, vol. 15, no. 3, Copyright © 1977 by Transaction, Inc.; p. 225. Sidney Lens, "What the President Didn't Tell Us." Reprinted by permission from the May 4, 1983 issue of *The Christian Century*, © 1983, Christian Century Foundation; p. 242. Robert Scheer, "Letting Go of the Cold War," *New Perspectives Quarterly*, Spring 1988. Reprinted with permission; p. 255. **Chapter 5:** Charles Krauthammer, "When to Call Off the Cold War," *The New Republic*, November 16, 1987. Reprinted by permission of *The New Republic*, © 1987, The New Republic, Inc.; p. 255. Richard J. Barnet, "A Balance Sheet: Lippmann, Kennan, and the Cold War," *Diplomatic History* (Spring 1992): 302-11; p. 277. Reprinted with permission. John Lewis Gaddis, "The Cold War, the Long Peace, and the Future," *Diplomatic History* 16 (Spring 1992): 234-46. Reprinted with permission; p. 267.

Library of Congress Cataloging-in-Publication Data

The Cold War : opposing viewpoints / William Dudley, book editor.
      p.   cm. — (American history series)
  Includes bibliographical references (p.) and index.
  ISBN 1-56510-009-3 (lib. bdg. : acid-free paper) : — ISBN
1-56510-008-5 (pbk. : acid-free paper) :
    1. United States—Foreign relations—1945-1989—Sources.
2. Cold War—History—Sources.   I. Dudley, William, 1964- .
II. Series: American history series (San Diego, Calif.)
E743.C587   1992   92-21797
327.73—dc20   CIP

Contents

Foreword

Aboard the *Arbella* as it lurched across the cold, gray Atlantic, John Winthrop was as calm as the waters surrounding him were wild. With the confidence of a born leader, Winthrop gathered his Puritan passengers around him. It was time to offer a sermon. England lay behind them, and years of strife and persecution for their religious beliefs were over, he said. But the Puritan abandonment of England, he reminded his followers, did not mean that England was beyond redemption. Winthrop wanted his followers to remember England even as they were leaving it behind. Their goal should be to create a new England, one far removed from the authority of the Anglican church and King Charles I. In Winthrop's words, their settlement in the New World ought to be a model society, a city upon a hill. He hoped his band would be able to create a just society in America for corrupt England to imitate.

Unable to find either peace or freedom within their home country, these Puritans were determined to provide England with a living example of a community that valued both. Across the hostile Atlantic Ocean would shine the bright light of a just, harmonious, and God-serving society. England may have been beset by sin and corruption, but Winthrop and the colonists believed they could still save England—and themselves. Together, they would coax out of the rocky New England soil not only food for their tables but many thriving communities dedicated to achieving harmony and justice.

On June 8, 1630, John Winthrop and his company of refugees had their first glimpse of what they came to call New England. High on the surrounding hills stood a welcoming band of fir trees whose fragrance drifted to the *Arbella* on a morning breeze. To Winthrop, the "smell off the shore [was] like the smell of a garden."

This new world would, in fact, often be compared to the Garden of Eden. In it, John Winthrop would have his opportunity to start life over again. So would his family and his shipmates. So would all those who would come after them. Victims of conflict in old England hoped to find peace in New England.

Winthrop, for one, had experienced much conflict in his life. As a Puritan, he was opposed to Catholicism and Anglicanism, both of which, he believed, were burdened by distracting rituals and distant hierarchies. A parliamentarian by conviction, he despised Charles I, who had spurned Parliament and created a private army to do his bidding. He believed in individual responsibility and fought against the loss of religious and political freedom. A gentleman landowner, he feared the rising economic power of a merchant class that seemed to value only money. Once Winthrop stepped aboard the *Arbella*, he hoped conflict would not be a part of his American future.

But his Puritan religion told Winthrop that human beings are fallen creatures and that perfection, whether communal or individual, is unachievable on this earth. Therefore, he was presented with a dilemma: On the one hand, his religion demanded that he attempt to live a perfect life in an imperfect world. On the other hand, it told him that he was destined to fail.

Soon after Winthrop disembarked from the *Arbella*, he came face-to-face with this maddening dilemma. He found himself presiding not over a utopia—an ideal community—but over a colony caught up in disputes as troubling as any that he had confronted in his English past.

John Winthrop, it seems, was not the only Puritan with a dream of perfection, with a vision of a heaven on earth. Others in the community saw the dream differently. They wanted greater political and religious freedom than their leader was prepared to grant. Often, Winthrop was able to handle this conflict diplomatically. He expanded, for example, participation in elections and allowed the voters of Massachusetts Bay greater power.

But religious conflict was another matter because it was a conflict of competing visions of the Puritan utopia. In Roger Williams and Anne Hutchinson, two of his fellow colonists, John Winthrop faced rivals unprepared to accept his definition of the perfect community. To Williams, perfection demanded that he separate himself from the Puritan institutions in his community and create an even "purer" church. Winthrop, however, disagreed and exiled Williams to Rhode Island. Hutchinson presumed that she could interpret God's will without a minister. Again, Winthrop did not agree. Hutchinson was tried on charges of heresy, convicted, and banished from Massachusetts.

John Winthrop's Massachusetts colony was the first, but far from the last, American attempt to build a unified, peaceful community that, in the end, only provoked discord. This glimpse at its history reveals what Winthrop confronted: the unavoidable presence of conflict in American life.

American Assumptions

From America's origins in the early seventeenth century, Americans have often held several interrelated assumptions about their country. First, people believe that to be American is to be free. Second, because Americans did not have to free themselves from feudal lords or an entrenched aristocracy, conflict is often considered foreign to American life. Finally, America has been seen as a perpetual haven from the troubles and disputes that are found in the Old World.

John Winthrop, for one, lived his life as though all of these assumptions were true. But the opposing viewpoints presented in the American History Series should reveal that for many Americans, these assumptions were and are myths. Indeed, for numerous Americans, liberty has not always been guaranteed, and conflict has been a necessary, sometimes welcome aspect of their life. To these Americans, the United States is less a sanctuary than it is one more battleground for old and new ideas.

Our American landscape has been torn apart again and again by a great variety of clashes—theological, ideological, political, economic, geographical, racial, gender-based, and class-based. But to discover such a landscape is not necessarily to come upon a hopelessly divided country. If the editors desire to prove anything during the course of this series, it is not that America has been destroyed by conflict but rather that America has been enlivened, enriched, and even strengthened by exchanges between Americans who have disagreed with one another.

Observers of American life, however, often see a country in which its citizens behave as though all of the basic questions of life have been settled. Over the years, they see generation after generation of Americans who seem to blithely agree with one another. In the nineteenth century, French traveler Alexis de Tocqueville called the typical American a "venturesome conservative." According to Tocqueville, this American was willing to risk money in the marketplace but otherwise presented the drab front of someone who thought, dressed, and acted just like everyone else. To Tocqueville, Americans were individualistic risk takers when it came to playing the game of capitalism but were victims of public opinion (which he defined as the "tyranny of the majority") when it came to otherwise expressing themselves.

In the twentieth century, sociologist David Riesman has registered his agreement with Tocqueville. He has defined the modern American as "other-directed." Perhaps willing to leap into the economic arena, this American is unwilling to take risks in the marketplace of ideas. The result is either silence or assent, either because this person is unsure of his or her own beliefs or because the mass media dictate beliefs—or a bit of both. The other-directed American is fearful of standing apart from the crowd.

The editors of this series would like to suggest that Tocqueville and Riesman were too narrow in their assessment of Americans. They have found innumerable Americans who have been willing to take the trouble to disagree.

Thomas Jefferson was one of the least confrontational of Americans, but he boldly and irrevocably enriched American life with his individualistic views. Like John Winthrop before him, he had a notion of an American Eden. Like Winthrop, he offered a vision of a harmonious society. And like Winthrop, he not only became enmeshed in conflict but eventually presided over a people beset by it. But unlike Winthrop, Jefferson believed this Eden was not located in a specific community but in each individual American. His Declaration of Independence from Great Britain could also be read as a declaration of independence for each individual in American society.

Jefferson's Ideal

Jefferson's ideal world was composed of "yeoman farmers," each of whom was roughly equal to the other in society's eyes, each of whom was free from the restrictions of both government and his fellow citizens. Throughout his life, Jefferson offered a continuing challenge to Americans: advance individualism and equality or see the death of the American experiment. Jefferson believed that the strength of this experiment depended upon a society of autonomous individuals and a society without great gaps between rich and poor. His challenge to his fellow Americans to create—and sustain—such a society has itself produced both economic and political conflict.

A society whose guiding document is the Declaration of Independence is a society assured of the freedom to dream—and to disagree. We know that Jefferson himself hated conflict, whether personal or political. His tendency was to avoid confrontations of any sort, to squirrel himself away and write rather than to stand up and speak his mind. It is only through his written words that we can grasp Jefferson's utopian dream of a society of independent farmers, all pursuing their private dreams and all leading lives of sufficient prosperity.

This man of wealth and intellect lived an essentially happy life in accord with his view that Americans ought to have the right to pursue "happiness." But Jefferson's public life was much more troublesome. From the first rumblings of the American Revolution in the 1760s to the North-South skirmishes of the 1820s that ultimately produced the Civil War, Jefferson was at or near the center of American political history. The issues were almost too many—and too crucial—for one lifetime. Jefferson had to choose between supporting or rejecting the path of revolution. During and after the ensuing war, he was at the forefront of the battle for religious liberty. After endorsing the Constitution, he opposed the economic plans of Alexander Hamilton. At the end of the century, he fought the infamous Alien and Sedition Acts, which limited civil liberties. As president, he opposed the Federalist court, conspiracies to divide the union, and calls for a new war against England.

Throughout his life, Thomas Jefferson, slaveholder, pondered the conflict between American freedom and American slavery. And from retirement at his Monticello retreat, he frowned at the rising spirit of commercialism that he feared was dividing Americans and destroying his dream of American harmony.

No matter the issue, however, Thomas Jefferson invariably supported the rights of the individual. Worried as he was about the excesses of commercialism, he accepted them because his main concern was to live in a society where liberty and individualism could flourish. To Jefferson, Americans had to be free to worship as they desired. They also deserved to be free from an overreaching government. To Jefferson, Americans should also be free to possess slaves.

Harmony, an Elusive Goal

Before reading the articles in this anthology, the editors ask readers to ponder the lives of John Winthrop and Thomas Jefferson. Each held a utopian vision, one based upon the demands of community and the other on the autonomy of the individual. Each dreamed of a country of perpetual new beginnings. Each found himself thrust into a position of leadership and found that conflict could not be avoided. And each lived long enough to face and express many opposing views. Harmony, whether communal or individual, was a forever elusive goal.

The opposing visions of Winthrop and Jefferson have been at the heart of many differences among Americans from many backgrounds through the whole of American history. Moreover, their visions have provoked important responses that have helped shape American society, the American character, and many an American battle.

Is the theme of community versus the individual the single defining theme in American history? No, but it is a recurring theme that provides us with a useful point of departure for showing that Americans have been more rambunctious and contentious than Tocqueville or Riesman found them to be, that blandness has not been the defining characteristic for all Americans.

In this age of mass media, the danger exists that the real issues that divide Americans will be, at best, distorted or, at worst, ignored. But by thinking honestly about the past, the real issues and real differences have often been of critical, even of life-and-death, importance to Americans. And they continue to be so today.

The editors of the American History Series have done extensive research to find representative opinions on the issues included in these volumes. They found numerous outstanding opposing viewpoints from people of all times, classes, and genders in American history. From those, they selected commentaries that best fit the nature and flavor of the period under consideration. Every attempt was made to include the most important and relevant viewpoints in each chapter. Obviously, not every notable viewpoint could be included. Therefore, a bibliography has been provided at the end of each book to aid readers in seeking out for themselves additional information.

The editors are confident that as this series reveals past conflicts, it will help revitalize the reader's views of the American present. In that spirit, the American History Series is dedicated to the proposition that American history is more complicated, more fascinating, and more troubling than John Winthrop, Thomas Jefferson, Alexis de Tocqueville, or David Riesman ever dared to imagine.

John C. Chalberg
Consulting Editor

Introduction

"The crucial debate of the Cold War can be reduced to this question: were there any legitimate alternatives to the anti-communist consensus? . . . Put differently, did the Cold War have to be fought at all, and if so, did it have to be fought for so many years and on so many fronts."

In February 1945, President Franklin Roosevelt journeyed to Yalta in the Crimea for his second wartime meeting with British prime minister Winston Churchill and Soviet head of state Joseph Stalin. Fifteen months earlier, the same three men had gathered in Tehran, Iran, to begin discussing what the world would look like following the defeat of Nazi Germany. With an Allied victory anticipated but not imminent, the three leaders had chosen to postpone all difficult political decisions. Left to be determined at a subsequent meeting were such critical matters as European boundaries, German reparations, and Polish elections. But fifteen months later, the Nazis faced defeat. The time had finally arrived to welcome victory—and to negotiate the terms of peace, a task made difficult by the nature of the relationship between the three powers.

Nearly four years earlier, the United States, the Soviet Union, and Great Britain had found themselves united against a common enemy. Adolf Hitler's decision in the spring of 1941 to attack the Soviet Union, combined with the Japanese attack on Pearl Harbor, had forged this coalition. The result was what American general John Deane called a "strange alliance" of partners with dissimilar histories and conflicting interests.

In the first place, an ideological gulf dating from the 1917 Bolshevik Revolution separated the Soviets from their Western allies. Ever since the Bolsheviks had gained power, the world witnessed a war of words between revolutionary communists and liberal capitalists. On one side of this ideological divide stood V. I. Lenin, who sought to call into being the international working class. Moreover, he called upon it to ignore national boundaries as well as the routine and fraud of elections by embracing Marxism. On the other side stood Woodrow Wilson, who offered to make the world safe for democracy without threatening the future health of either the nation-state system or the capitalistic marketplace.

This ideological conflict between East and West briefly erupted into open war when British, French, and American troops entered the Russian civil war of 1918-1921 on the side of the anticommunists. But after the Bolsheviks solidified their position, the conflict reverted to a war of words—until the menace of Hitler created this "strange" wartime alliance.

By the end of World War II, what divided the Soviet Union from the United States and Great Britain was less ideology than their various beliefs about what should happen to Germany and occupied Europe. For example, Stalin wanted Germany de-Nazified and dismembered. Churchill favored the former but not the latter. This left Roosevelt to play the role of the great compromiser. He wanted Churchill and Stalin to arrive at a grand Rooseveltian consensus, thereby ensuring their cooperation in the postwar world.

Roosevelt's Goals

Roosevelt also wanted his quarrelsome allies—and the world —to see that he was opposed to both communism and imperialism. As an anticommunist, he would sometimes side with the conservative Churchill. As an anti-imperialist, he make certain that Stalin understood that the sun was about to set on the British empire. And whenever the discussion turned specifically to postwar Germany, Roosevelt hoped somehow to please both Churchill, who desired a strong Germany as a bulwark against communism, and Stalin, who was determined to eliminate Germany as a rival to Soviet power. It proved to be an impossible task.

As for the remainder of Europe, Roosevelt and Churchill presumed that free and open elections would be held in all countries under the control of Allied armies. Stalin, however, did not have a similar regard for the ballot box. This was especially the case in Central Europe and particularly in Poland, which had been in the middle of the invasion route for Hitler's armies. There, the uncertainty of free elections was subverted by the Soviet need for control.

Roosevelt hoped that the Yalta Declaration on Liberated Europe would guarantee free elections in Poland and elsewhere. But by early 1945, either the Red Army had swept through much of Central Europe or pro-Soviet partisans had borne the brunt of the fight against Hitler. The result was Soviet dominance in Poland, Czechoslovakia, Hungary, Romania, Yugoslavia, and Bulgaria. Therefore, Stalin's troops were able to dictate the political future of Poland and other Soviet-occupied countries.

Did Roosevelt truly intend to hold the Soviets to the pledges contained in the Yalta declaration? No definitive answer to this crucial question is possible because within two months of the Yalta meeting, the American president was dead. We do know that Roosevelt had based his postwar foreign policy plans on continued cooperation with the Soviet Union. But some evidence suggests that the post-Yalta Roosevelt was increasingly suspicious of

Soviet intentions and correspondingly doubtful that any cooperative spirit would survive. For the new American president, Harry S Truman, those suspicions and doubts soon multiplied.

Within days of becoming president, Truman made it clear that he was not pleased with the Soviet stance toward Europe. The Red Army's continued presence in Poland signaled that free elections were not a possibility in that beleaguered country. Truman used his first meeting with Soviet foreign minister Vyacheslav Mikhaylovich Molotov to express his disapproval. In coarse language, the president informed Stalin's representative that he expected the Soviets to honor the Yalta agreement by permitting free elections to take place. This calculated tirade signaled that the Truman administration was not necessarily committed to the Roosevelt policy of postwar Soviet-American cooperation.

A White House Debate

Through the remainder of 1945 and the start of 1946, a debate raged within the White House. The immediate issue was the fate of Poland. The larger issue was the state of Soviet-American relations. On one side were advocates of what historian Daniel Yergin calls the "Yalta axioms." These Roosevelt loyalists argued for the continuation of Soviet-American cooperation at virtually all costs. In their view, world peace depended upon the ability of Washington and Moscow to perpetuate their wartime friendship. Opposed to those who advocated cooperation were primarily State Department foreign service officers who had long been suspicious of Stalin's intentions.

We now know that these hard-line anti-Soviet advisers were able to convince Truman to follow their lead. But at the time, they were worried that the new president would take a soft approach to Soviet expansionism. They feared that Truman would endorse the rapid demobilization of U.S. troops and the corresponding retreat from Europe that the American people desired. Exhausted by four years of war and anxious to spend money saved during the war, Americans of all descriptions pressured Congress to "bring the boys home" quickly. As American ambassador to Moscow Averell Harriman put it, "All the American people want to do is go to movies and drink coke."

After sending a series of mixed signals to the Soviets in the early months of his administration, Truman settled into a solidly anti-Soviet stance by early 1946. After dispatching Roosevelt aide Harry Hopkins to Moscow early in his presidency, Truman sent no more friendly emissaries to meet with Stalin. He also abandoned aid and scratched all proposals to extend low-interest loans to the Soviets. He was "tired of babying the Soviets," Truman said, and he moved instead to end negotiations with

Moscow rather than formally accede to the Soviet domination of Central Europe.

A recently defeated British politician agreed with the new American president. In February 1946, Winston Churchill traveled to Fulton, Missouri, to deliver a speech. Accompanied by Truman, Churchill chose small Westminster College in his host's home state to declare that from "Stettin in the Baltic to Trieste in the Adriatic an 'Iron Curtain' had descended across the continent of Europe."

To many observers, this ideologically charged speech was the opening salvo of the West's belated challenge to Soviet dominance in Central and Eastern Europe. During the next year, the president refused to sign any treaty that would mark the formal end of World War II and the formal onset of Soviet control of Central and Eastern Europe. Worried that Stalin was poised to march the Red Army into the heart of Europe, Truman also purged those who desired cooperation with the Soviets, such as Commerce Secretary Henry Wallace, from his administration.

The Truman Doctrine

If there were any doubts that the hot war against Germany had been replaced by a cold war—continuous confrontation short of military action—they were eliminated when Truman appeared before a joint session of Congress in March 1947. The occasion was the president's declaration of what has come to be called the Truman Doctrine. In that single speech, Truman publicly challenged the Soviet Union by making clear his willingness to engage in the Cold War.

In the late winter of 1947, no gunfire was exchanged between Americans and Soviets, but a war between Washington and Moscow was being waged nonetheless. It marked a return to the post-1917 war of rival ideologies. As such, it was a war for the allegiance of peoples and nations everywhere. But it was also a struggle for international political, military, and economic supremacy. It was, at times, a secret war of two intelligence bureaucracies. At other times, it erupted into real wars fought by proxies for one side or the other. (In the 1960s and 1970s, for example, the United States was stuck in Vietnam, indirectly fighting the Soviet Union and directly fighting Moscow's ally, North Vietnam. In the 1980s, the Cold War flared once again into a hot war. This time the site was Afghanistan, where the Soviet Union was defeated by the Afghani rebels, representing the United States.)

But in 1947, the immediate battleground was Greece. For nearly four years, a civil war between left-and right-wing forces had torn that country apart. During that time, Great Britain had bankrolled the anticommunists, but in the winter of 1946-47, it decided that it could no longer afford this economic burden. The British government delivered this news to the Truman administration at a propitious moment. Having already decided to block further Soviet military moves in Europe, Truman needed to build public support for his anticommunist foreign policy. As Senator Arthur Vandenberg, a one-time isolationist, put it directly to Truman, the time had come to "scare hell"out of the American people with tales of communism on the march.

Truman, therefore, used the Greek issue to divert the attention of moviegoing and coke-drinking Americans. In the president's view, too many countries had already been lost to Moscow and communism. But no more. In his speech to Congress, Truman not only called for American aid to Greece and its neighbor Turkey but promised American support for free peoples everywhere in their separate struggles against totalitarianism.

By the spring of 1947, therefore, the Cold War was fully underway. Before the year was out, the Truman administration had steered the Marshall Plan through Congress, making billions of dollars available to rebuild Western Europe and to block the presumed expansion of communism at the same time. Later that same year, Congress, at Truman's request, created the Central Intelligence Agency, which gave the United States its first peacetime spying capability. Before the year was out, Truman also moved to reorganize the military by bringing all branches of service under the umbrella of a reconstituted Defense Department.

Kennan's Contribution

All that was needed to win the Cold War was a theory and a plan of action. Both were provided by an obscure foreign service officer name George F. Kennan. First in a now-famous telegram from the American embassy in Moscow and subsequently in an anonymous article for *Foreign Affairs Quarterly*, Kennan outlined what has come to be called the containment doctrine. With an eye toward saving Western Europe from communism, Kennan advised the American government to block any further Soviet moves toward the West and to wait for communism to crumble on its own. In his view, there was no need for the United States to send an army to liberate Central and Eastern Europe. Washington had only to draw a line, make clear its willingness to enforce that line, and bide its time until communism withered away. In a curious reversal of Marx, Kennan contended that it was the communist East, not the capitalist West, that was destined to die as a result of it own internal contradictions. Communism would collapse for one of two reasons: either the regime would provide consumer goods to its people, who would then lose their revolutionary fervor, or the regime would not deliver its promised utopia and the people would rebel. In any event, the United States had only to be vigilant and patient.

With an intellectual rationale and an intelligence apparatus, not to mention a reconstituted military and a revitalized American public, the Truman administration was ready to settle in for whatever the duration of the Cold War might be. A hot war, of course, was always a possibility the United States would have to be prepared for. But the immediate reality was the Cold War, which the United States was already waging.

Was it necessary for the United States to engage in this long war? That question has bedeviled American policymakers for nearly half a century. Just what were Stalin's intentions? Was he a defensive nationalist who was interested only in a secure sphere of influence? Or was he preparing to pounce on the rest of Europe? As of 1947, no one in the West could be sure. Perhaps now that the Cold War is over and archives are finally being opened, we can arrive at a more definitive answer.

Until then, we should consider the thoughts of Hungarian-American historian John Lukacs. In his opinion, both the United States and the Soviet Union overreacted between 1945 and 1947. Moscow wrongly thought that Washington was bent on the forceful deliverance of Central Europe from Soviet control. And Washington mistakenly assumed that Stalin was determined to send the Red Army crashing into Western Europe.

In building its case against Soviet expansionism, Lukacs believes, the United States concluded that fascism and communism were similar, that communism was a sort of "red fascism," and that it was time to make an uncompromising stand against totalitarianism. By 1947, the result was a Cold War of international dimensions. And with it came two hot wars in Asia, numerous smaller conflicts around the globe, a voracious arms race, and the creation of a kind of garrison-state mentality on both sides of the iron curtain.

From the perspective of the 1990s and the collapse of communism, it seems easy for Americans to conclude that it was worth all of the blood and dollars invested over the past half century. But questions do remain. Is Lukacs correct? Do the origins of the Cold War reside in a gigantic misunderstanding? Even if he is wrong, could the recent triumph of the West have been obtained without the staggering costs? Moreover, did this conflict over the future of Central Europe necessarily have to be transformed into a titanic international struggle?

There were also plenty of opposing views among those who agreed that a Cold War had to be fought. They debated whether the weapon of choice should be the word, the pocketbook, or the missile; whether those missiles should have been nuclear warheads; what the roles of arms negotiations, summitry, and the United Nations should be; when and how the United States should be confrontational; when and how it should practice détente; and under what circumstances the Cold War should become a hot war.

More precisely, they debated just how the United States should have responded to many crucial events that occurred during the half century of the Cold War, events such as the blockade of Berlin, the triumph of Mao Tse-tung in China, the attack on South Korea, the death of Stalin, the French requests for aid in Indochina, the Hungarian pleas for help as Soviet tanks rumbled through Budapest, the flight of Sputnik, the fiasco of the U-2 crisis, the arrival of Soviet missiles in Cuba, the naval skirmishes in the Gulf of Tonkin, Nikita Krushchev's removal from power, Moscow's crushing of the "Prague spring," the repeated wars in the Middle East, the Sandinista revolution in Nicaragua, the Soviet invasion of Afghanistan, the death of Leonid Brezhnev, the pressure from the left for arms reductions, the pressure from the right for arms buildup, the coming to power of Mikhail Gorbachev, the birth of *glasnost* and *perestroika*, and the demise of communism and the Soviet Union.

Liberal Anticommunism

During the first half of the Cold War, the American government wrestled with many of these questions from the perspective of liberal anticommunism. Before and during World War II, many liberals had joined forces with socialists and communists in a coalition against fascism. Under the banner of the Popular Front, liberals decided that they ought to have "no enemies to the left." All progressive forces should be unified against Hitler and fascism. By 1947, the Popular Front was virtually dead. Suddenly, it was important that liberals divorce themselves from their communist allies. True liberals were not communists. True liberals believed in civil liberties, democratic elections, and reform.

From Harry Truman through Lyndon Johnson (with a brief exile during the Eisenhower years), liberals and the Democratic party controlled the White House and fought the Cold War. These Democrats believed in spending money to advance social programs *and* to block communism. They argued that it was Washington's job to advance civil rights in Mississippi and to build a democratic government in South Vietnam. Of course, there were critics on the left and the right. For example, in the name of preserving the Popular Front, Henry Wallace was prepared to concede Moscow its sphere of influence in Europe. Conservative intellectuals, such as James Burnham, wanted to roll back communism rather than just draw lines of containment in either Europe or Asia. And conservative politicians, such as Senator Joseph Mc-Carthy, preferred to hunt for communists at home rather than face the reality of the Red Army abroad. But essentially, the liberal anticommunists had formed a consensus.

Ironically, that consensus came apart over the war in Vietnam, which was fought in the name of anticommunism. The failure of that war in turn contributed to the death of liberal anticommunism and to the revival of a kind of liberal isolationism.

The Cold War and Republicans

The second half of the Cold War was in the hands of Republicans (who faced an even briefer exile during the Carter years). From Richard Nixon, who came to power as a result of Democratic divisions over Vietnam, through George Bush, who held power at the historic moment when communism lost power in Central Europe and the Soviet Union, a version of what might be called conservative anticommunism prevailed. More suspicious of spending money at home, these Republican presidents were nonetheless willing to invest heavily abroad. Once again, the anticommunist consensus held.

But opposition to that consensus existed. Under attack constantly from the left, Richard Nixon had to defend his administration against what he thought were premature calls for America to "come home" from the war in Vietnam. He also faced criticism from the right for pursuing arms agreements and a strategy of detente with the Soviet Union. Early in his presidency, Ronald Reagan had to fend off the nuclear freeze movement and defend his refusal to engage in summit diplomacy with the Soviets. Later in his administration, Reagan faced charges of betrayal from the right for his sudden fascination with arms limitations and his cozy relationship with Mikhail Gorbachev.

In the end, however, these disputes and even battles between the American left and the American right are of relatively minor importance. The crucial debate of the Cold War can be reduced to this question: Were there any legitimate alternatives to the anticommunist consensus, whether led initially by liberals or more recently by conservatives? Put differently, did the Cold War have to be fought at all, and if so, did it have to be fought for so many years and on so many fronts? Whatever the reader's answer, the Cold War has been a costly affair, not only in terms of lives and dollars but also in terms of time and energy. The Cold War was long with us. Need that have been the case?

John C. Chalberg
Consulting Editor

CHAPTER 1

From Allies to Enemies: The Origins of the Cold War

Chapter Preface

The Cold War began in the turbulent years immediately follow-ing World War II when the alliance between the United States and the Soviet Union, victorious over Nazi Germany and Japan, fell apart over disagreements on re-creating the world order and, especially, over the future of Europe. These disagreements even-tually hardened into a lengthy period of ideological and political deadlock that was to last for more than forty years. Whether or not such a transformation of World War II allies to Cold War ene-mies was inevitable was hotly debated within the U.S. govern-ment at the time and continues to be debated by historians today.

Tensions in Soviet-American relations go back at least as far as the Bolshevik Revolution of October 1917, which brought the Bol-shevik communists to power in Russia. Under the leadership of Vladimir Lenin, the communists espoused a worldwide anticapi-talist revolution. The United States under President Woodrow Wilson refused to recognize the new regime, which for the next few years was caught up in a civil war with anti-Bolshevik forces. In an attempt to contain or topple the Bolsheviks, the United States engaged in an economic boycott, refused to let Russia par-ticipate in the Paris peace conference following World War I, pro-vided aid to non-Bolshevik forces, and even intervened with U.S. troops in Siberia and northern Russia. Despite these efforts, the communists were victorious in their civil war and established the Union of Soviet Socialist Republics in 1922. The United States re-fused to extend diplomatic recognition to the Soviet Union until 1933.

The Soviet-Nazi pact of 1939 further worsened U.S.-Soviet rela-tions. But two years later the two countries found themselves on the same side as they both came under attack from the Axis pow-ers of Germany and Japan. The United States gave the Soviet Union more than $11 billion in aid under the Lend-Lease Act over the course of the war, and the Soviet Union was portrayed favor-ably in the American news media as heroically resisting Nazi ag-gression. However, the alliance was strained by American fears that the Soviet Union might make a separate settlement with Ger-many (as they had in World War I) and by Soviet frustrations over delays in the American and British joint invasion of Europe from the west, which finally occurred in June 1944.

As victory over Germany appeared more and more likely, fric-tion in the alliance between Great Britain, the United States, and the Soviet Union increased. The Soviet Union had been invaded through Poland twice in thirty years and had lost 20 million people in World War II. Consequently, it was determined to take advantage of its army's advances into Europe to set up friendly governments in the region and to destroy Germany's capacity to wage another war. The U.S. postwar goals included self-determination for European countries and a rebuilt, capitalist Europe with a revitalized Germany at its center. The February 1945 Yalta Conference between U.S. president Franklin D. Roosevelt, Soviet premier Joseph Stalin, and British prime minister Winston Churchill resulted in the division of Germany into four occupation zones (with France the fourth occupying power) and a Soviet promise to hold free elections in Eastern Europe. The free elections were never held, and the Soviet zone eventually became the separate communist nation of East Germany.

On April 12, 1945, President Roosevelt died. Harry S Truman, a former senator from Missouri with little foreign policy experience, suddenly found himself faced with several momentous decisions. Immediate attention was devoted to the defeat of Germany and Japan and determining whether to use the newly developed atomic bomb. But looking ahead to the end of World War II, Truman also faced a devastated Europe, a war-weary American populace, an increasingly threatening Soviet Union, and a U.S. government divided on what to do next.

Debate on relations with the Soviet Union focused on several fundamental issues: what Soviet intentions and capabilities were, whether the United States should become intimately involved in affairs outside its immediate borders, whether the newly created United Nations could serve as a guarantor of world order, and whether the United States could successfully pursue aggressive policies against the Soviet Union short of total war. Many of these questions remained areas of controversy throughout the history of the Cold War.

VIEWPOINT 1

"The real peace treaty we now need is between the United States and Russia."

The U.S. Should Seek Peace with the Soviet Union

Henry A. Wallace (1888-1960)

The year following the end of World War II was marked by increasing confrontation and tension between the United States and the Soviet Union. Soviet and U.S. forces confronted each other in Iran, with the Soviets eventually relinquishing claims to the northern portion of the country. Negotiations over the fate of Germany faltered, and the prospect of a permanently divided Germany seemed more and more likely. On March 6, 1946, Winston Churchill captured the attention of Americans when he said in a speech in Fulton, Missouri, that the Soviet Union was creating an "iron curtain" around Eastern Europe.

Many historians have wondered how the United States might have responded to such situations had Henry A. Wallace been president. Wallace was vice president of the United States under Franklin D. Roosevelt from 1941 to 1945. He previously served Roosevelt as secretary of agriculture. Wallace was replaced as vice president by Harry S Truman for Roosevelt's fourth election in 1944, and he became secretary of commerce shortly before Roosevelt's death and Truman's ascension to the presidency in April 1945.

Wallace differed with many in the Truman administration over U.S. policies toward the Soviet Union, which he regarded as too harsh. On September 12, 1946, in a speech at Madison Square Garden in New York City, Wallace called for a higher priority on improving relations with the USSR. In the speech, taken from the October 1, 1946 issue of *Vital Speeches of the Day*, he asserts that the United States should not interfere too much within the Soviet Union's "sphere of influence," which he defines to include Eastern Europe.

Wallace's speech angered many within the Truman administration and led to his resignation from government. He ran for president in 1948 under the newly formed Progressive Party, calling for disarmament and the end of the Cold War. Wallace received more than one million votes but failed to carry a single state.

Tonight I want to talk about peace—and how to get peace. Never have the common people of all lands so longed for peace. Yet, never in a time of comparative peace have they feared war so much.

Up till now peace has been negative and unexciting. War has been positive and exciting. Far too often, hatred and fear, intolerance and deceit have had the upper hand over love and confidence, trust and joy. Far too often, the law of nations has been the law of the jungle; and the constructive spiritual forces of the Lord have bowed to the destructive forces of Satan.

The Atom Bomb

During the past year or so, the significance of peace has been increased immeasurably by the atom bomb, guided missiles and airplanes which soon will travel as fast as sound. Make no mistake about it—another war would hurt the United States many times as much as the last war. We cannot rest in the assurance that we invented the atom bomb—and therefore that this agent of destruction will work best for us. He who trusts in the atom bomb will sooner or later perish by the atom bomb—or something worse.

I say this as one who steadfastly backed preparedness throughout the Thirties. We have no use for namby-pamby pacifism. But we must realize that modern inventions have now made peace the most exciting thing in the world—and we should be willing to pay a just price for peace. If modern war can cost us $400 billion, we should be willing and happy to pay much more for peace. But certainly, the cost of peace is to be measured not in dollars but in the hearts and minds of men. . . .

I plead for an America vigorously dedicated to peace—just as I plead for opportunities for the next generation throughout the

British prime minister Winston Churchill, U.S. president Harry S Truman, and Soviet premier Joseph Stalin in Potsdam, Germany. The July 1945 meeting is the last of the summits between the leaders of the principal Allies of World War II.

world to enjoy the abundance which now, more than ever before, is the birthright of man.

To achieve lasting peace, we must study in detail just how the Russian character was formed—by invasions of Tartars, Mongols, Germans, Poles, Swedes, and French; by the czarist rule based on ignorance, fear and force; by the intervention of the British, French and Americans in Russian affairs from 1919 to 1921; by the geography of the huge Russian land mass situated strategically between Europe and Asia; and by the vitality derived from the rich Russian soil and the strenuous Russian climate. Add to all this the tremendous emotional powers which Marxism and Leninism give to the Russian leaders—and then we can realize that we are reckoning with a force which cannot be handled successfully by a "Get tough with Russia" policy. "Getting tough" never bought anything real and lasting—whether for schoolyard bullies or businessmen or world powers. The tougher we get, the tougher the Russians will get.

Throughout the world there are numerous reactionary elements which had hoped for Axis victory—and now profess great friendship for the United States. Yet these enemies of yesterday and false friends of today continually try to provoke war between the United States and Russia. They have no real love of the United States. They only long for the day when the United States and Russia will destroy each other.

We must not let our Russian policy be guided or influenced by those inside or outside the United States who want war with Russia. This does not mean appeasement.

We must earnestly want peace with Russia—but we want to be met half way. We want cooperation. And I believe that we can get cooperation once Russia understands that our primary objective is neither saving the British Empire nor purchasing oil in the Near East with the lives of American soldiers. We cannot allow national oil rivalries to force us into war. All of the nations producing oil, whether inside or outside of their own boundaries, must fulfill the provisions of the United Nations Charter and encourage the development of world petroleum reserves so as to make the maximum amount of oil available to all nations of the world on an equitable peaceful basis—and not on the basis of fighting the next war.

For her part, Russia can retain our respect by cooperating with the United Nations in a spirit of openminded and flexible give-and-take.

The Peace Treaty We Need

The real peace treaty we now need is between the United States and Russia. On our part, we should recognize that we have no more business in the *political* affairs of Eastern Europe than Russia has in the *political* affairs of Latin America, Western Europe and the United States. We may not like what Russia does in Eastern Europe. Her type of land reform, industrial expropriation, and suppression of basic liberties offends the great majority of the people of the United States. But whether we like it or not the Russians will try to socialize their sphere of influence just as we try to democratize our sphere of influence. This applies also to Germany and Japan. We are striving to democratize Japan and our area of control in Germany, while Russia strives to socialize eastern Germany.

As for Germany, we all must recognize that an equitable settlement, based on a unified German nation, is absolutely essential to any lasting European settlement. This means that Russia must be assured that never again can German industry be converted into military might to be used against her—and Britain, Western Europe and the United States must be certain that Russia's German policy will not become a tool of Russian design against Western Europe.

The Russians have no more business in stirring up native communists to political activity in Western Europe, Latin America and the United States than we have in interfering in the politics of Eastern Europe and Russia. We know what Russia is up to in Eastern Europe, for example, and Russia knows what we are up to. We cannot permit the door to be closed against our trade in

28

We Can Get Along with the Russians

During World War II many Americans, including President Franklin Delano Roosevelt, expressed optimism about the future of U.S.-Soviet relations. This excerpt from one of Roosevelt's "Fireside Chats" was broadcast December 24, 1943, shortly after Roosevelt, Soviet leader Joseph Stalin, and British prime minister Winston S. Churchill met in a conference in Teheran, Iran.

During the last two days at Teheran, Marshal Stalin, Mr. Churchill, and I looked ahead to the days and months and years that will follow Germany's defeat. We were united in determination that Germany must be stripped of her military might and be given no opportunity within the foreseeable future to regain that might. . . .

We did discuss international relationships from the point of view of big, broad objectives, rather than details. But on the basis of what we did discuss, I can say even today that I do not think any insoluble differences will arise among Russia, Great Britain, and the United States.

In these conferences we were concerned with basic principles—principles which involve the security and the welfare and the standard of living of human beings in countries large and small.

To use an American and somewhat ungrammatical colloquialism, I may say that I "got along fine" with Marshal Stalin. He is a man who combines a tremendous, relentless determination with a stalwart good humor. I believe he is truly representative of the heart and soul of Russia; and I believe that we are going to get along very well with him and the Russian people—very well indeed.

Britain, Russia, China, and the United States and their allies represent more than three-quarters of the total population of the earth. As long as these four Nations with great military power stick together in determination to keep the peace there will be no possibility of an aggressor Nation arising to start another world war.

Eastern Europe any more than we can in China. But at the same time we have to recognize that the Balkans are closer to Russia than to us—and that Russia cannot permit either England or the United States to dominate the politics of that area.

China is a special case and although she holds the longest frontier in the world with Russia, the interests of world peace demand that China remain free from any sphere of influence, either politically or economically. We insist that the door to trade and economic development opportunities be left wide open in China as in all the world. However, the open door to trade and opportunities for economic development in China are meaningless unless there is a unified and peaceful China—built on the cooperation of the various groups in that country and based on a hands-off policy of the outside powers.

We are still arming to the hilt. Our excessive expenses for military purposes are the chief cause for our unbalanced budget. If taxes are to be lightened we must have the basis of a real peace with Russia—a peace that cannot be broken by extremist propagandists. We do not want our course determined for us by master minds operating out of London, Moscow or Nanking.

A Friendly Cooperation

Russian ideas of social-economic justice are going to govern nearly a third of the world. Our ideas of free enterprise democracy will govern much of the rest. The two ideas will endeavor to prove which can deliver the most satisfaction to the common man in their respective areas of political dominance. But by mutual agreement, this competition should be put on a friendly basis and the Russians should stop conniving against us in certain areas of the world just as we should stop scheming against them in other parts of the world. Let the results of the two systems speak for themselves.

Meanwhile, the Russians should stop teaching that their form of communism must, by force if necessary, ultimately triumph over democratic capitalism—while we should close our ears to those among us who would have us believe that Russian communism and our free enterprise system cannot live, one with another, in a profitable and productive peace.

Under friendly peaceful competition the Russian world and the American world will gradually become more alike. The Russians will be forced to grant more and more of the personal freedoms; and we shall become more and more absorbed with the problems of social-economic justice.

Russia must be convinced that we are not planning for war against her and we must be certain that Russia is not carrying on territorial expansion or world domination through native communists faithfully following every twist and turn in the Moscow party line. But in this competition, we must insist on an open door for trade throughout the world. There will always be an ideological conflict—but that is no reason why diplomats cannot work out a basis for both systems to live safely in the world side by side.

The United Nations

Once the fears of Russia and the United States Senate have been allayed by practical regional political reservations, I am sure that concern over the veto power would be greatly diminished. Then the United Nations would have a really great power in those areas which are truly international and not regional. In the worldwide, as distinguished from the regional field, the armed might of the United Nations should be so great as to make opposition useless. Only the United Nations should have atomic bombs and its military establishment should give special emphasis to air power. It should have control of the strategically located air bases with which the United States and Britain have encircled the world. And not only should individual nations be prohibited from manufacturing atomic bombs, guided missiles and military aircraft for bombing purposes, but no nation should be allowed to spend on its military establishment more than perhaps 15 per cent of its budget. . . .

In brief, as I see it today, the World Order is bankrupt—and the United States, Russia and England are the receivers. These are the hard facts of power politics on which we have to build a functioning, powerful United Nations and a body of international law. And as we build, we must develop fully the doctrine of the rights of small peoples as contained in the United Nations Charter. This law should ideally apply as much to Indonesians and Greeks as to Bulgarians and Poles—but practically, the application may be delayed until both British and Russians discover the futility of their methods.

In the full development of the rights of small nations, the British and Russians can learn a lesson from the Good Neighbor policy of Franklin Roosevelt. For under Roosevelt, we in the Western Hemisphere built a workable system of regional internationalism that fully protected the sovereign rights of every nation—a system of multilateral action that immeasurably strengthened the whole of world order.

Organizing for Peace

In the United States an informed public opinion will be all-powerful. Our people are peace-minded. But they often express themselves too late—for events today move much faster than public opinion. The people here, as everywhere in the world, must be convinced that another war is not inevitable. And through mass meetings such as this, and through persistent pamphleteering, the people can be organized for peace—even though a large segment of our press is propagandizing our people for war in the hope of scaring Russia. And we who look on this war-with-Russia talk as criminal foolishness must carry our message direct to the people—even though we may be called communists because we dare to speak out.

I believe that peace—the kind of peace I have outlined tonight—is the basic issue, both in the Congressional campaign this fall and right on through the Presidential election in 1948. How we meet this issue will determine whether we live not in "one world" or "two worlds"—but whether we live at all.

31

VIEWPOINT 2

"It is highly dangerous to conclude that hope of international peace lies only in 'accord,' 'mutual understanding,' or 'solidarity' with the Soviet Union."

The U.S. Should Not Seek Peace with the Soviet Union

Clark M. Clifford (1906-)

Clark M. Clifford served as policy adviser for Presidents Truman, Kennedy, and Johnson, and played an important role in the formulation and implementation of U.S. foreign policy. He served as secretary of defense from 1968-1969, heading the department he helped to create in 1947.

In 1946, serving as special counsel to President Harry S Truman, Clifford prepared a secret report to the president on U.S. relations with the Soviet Union. The report was based on consultations with the secretary of state, the attorney general, the Joint Chiefs of Staff, and other officials. It was written at a time when relations between the two World War II allies were foundering over disputes over Europe and other matters.

In his report Clifford states that aggressive military actions and threats by the Soviet Union endanger the United States. He argues against placating the Soviet Union, asserting that such a policy would be dangerous. He also urges that the United States be prepared to use atomic and biological weapons against the Soviet Union, if only as a deterrent to further Soviet aggression. Clifford concludes that the United States should restrain the Soviet Union from expanding its military influence to additional areas, and that the United States should provide economic and military assistance to countries outside the Soviet sphere. The ideas expressed in Clifford's report were carried out with the proclamation of the Truman Doctrine in 1947, in which the United States pledged to assist "free peoples who are resisting attempted subjugation by armed minorities or by outside pressures."

The following excerpt is taken from the conclusion of Clifford's secret report which was reprinted in *Containment: Documents on American Policy and Strategy*, edited by Thomas H. Etzold and John Lewis Gaddis (NY: Columbia University Press, 1978).

The primary objective of United States policy toward the Soviet Union is to convince Soviet leaders that it is in their interest to participate in a system of world cooperation, that there are no fundamental causes for war between our two nations, and that the security and prosperity of the Soviet Union, and that of the rest of the world as well, is being jeopardized by aggressive militaristic imperialism such as that in which the Soviet Union is now engaged.

Aggressive Soviet Leaders

However, these same leaders with whom we hope to achieve an understanding on the principles of international peace appear to believe that a war with the United States and the other leading capitalistic nations is inevitable. They are increasing their military power and the sphere of Soviet influence in preparation for the "inevitable" conflict, and they are trying to weaken and subvert their potential opponents by every means at their disposal. So long as these men adhere to these beliefs, it is highly dangerous to conclude that hope of international peace lies only in "accord," "mutual understanding," or "solidarity" with the Soviet Union.

Adoption of such a policy would impel the United States to make sacrifices for the sake of Soviet-U.S. relations, which would only have the effect of raising Soviet hopes and increasing Soviet demands, and to ignore alternative lines of policy, which might be much more compatible with our own national and international interests.

The Soviet Government will never be easy to "get along with." The American people must accustom themselves to this thought, not as a cause for despair, but as a fact to be faced objectively and courageously. If we find it impossible to enlist Soviet cooperation in the solution of world problems, we should be prepared to join with the British and other Western countries in an attempt to build up a world of our own which will pursue its own objectives and will recognize the Soviet orbit as a distinct entity with which conflict is not predestined but with which we cannot pursue common aims.

Hopes for Russian Cooperation Are Illusions

Among the most influential critics of Henry A. Wallace and others who called for U.S.-Soviet cooperation was the theologian and political philosopher Reinhold Niebuhr. In this excerpt from a 1946 Life *magazine article, Niebuhr, just returned from a trip to Germany, attacks Wallace's argument that Russian aggressiveness is caused by U.S. policies.*

Wallace believes that Russian fears are prompted primarily by our own strategic preparations for a possible conflict. It would be idle to deny that the Russian-Western tension, like all such tensions, generates a vicious circle of mutual mistrust in which the defensive strategy of each side seems to be purely offensive from the standpoint of the other and thus prompts counterdefensive measures. It may even be true that at the end of the war we made some mistakes which set Russia upon her present course. I am increasingly forced to doubt this latter thesis, however, because evidence accumulates that Russia was excessively suspicious during the war, even while we were rendering her maximum aid, and that some of the rather too generous concessions which Roosevelt made were prompted by the hope of allaying those fears. The hope proved illusory. We withdrew our armies, for instance, to allow the Russians to occupy a wide zone, completely surrounding Berlin. The Russians have since pulled up all double railroad tracks between Berlin and our zone to make our occupation of Berlin as difficult as possible through the inconveniences of a single-track road. Confronted with this kind of politics there is no possible strategy which can absolutely guarantee peace. But there is certainly no hope in a policy which assumes that Russian truculence is merely the consequence of fears aroused by our defensive measures.

As long as the Soviet Government maintains its present foreign policy, based upon the theory of an ultimate struggle between Communism and Capitalism, the United States must assume that the U.S.S.R. might fight at any time for the twofold purpose of expanding the territory under communist control and weakening its potential capitalist opponents. The Soviet Union was able to flow into the political vacuum of the Balkans, Eastern Europe, the Near East, Manchuria and Korea because no other nation was both willing and able to prevent it. Soviet leaders were encouraged by easy success and they are now preparing to take over new areas in the same way. The Soviet Union, as Stalin euphemistically phrased it, is preparing "for any eventuality."

Unless the United States is willing to sacrifice its future security for the sake of "accord" with the U.S.S.R. now, this government must, as a first step toward world stabilization, seek to prevent additional Soviet aggression. The greater the area controlled by the Soviet Union, the greater the military requirements of this country will be. Our present military plans are based on the assumption that, for the next few years at least, Western Europe, the Middle East, China and Japan will remain outside the Soviet sphere. If the Soviet Union acquires control of one or more of these areas, the military forces required to hold in check those of the U.S.S.R. and prevent still further acquisitions will be substantially enlarged. That will also be true if any of the naval and air bases in the Atlantic and Pacific, upon which our present plans rest, are given up. This government should be prepared, while scrupulously avoiding any act which would be an excuse for the Soviets to begin a war, to resist vigorously and successfully any efforts of the U.S.S.R. to expand into areas vital to American security.

The language of military power is the only language which disciples of power politics understand. The United States must use that language in order that Soviet leaders will realize that our government is determined to uphold the interests of its citizens and the rights of small nations. Compromise and concessions are considered, by the Soviets, to be evidences of weakness and they are encouraged by our "retreats" to make new and greater demands.

The main deterrent to Soviet attack on the United States, or to attack on areas of the world which are vital to our security, will be the military power of this country. It must be made apparent to the Soviet Government that our strength will be sufficient to repel any attack and sufficient to defeat the U.S.S.R. decisively if a war should start. The prospect of defeat is the only sure means of deterring the Soviet Union.

Soviet Weaknesses

The Soviet Union's vulnerability is limited due to the vast area over which its key industries and natural resources are widely dispersed, but it is vulnerable to atomic weapons, biological warfare, and long-range air power. Therefore, in order to maintain our strength at a level which will be effective in restraining the Soviet Union, the United States must be prepared to wage atomic and biological warfare. A highly mechanized army, which can be moved either by sea or by air, capable of seizing and holding strategic areas, must be supported by powerful naval and air forces. A war with the U.S.S.R. would be "total" in a more horrible sense than any previous war and there must be constant research for both offensive and defensive weapons.

Whether it would actually be in this country's interest to employ atomic and biological weapons against the Soviet Union in the event of hostilities is a question which would require careful consideration in the light of the circumstances prevailing at the time. The decision would probably be influenced by a number of factors, such as the Soviet Union's capacity to employ similar weapons, which can not now be estimated. But the important point is that the United States must be prepared to wage atomic and biological warfare if necessary. The mere fact of preparedness may be the only powerful deterrent to Soviet aggressive action and in this sense the only sure guaranty of peace.

The United States, with a military potential composed primarily of highly effective technical weapons, should entertain no proposal for disarmament or limitation of armament as long as the possibility of Soviet aggression exists. Any discussion on the limitation of armaments should be pursued slowly and carefully with the knowledge constantly in mind that proposals on outlawing atomic warfare and long-range offensive weapons would greatly limit United States strength, while only moderately affecting the Soviet Union. The Soviet Union relies primarily on a large infantry and artillery force and the result of such arms limitation would be to deprive the United States of its most effective weapons without impairing the Soviet Union's ability to wage a quick war of aggression in Western Europe, the Middle East or the Far East.

The Soviet Government's rigid controls on travellers, and its internal security measures, enable it to develop military weapons and build up military forces without our knowledge. The United States should not agree to arms limitations until adequate intelligence of events in the U.S.S.R. is available and, as long as this situation prevails, no effort should be spared to make our forces adequate and strong. Unification of the services and the adoption of universal military training would be strong aids in carrying out a forthright United States policy. In addition to increasing the efficiency of our armed forces, this program would have a salutary psychological effect upon Soviet ambitions.

Sharing Technological Information

Comparable to our caution in agreeing to arms limitation, the United States should avoid premature disclosure of scientific and technological information relating to war materiel until we are assured of either a change in Soviet policies or workable international controls. Any disclosure would decrease the advantage the United States now has in technological fields and diminish our strength in relation to that of the U.S.S.R.

In addition to maintaining our own strength, the United States should support and assist all democratic countries which are in any way menaced or endangered by the U.S.S.R. Providing military support in case of attack is a last resort; a more effective barrier to communism is strong economic support. Trade agreements, loans and technical missions strengthen our ties with friendly nations and are effective demonstrations that capitalism is at least the equal of communism. The United States can do much to ensure that economic opportunities, personal freedom and social equality are made possible in countries outside the Soviet sphere by generous financial assistance. Our policy on reparations should be directed toward strengthening the areas we are endeavoring to keep outside the Soviet sphere. Our efforts to break down trade barriers, open up rivers and international waterways, and bring about economic unification of countries, now divided by occupation armies, are also directed toward the re-establishment of vigorous and healthy noncommunist economies.

The Soviet Union recognizes the effectiveness of American economic assistance to small nations and denounces it bitterly by constant propaganda. The United States should realize that Soviet propaganda is dangerous (especially when American "imperialism" is emphasized) and should avoid any actions which give an appearance of truth to the Soviet charges. A determined effort should be made to expose the fallacies of such propaganda.

There are some trouble-spots which will require diligent and considered effort on the part of the United States if Soviet penetration and eventual domination is to be prevented. In the Far East, for example, this country should continue to strive for a unified and economically stable China, a reconstructed and democratic Japan, and a unified and independent Korea. We must ensure Philippine prosperity and we should assist in the peaceful solution, along noncommunistic lines, of the political problems of Southeast Asia and India.

The United Nations

With respect to the United Nations, we are faced with the fact that the U.S.S.R. uses the United Nations as a means of achieving its own ends. We should support the United Nations and all other organizations contributing to international understanding, but if the Soviet Union should threaten to resign at any time because it fails to have its own way, the United States should not oppose Soviet departure. It would be better to continue the United Nations as an association of democratic states than to sacrifice our principles to Soviet threats.

Since our difficulties with the Soviet Union are due primarily to

The Speaker's Platform

the doctrines and actions of a small ruling clique and not the Soviet people, the United States should strive energetically to bring about a better understanding of the United States among influential Soviets and to counteract the anti-American propaganda which the Kremlin feeds to the Soviet people. To the greatest extent tolerated by the Soviet Government, we should distribute books, magazines, newspapers and movies among the Soviets, beam radio broadcasts to the U.S.S.R., and press for an exchange of tourists, students and educators. We should aim, through intellectual and cultural contacts, to convince Soviet leaders that the United States has no aggressive intentions and that the nature of our society is such that peaceful coexistence of capitalistic and communistic states is possible.

A long-range program of this sort may succeed where individual high-level conversations and negotiations between American and Soviet diplomats may fail in bringing about any basic change in the Soviet outlook. The general pattern of the Soviet system is too firmly established to be altered suddenly by any individual—even Stalin. Conferences and negotiations may continue to attain individual objectives but it appears highly improbable that we can persuade the Soviets, by conferences alone, to change the character of their philosophy and society. If they can be influenced in ways beneficial to our interests, it will be primarily by what we do rather than by what we say, and it is likely to be a slow and laborious process.

Our best chances of influencing Soviet leaders consist in making it unmistakably clear that action contrary to our conception of a decent world order will redound to the disadvantage of the Soviet regime whereas friendly and cooperative action will pay dividends. If this position can be maintained firmly enough and long enough, the logic of it must permeate eventually into the Soviet system.

Trade with the Soviets

Cooperation by the Soviets can result in increased trade. The United States Government must always bear in mind, however, that questions as to the extent and nature of American trade should be determined by the overall interests of this country. It should also bear in mind that, while Soviet policy can conceivably be influenced by the hope of obtaining greater economic assistance from this country, it is unlikely that the Soviet Government will entertain sentiments of gratitude for aid once it has been granted and it is unlikely to be induced by goodwill gifts to modify its general policies. For the time being, economic aid granted to the Soviet Government or other governments within its sphere, and the fruits of private trade with persons inside these countries, will go to strengthen the entire world program of the Kremlin. . . .

Within the United States, communist penetration should be exposed and eliminated whenever the national security is endangered. The armed forces, government agencies and heavy industries are the principal targets for communistic infiltration at present.

Because the Soviet Union is a highly-centralized state, whose leaders exercise rigid discipline and control of all governmental functions, its government acts with speed, consistency, and boldness. Democratic governments are usually loosely organized, with a high degree of autonomy in government departments and agencies. Government policies at times are confused, misunderstood, or disregarded by subordinate officials. The United States can not afford to be uncertain of its policies toward the Soviet Union. There must be such effective coordination within the government that our military and civil policies concerning the U.S.S.R., her satellites, and our Allies are consistent and forceful. Any uncertainty or discrepancy will be seized immediately by the Soviets and exploited at our cost.

Our policies must also be global in scope. By time-honored custom, we have regarded "European Policy," "Near Eastern Policy," "Indian Policy" and "Chinese Policy" as separate problems to be handled by experts in each field. But the areas involved, far removed from each other by our conventional standards, all border on the Soviet Union and our actions with respect to each must be considered in the light of overall Soviet objectives.

Only a well-informed public will support the stern policies which Soviet activities make imperative and which the United States Government must adopt. The American people should be fully informed about the difficulties in getting along with the Soviet Union, and the record of Soviet evasion, misrepresentation, aggression and militarism should be made public.

In conclusion, as long as the Soviet Government adheres to its present policy, the United States should maintain military forces powerful enough to restrain the Soviet Union and to confine Soviet influence to its present area. All nations not now within the Soviet sphere should be given generous economic assistance and political support in their opposition to Soviet penetration. Economic aid may also be given to the Soviet Government and private trade with the U.S.S.R. permitted provided the results are beneficial to our interests and do not simply strengthen the Soviet program. We should continue to work for cultural and intellectual understanding between the United States and the Soviet Union but that does not mean that, under the guise of an exchange program, communist subversion and infiltration in the United States will be tolerated. In order to carry out an effective policy toward the Soviet Union, the United States Government should coordinate its own activities, inform and instruct the American people about the Soviet Union, and enlist their support based upon knowledge and confidence. These actions by the United States are necessary before we shall ever be able to achieve understanding and accord with the Soviet Government on any terms other than its own.

Even though Soviet leaders profess to believe that the conflict between Capitalism and Communism is irreconcilable and must eventually be resolved by the triumph of the latter, it is our hope that they will change their minds and work out with us a fair and equitable settlement when they realize that we are too strong to be beaten and too determined to be frightened.

VIEWPOINT 3

"I consider the problem of our satisfactory relations with Russia as not merely connected with but as virtually dominated by the problem of the atomic bomb."

The U.S. Should Cooperate with the Soviet Union over the Development of Atomic Weapons

Henry L. Stimson (1867-1950)

The beginning of the Cold War coincided with the development of nuclear weapons, which, as the world saw when the United States used them on Japan in 1945, were many times more destructive than all previous weapons. The awful specter of nuclear war was an ever-present possibility throughout the Cold War. The United States was the first country to develop nuclear weapons, and, for a few years, held a monopoly on their possession. An important early debate in the Cold War involved whether the United States should share information on the atom bomb with the Soviet Union in an effort to seek their cooperation in the control of the weapons.

One of the key participants in this debate was Henry L. Stimson, a lawyer and statesman who during his long career served in many government posts. He was secretary of state from 1929 to 1933 under President Herbert Hoover, and he served as secretary of war twice, from 1911 to 1913 and from 1940 to 1945 during World War II. In addition to his duties supervising the mobilization and training of U.S. armed forces, Stimson served as chief presidential adviser on atomic policy. He recommended to President Harry S Truman that the United States drop the atomic bomb on Japan.

The following viewpoint is taken from a memorandum for President Truman, written a week before Stimson's retirement on September 11, 1945, about a month after the United States dropped two atomic bombs on Japan and shortly after Japan's surrender. Stimson argues in the memorandum reprinted in *Foreign Relations of the United States, 1945, Volume II, General: Political and Economic Matters* (Washington, DC: Government Printing Office, 1967), that the development of atomic weapons increases the importance of the United States and Soviet Union building relations of mutual confidence and understanding. He calls for direct negotiations between the United States and the Soviet Union to limit atomic bomb production and develop peaceful uses of atomic power, and he argues against U.S. efforts to use the atomic bomb as a military threat for diplomatic leverage. Stimson asserts that the new weapons make it all the more important for the two nations to develop trust with each other.

The advent of the atomic bomb has stimulated great military and probably even greater political interest throughout the civilized world. In a world atmosphere already extremely sensitive to power, the introduction of this weapon has profoundly affected political considerations in all sections of the globe.

In many quarters it has been interpreted as a substantial offset to the growth of Russian influence on the continent. We can be certain that the Soviet Government has sensed this tendency and the temptation will be strong for the Soviet political and military leaders to acquire this weapon in the shortest possible time. Britain in effect already has the status of a partner with us in the development of this weapon. Accordingly, unless the Soviets are voluntarily invited into the partnership upon a basis of cooperation and trust, we are going to maintain the Anglo-Saxon bloc over against the Soviet in the possession of this weapon. Such a condition will almost certainly stimulate feverish activity on the part of the Soviet toward the development of this bomb in what will in effect be a secret armament race of a rather desperate character. There is evidence to indicate that such activity may have already commenced.

If we feel, as I assume we must, that civilization demands that some day we shall arrive at a satisfactory international arrangement respecting the control of this new force, the question then is how long we can afford to enjoy our momentary superiority in the hope of achieving our immediate peace council objectives.

Russia and America Should Be Partners

Whether Russia gets control of the necessary secrets of production in a minimum of say four years or a maximum of twenty years is not nearly as important to the world and civilization as to make sure that when they do get it they are willing and co-operative partners among the peace-loving nations of the world. It is true if we approach them now, as I would propose, we may be gambling on their good faith and risk their getting into production of bombs a little sooner than they would otherwise.

To put the matter concisely, I consider the problem of our satisfactory relations with Russia as not merely connected with but as virtually dominated by the problem of the atomic bomb. Except for the problem of the control of that bomb, those relations, while vitally important, might not be immediately pressing. The establishment of relations of mutual confidence between her and us could afford to await the slow progress of time. But with the discovery of the bomb, they became immediately emergent. Those relations may be perhaps irretrievably embittered by the way in which we approach the solution of the bomb with Russia. For if we fail to approach them now and merely continue to negotiate with them, having this weapon rather ostentatiously on our hip, their suspicions and their distrust of our purposes and motives will increase. It will inspire them to greater efforts in an all-out effort to solve the problem. If the solution is achieved in that spirit, it is much less likely that we will ever get the kind of covenant we may desperately need in the future. This risk is, I believe, greater than the other, inasmuch as our objective must be to get the best kind of international bargain we can—one that has some chance of being kept and saving civilization not for five or for twenty years, but forever.

The chief lesson I have learned in a long life is that the only way you can make a man trustworthy is to trust him; and the surest way to make him untrustworthy is to distrust him and show your distrust.

A New Force

If the atomic bomb were merely another though more devastating military weapon to be assimilated into our pattern of international relations, it would be one thing. We could then follow the old custom of secrecy and nationalistic military superiority relying on international caution to prescribe the future use of the weapon as we did with gas. But I think the bomb instead constitutes merely a first step in a new control by man over the forces of nature too revolutionary and dangerous to fit into the old concepts. I think it really caps the climax of the race between man's growing technical power for destructiveness and his psychological power of self-control and group control—his moral power. If so, our method of approach to the Russians is a question of the most vital importance in the evolution of human progress.

The Need for International Cooperation

President Harry S Truman gave his first major foreign policy address of his presidency on October 27, 1945, at a New York City Navy Day celebration. At this time he still expressed hopes for U.S.-Soviet cooperation, which he stated was all the more important because of the development of atomic weapons.

We are now passing through a difficult phase of international relations. Unfortunately it has always been true after past wars that the unity among Allies, forged by their common peril, has tended to wear out as the danger passed.

The world can not afford any let-down in the united determination of the Allies in this war to accomplish a lasting peace. The world can not afford to let the cooperative spirit of the Allies in this war disintegrate. The world simply can not allow this to happen. The people in the United States, in Russia and Britain, in France and China, in collaboration with all other peace-loving people, must take the course of current history into their own hands and mould it in a new direction—the direction of continued cooperation. It was a common danger which united us before victory. Let it be a common hope which continues to draw us together in the years to come.

The atomic bombs that fell on Hiroshima and Nagasaki must be made a signal, not for the old process of falling apart but for a new era—an era of ever closer unity and ever closer friendship among peaceful nations. . . .

The immediate, the greatest threat to us is the threat of disillusionment, the danger of an insidious skepticism—a loss of faith in the effectiveness of international cooperation. Such a loss of faith would be dangerous at any time. In an atomic age it would be nothing short of disastrous.

Since the crux of the problem is Russia, any contemplated action leading to the control of this weapon should be primarily directed *to* Russia. It is my judgment that the Soviet would be more apt to respond sincerely to a direct and forthright approach made by the United States on this subject than would be the case if the approach were made as a part of a general international scheme, or if the approach were made after a succession of express or implied threats or near threats in our peace negotiations.

My idea of an approach to the Soviets would be a direct proposal after discussion with the British that we would be prepared in effect to enter an arrangement with the Russians, the general purpose of which would be to control and limit the use of the atomic bomb as an instrument of war and so far as possible to direct and encourage the development of atomic power for peaceful and humanitarian purposes. Such an approach might more specifically lead to the proposal that we would stop work on the further improvement in, or manufacture of, the bomb as a military weapon, provided the Russians and the British would agree to do likewise. It might also provide that we would be willing to impound what bombs we now have in the United States provided the Russians and the British would agree with us that in no event will they or we use a bomb as an instrument of war unless all three Governments agree to that use. We might also consider including in the arrangement a covenant with the U.K. and the Soviets providing for the exchange of benefits of future developments whereby atomic energy may be applied on a mutually satisfactory basis for commercial or humanitarian purposes.

I would make such an approach just as soon as our immediate political considerations make it appropriate.

A United States Action

I emphasize perhaps beyond all other considerations the importance of taking this action with Russia as a proposal of the United States—backed by Great Britain but peculiarly the proposal of the United States. Action of any international group of nations, including many small nations who have not demonstrated their potential power or responsibility in this war would not, in my opinion, be taken seriously by the Soviets. The loose debates which would surround such proposal, if put before a conference of nations, would provoke but scant favor from the Soviet. As I say, I think this is the most important point in the program.

After the nations which have won this war have agreed to it, there will be ample time to introduce France and China into the covenants and finally to incorporate the agreement into the scheme of the United Nations. The use of this bomb has been accepted by the world as the result of the initiative and productive capacity of the United States, and I think this factor is a most potent lever toward having our proposals accepted by the Soviets, whereas I am most skeptical of obtaining any tangible results by way of any international debate. I urge this method as the most realistic means of accomplishing this vitally important step in the history of the world.

VIEWPOINT 4

"It appears impossible for the United States, even though it continues to seek a solution, to agree with the USSR on a plan for the international control of atomic energy."

U.S.-Soviet Cooperation over Atomic Weapons Is Unrealistic

U.S. State Department Policy Planning Staff

The Policy Planning Staff was founded within the U.S. State Department on May 5, 1947, in order to formulate and develop long-term strategies and programs for U.S. foreign affairs. Under its first director, George F. Kennan, the PPS and the reports it generated played major roles in U.S. policy toward the Soviet Union following World War II.

The following viewpoint is taken from a top secret PPS report presented on August 21, 1947. By this time, the United States and the Soviet Union had been engaged in negotiations over the international control of atomic energy with little result. The report argues that the Soviet Union is using the negotiations as a delaying tactic until they can develop their own atomic weapons, and that further negotiations with the Soviet Union over these matters may not be in the best interests of the United States. The report calls for the United States to improve its civil defense programs in order to convince the Soviet Union of its willingness to use atomic weapons if necessary.

After fourteen months of negotiations in the United Nations Atomic Energy Commission (UNAEC) the impasse continues. . . . Several basic differences divide the Soviet Union and Poland from the other ten members of the AEC. While these differences include, of course, the mechanics of inspection and the relation of the veto to the use of sanctions, there are two points of disagreement which are basic and which have become even more significant.

Basic Disagreements

First, the majority believes that outlawry of atomic weapons should be accomplished only as part of an international agreement providing for the development, by stages, of an adequate system of control, with safeguards necessary to protect complying states against the hazards of violations and evasions. The Soviet Union, on the other hand, evidently does not intend to abandon its insistence on the destruction of atomic bomb stocks before adoption of an international control convention, or at least before it can become reasonably effective.

Second, the United States and most other UNAEC countries believe that an international control plan would afford no security unless it envisaged an atomic development authority endowed with broad powers over practically all operations connected with the production of atomic energy. Its powers would be those which, in Western nomenclature at least, are usually subsumed in the term ownership. The Soviet Union has repeatedly rejected the idea of such an authority, claiming to see in it an instrument for interference with the internal affairs of sovereign states.

Without a settlement on these two points it appears impossible for the United States, even though it continues to seek a solution, to agree with the USSR on a plan for the international control of atomic energy.

Basic Requirements of Future U.S. Policy

In the face of these fundamental differences the United States must begin to develop a policy which does not appear to place all our eggs in the UN Atomic Energy Commission basket. . . .

A due regard for United States security does not permit us to stand idly by while the Soviet Union continues its filibuster in the UNAEC. The Russians are using delaying tactics in the Commission while they pursue specific objectives outside the meeting hall. These include:

a. Hastening their own development of atomic bombs;

b. Dividing opinion in other United Nations, particularly

A U.S. Proposal for International Control of the Atom

On June 14, 1946, at the United Nations, the United States presented to the world its proposal for placing atomic weapons under international control. Bernard M. Baruch, U.S. representative to the United Nations Atomic Energy Commission, called for the creation of an International Atomic Development Authority to control all aspects of producing atomic bombs. The United States would turn over its own atomic bombs and facilities—but only after negotiations were fully completed. This proposal never came to fruition, in part because of Soviet objections that it was weighted in favor of the United States.

The United States proposes the creation of an International Atomic Development Authority, to which should be entrusted all phases of the development and use of atomic energy, starting with the raw material and including—

1. Managerial control or ownership of all atomic-energy activities potentially dangerous to world security.
2. Power to control, inspect, and license all other atomic activities.
3. The duty of fostering the beneficial uses of atomic energy.
4. Research and development responsibilities of an affirmative character intended to put the Authority in the forefront of atomic knowledge and thus to enable it to comprehend, and therefor to detect, misuse of atomic energy. To be effective, the Authority must itself be the world's leader in the field of atomic knowledge and development and thus supplement its legal authority with the great power inherent in possession of leadership in knowledge.

I offer this as a basis for beginning our discussion.

But I think the peoples we serve would not believe—and without faith nothing counts—that a treaty, merely outlawing possession or use of the atomic bomb, constitutes effective fulfillment of the instructions to this Commission. Previous failures have been recorded in trying the method of simple renunciation, unsupported by effective guaranties of security and armament limitation. No one would have faith in that approach alone.

Now, if ever, is the time to act for the common good. Public opinion supports a world movement toward security. If I read the signs aright, the peoples want a program not composed merely of pious thoughts but of enforceable sanctions—an international law with teeth in it.

those having atomic energy resources or skills;

c. Infiltration of research and control programs in any or all other countries;

d. Breaking down existing secret US arrangements for procurement of raw materials outside the United States;

e. Extension of their area of effective political domination by infiltration or direct pressure.

This enumeration demonstrates that we cannot consider the debate in the AEC as taking place in a vacuum. The extent to which Soviet strategic and diplomatic objectives are furthered by delay in the Commission is obvious, and too pat for mere coincidence. We must consider Soviet tactics in the AEC as part of the Kremlin's general strategy; and we must be able to recognize the end of the line when we come to it.

Alternative Measures Needed

We are now faced with the basic fact that under present circumstances the effort to achieve international control affords less hope for protecting our national security than other means. We must begin, therefore, to take alternative measures which, while they would not provide as high a degree of security as effective international control, would at least materially improve the United States position in a world in which others possess atomic weapons.

This means that we turn a corner in our thinking and this turning-point must soon be made unmistakable to the peoples of the United States, the Soviet Union and the rest of the world.

This does not mean, however, that there is any necessity for terminating the work of the Commission at this point. On the contrary it is desirable that the door be left open to further negotiation with the Russians *subsequent* to the taking of these alternative measures. For although the measures would be taken primarily in the interests of our own security, they might just possibly have some effect in inclining the Russians toward the plan of the other UNAEC nations. This is so for the following reasons:

The Russians are trained to reason dialectically. Their diplomatic history shows that they seldom approach an objective along one course without at the same time having in reserve an alternative and sometimes entirely dissimilar course. In pressing their own demands, they are quick to take into account the extent to which their opponent has alternatives to the acceptance of their demands. If they think he has no acceptable alternative, they are insistent and intractable.

Thus far, we have not demonstrated to the Russians that we have any alternative to the present course of basing our future atomic security on general international agreement. On the contrary, we have tended to labor the point that there is no effective means of defense against atomic weapons. The Russians have probably concluded from this that we see no alternative to international agreement. This has put them in a position where they feel at liberty to stall the negotiations indefinitely, believing that as long as they refuse to reach agreement with us their basic secu-

49

rity position will not deteriorate, because little will be done here to reduce our vulnerability and to increase our retaliatory power in the face of atomic attack.

The Russians are probably negotiating under the impression that this country has not taken, nor even seriously contemplated, any serious measures of civilian defense. This being the case, the possibility of being able, in the event of a military conflict, to cause great damage and panic by a surprise attack must be an appealing one to them. It must put a premium, in their minds, on the possibility that they may some day be able to use the weapon against us.

There is no intention here to make light of the damage which can be done by the atomic weapon or the difficulties of defense against it. Nor is there any disposition to minimize the importance of the planning for atomic warfare and defense which has already been done in the military establishments. But there must be degrees in vulnerability to atomic attack; and there are certainly degrees in determination and effectiveness of retaliatory force.

Strengthening Our Bargaining Position

If it were clearly established in the Russian mind that there was no possibility of this country's being a push-over in the face of surprise atomic attack—that there existed in this country mechanisms which would enable us to recuperate with relative promptness and to impose swift retribution, even in the face of the heaviest blow; and that we were ready to depart from traditional American policy in the direction of effective international understandings which increase our retaliatory power—then there could be no doubt that the prospect of the atomic age would take on a somewhat different color to Russian eyes.

It cannot be said with any assurance that the effect thus achieved would be strong enough to overcome the inhibitions on the Russian side which stand in the way of Soviet acceptance of our atomic energy proposals. Indeed, the odds are probably rather on the other side. But the possibility that their attitude might be affected to some extent by such a state of affairs is a strong one; and unless that possibility had been explored before the work of the Atomic Energy Commission was permitted to come to a final end, it would not be possible for us to say that we had exhausted every possibility of bringing the Russians near to our point of view.

50

VIEWPOINT 5

"The main element of any United States policy toward the Soviet Union must be that of a long-term, patient but firm and vigilant containment of Russian expansive tendencies."

The U.S. Should Contain Soviet Expansion

George F. Kennan (1904-)

In July 1947 an article attributed only to "X," entitled "The Sources of Soviet Conflict," appeared in *Foreign Affairs*, a quarterly journal on world affairs and U.S. foreign policy that remains influential today. Published at a time of growing tensions between the United States and the U.S.S.R., the article became one of the most widely discussed and reprinted articles ever published on foreign affairs. Its analysis of the Soviet Union and its calls for U.S. containment of Soviet expansion formed a basis for U.S. Cold War policy for the next forty years.

"X" was eventually revealed to be George F. Kennan, the director of the Policy Planning Staff at the U.S. State Department in Washington. Kennan had recently returned from the Soviet Union, where he had worked at the U.S. embassy in Moscow and was one of the first U.S. diplomats to express pessimism about continuing the cooperation with the Soviet Union that had begun during World War II. Kennan later became the U.S. ambassador to the Soviet Union, and, following his retirement from government, he became a noted author, scholar, and teacher on the Soviet Union and on U.S. foreign policy.

Kennan begins his "X" article by examining the leadership of the Soviet Union. He argues that their ideology and dictatorial positions compel the Soviet Union to seek increasing international domination and to take an adversarial stance toward the United States. To counter these threats, Kennan advocates a policy of containment—of preventing Soviet power and its communist ideology from spreading to additional countries. He argues that the United States should not risk open war by forcing the Soviet Union to withdraw from Eastern Europe or by otherwise directly challenging them, but it should take steps, he says, to ensure that the Soviet Union does not expand its military influence to other areas of the world. Kennan asserts that weaknesses within the Soviet Union would, over the next ten or fifteen years, force its leaders to reduce their threatening stance toward the United States.

The political personality of Soviet power as we know it today is the product of ideology and circumstances: ideology inherited by the present Soviet leaders from the movement in which they had their political origin, and circumstances of the power which they now have exercised for nearly three decades in Russia. There can be few tasks of psychological analysis more difficult than to try to trace the interaction of these two forces and the relative rôle of each in the determination of official Soviet conduct. Yet the attempt must be made if that conduct is to be understood and effectively countered.

Soviet Ideology

It is difficult to summarize the set of ideological concepts with which the Soviet leaders came into power. Marxian ideology, in its Russian-Communist projection, has always been in process of subtle evolution. The materials on which it bases itself are extensive and complex. But the outstanding features of Communist thought as it existed in 1916 may perhaps be summarized as follows: (a) that the central factor in the life of man, the factor which determines the character of public life and the "physiognomy of society," is the system by which material goods are produced and exchanged; (b) that the capitalist system of production is a nefarious one which inevitably leads to the exploitation of the working class by the capital-owning class and is incapable of developing adequately the economic resources of society or of distributing fairly the material goods produced by human labor; (c) that capitalism contains the seeds of its own destruction and must, in view

The Long Telegram

Months before publication of his "X" article, George F. Kennan's views were already widely known and accepted within the U.S. government. This was primarily due to his famous "long telegram," an eight thousand-word report Kennan cabled from the U.S. embassy in Moscow on February 22, 1946. Kennan's views on the Soviet Union greatly influenced subsequent U.S. foreign policy.

In summary, we have here a political force committed fanatically to the belief that with US there can be no permanent *modus vivendi*, that it is desirable and necessary that the internal harmony of our society be disrupted, our traditional way of life be destroyed, the international authority of our state be broken, if Soviet power is to be secure. This political force has complete power of disposition over energies of one of world's greatest peoples and resources of world's richest national territory, and is borne along by deep and powerful currents of Russian nationalism. In addition, it has an elaborate and far flung apparatus for exertion of its influence in other countries, an apparatus of amazing flexibility and versatility, managed by people whose experience and skill in underground methods are presumably without parallel in history. Finally, it is seemingly inaccessible to considerations of reality in its basic reactions. For it, the vast fund of objective fact about human society is not, as with us, the measure against which outlook is constantly being tested and reformed, but a grab bag from which individual items are selected arbitrarily and tendenciously to bolster an outlook already preconceived. This is admittedly not a pleasant picture. Problem of how to cope with this force is undoubtedly greatest task our diplomacy has ever faced and probably greatest it will ever have to face.

of the inability of the capital-owning class to adjust itself to economic change, result eventually and inescapably in a revolutionary transfer of power to the working class; and (d) that imperialism, the final phase of capitalism, leads directly to war and revolution. . . .

The circumstances of the immediate post-revolution period—the existence in Russia of civil war and foreign intervention, together with the obvious fact that the Communists represented only a tiny minority of the Russian people—made the establishment of dictatorial power a necessity. . . .

Now the outstanding circumstance concerning the Soviet régime is that down to the present day . . . the men in the Kremlin have continued to be predominantly absorbed with the struggle to secure and make absolute the power which they seized in November 1917. They have endeavored to secure it primarily against forces at home, within Soviet society itself. But they have also endeavored to secure it against the outside world. . . .

As long as remnants of capitalism were officially recognized as existing in Russia, it was possible to place on them, as an internal element, part of the blame for the maintenance of a dictatorial form of society. But as these remnants were liquidated, little by little, this justification fell away; and when it was indicated officially that they had been finally destroyed, it disappeared altogether. And this fact created one of the most basic of the compulsions which came to act upon the Soviet régime: since capitalism no longer existed in Russia and since it could not be admitted that there could be serious or widespread opposition to the Kremlin springing spontaneously from the liberated masses under its authority, it became necessary to justify the retention of the dictatorship by stressing the menace of capitalism abroad. . . .

By the same token, tremendous emphasis has been placed on the original Communist thesis of a basic antagonism between the capitalist and Socialist worlds. It is clear, from many indications, that this emphasis is not founded in reality. The real facts concerning it have been confused by the existence abroad of geniune resentment provoked by Soviet philosophy and tactics and occasionally by the existence of great centers of military power, notably the Nazi régime in Germany and the Japanese Government of the late 1930's, which did indeed have aggressive designs against the Soviet Union. But there is ample evidence that the stress laid in Moscow on the menace confronting Soviet society from the world outside its borders is founded not in the realities of foreign antagonism but in the necessity of explaining away the maintenance of dictatorial authority at home. . . .

Soviet Policy

So much for the historical background. What does it spell in terms of the political personality of Soviet power as we know it today?

Of the original ideology, nothing has been officially junked. Belief is maintained in the basic badness of capitalism, in the inevitability of its destruction, in the obligation of the proletariat to assist in that destruction and to take power into its own hands. But stress has come to be laid primarily on those concepts which relate most specifically to the Soviet régime itself: to its position as the sole truly Socialist régime in a dark and misguided world, and to the relationships of power within it.

The first of these concepts is that of the innate antagonism between capitalism and Socialism. We have seen how deeply that concept has become imbedded in foundations of Soviet power. It has profound implications for Russia's conduct as a member of international society. It means that there can never be on Moscow's side any sincere assumption of a community of aims between the Soviet Union and powers which are regarded as capitalist. It must invariably be assumed in Moscow that the aims of the capitalist world are antagonistic to the Soviet régime, and therefore to the interests of the peoples it controls. If the Soviet Government occasionally sets its signature to documents which would indicate the contrary, this is to be regarded as a tactical manœuvre permissable in dealing with the enemy (who is without honor) and should be taken in the spirit of *caveat emptor*. Basically, the antagonism remains. It is postulated. And from it flow many of the phenomena which we find disturbing in the Kremlin's conduct of foreign policy: the secretiveness, the lack of frankness, the duplicity, the wary suspiciousness, and the basic unfriendliness of purpose. These phenomena are there to stay, for the foreseeable future. There can be variations of degree and of emphasis. When there is something the Russians want from us, one or the other of these features of their policy may be thrust temporarily into the background; and when that happens there will always be Americans who will leap forward with gleeful announcements that "the Russians have changed," and some who will even try to take credit for having brought about such "changes." But we should not be misled by tactical manœuvres. These characteristics of Soviet policy, like the postulate from which they flow, are basic to the internal nature of Soviet power, and will be with us, whether in the foreground or the background, until the internal nature of Soviet power is changed.

This means that we are going to continue for a long time to find the Russians difficult to deal with. It does not mean that they should be considered as embarked upon a do-or-die program to overthrow our society by a given date. The theory of the inevitability of the eventual fall of capitalism has the fortunate connotation that there is no hurry about it. The forces of progress can take their time in preparing the final *coup de grâce*. Meanwhile, what is vital is that the "Socialist fatherland"—that oasis of power which has been already won for Socialism in the person of the Soviet Union—should be cherished and defended by all good Communists at home and abroad, its fortunes promoted, its enemies badgered and confounded. The promotion of premature, "adventuristic" revolutionary projects abroad which might embarrass Soviet power in any way would be an inexcusable, even a counter-revolutionary act. The cause of Socialism is the support and promotion of Soviet power, as defined in Moscow.

Kremlin Authority

This brings us to the second of the concepts important to contemporary Soviet outlook. That is the infallibility of the Kremlin. The Soviet concept of power, which permits no focal points of organization outside the Party itself, requires that the Party leadership remain in theory the sole repository of truth. For if truth were to be found elsewhere, there would be justification for its expression in organized activity. But it is precisely that which the Kremlin cannot and will not permit. . . .

But we have seen that the Kremlin is under no ideological compulsion to accomplish its purposes in a hurry. Like the Church, it is dealing in ideological concepts which are of long-term validity, and it can afford to be patient. It has no right to risk the existing achievements of the revolution for the sake of vain baubles of the future. The very teachings of Lenin himself require great caution and flexibility in the pursuit of Communist purposes.

Again, these precepts are fortified by the lessons of Russian history: of centuries of obscure battles between nomadic forces over the stretches of a vast unfortified plain. Here caution, circumspection, flexibility and deception are the valuable qualities; and their value finds natural appreciation in the Russian or the oriental mind. Thus the Kremlin has no compunction about retreating in the face of superior force. And being under the compulsion of no timetable, it does not get panicky under the necessity for such retreat. Its political action is a fluid stream which moves constantly, wherever it is permitted to move, toward a given goal. Its main concern is to make sure that it has filled every nook and cranny available to it in the basin of world power. But if it finds unassailable barriers in its path, it accepts these philosophically and accommodates itself to them. The main thing is that there should always be pressure, unceasing constant pressure, toward the desired goal. There is no trace of any feeling in Soviet psychology that that goal must be reached at any given time.

Soviet Diplomacy

These considerations make Soviet diplomacy at once easier and more difficult to deal with than the diplomacy of individual aggressive leaders like Napoleon and Hitler. On the one hand it is more sensitive to contrary force, more ready to yield on individual sectors of the diplomatic front when that force is felt to be too strong, and thus more rational in the logic and rhetoric of power. On the other hand it cannot be easily defeated or discouraged by a single victory on the part of its opponents. And the patient persistence by which it is animated means that it can be effectively countered not by sporadic acts which represent the momentary whims of democratic opinion but only by intelligent long-range policies on the part of Russia's adversaries—policies no less steady in their purpose, and no less variegated and resourceful in their application, than those of the Soviet Union itself.

In these circumstances it is clear that the main element of any

United States policy toward the Soviet Union must be that of a long-term, patient but firm and vigilant containment of Russian expansive tendencies. It is important to note, however, that such a policy has nothing to do with outward histrionics: with threats or blustering or superfluous gestures of outward "toughness." While the Kremlin is basically flexible in its reaction to political realities, it is by no means unamenable to considerations of prestige. Like almost any other government, it can be placed by tactless and threatening gestures in a position where it cannot afford to yield even though this might be dictated by its sense of realism. The Russian leaders are keen judges of human psychology, and as such they are highly conscious that loss of temper and of self-control is never a source of strength in political affairs. They are quick to exploit such evidences of weakness. For these reasons, it is a *sine qua non* of successful dealing with Russia that the foreign government in question should remain at all times cool and collected and that its demands on Russian policy should be put forward in such a manner as to leave the way open for a compliance not too detrimental to Russian prestige.

In the light of the above, it will be clearly seen that the Soviet pressure against the free institutions of the western world is something that can be contained by the adroit and vigilant application of counter-force at a series of constantly shifting geographical and political points, corresponding to the shifts and manœuvres of Soviet policy, but which cannot be charmed or talked out of existence. The Russians look forward to a duel of infinite duration, and they see that already they have scored great successes. It must be borne in mind that there was a time when the Communist Party represented far more of a minority in the sphere of Russian national life than Soviet power today represents in the world community.

But if ideology convinces the rulers of Russia that truth is on their side and that they can therefore afford to wait, those of us on whom that ideology has no claim are free to examine objectively the validity of that premise. The Soviet thesis not only implies complete lack of control by the west over its own economic destiny, it likewise assumes Russian unity, discipline and patience over an infinite period. Let us bring this apocalyptic vision down to earth, and suppose that the western world finds the strength and resourcefulness to contain Soviet power over a period of ten to fifteen years. What does that spell for Russia itself?

Predicting the Soviet Future

The Soviet leaders, taking advantage of the contributions of modern technique to the arts of despotism, have solved the question of obedience within the confines of their power. Few chal-

The Truman Doctrine

The Truman Doctrine was a major turning point in American foreign policy, and one of the key events in starting the Cold War. It was proclaimed March 12, 1947, when President Truman asked Congress to appropriate money to assist Greece and Turkey, two nations in social turmoil and, in the case of Greece, faced with communist-led insurgencies. Truman justified this request with rhetoric describing a worldwide struggle between the free world and totalitarianism.

I am fully aware of the broad implications involved if the United States extends assistance to Greece and Turkey, and I shall discuss these implications with you at this time.

One of the primary objectives of the foreign policy of the United States is the creation of conditions in which we and other nations will be able to work out a way of life free from coercion. This was a fundamental issue in the war with Germany and Japan. Our victory was won over countries which sought to impose their will, and their way of life, upon other nations.

To ensure the peaceful development of nations, free from coercion, the United States has taken a leading part in establishing the United Nations. The United Nations is designed to make possible lasting freedom and independence for all its members. We shall not realize our objectives, however, unless we are willing to help free peoples to maintain their free institutions and their national integrity against aggressive movements that seek to impose upon them totalitarian regimes. This is no more than a frank recognition that totalitarian regimes imposed upon free peoples, by direct or indirect aggression, undermine the foundations of international peace and hence the security of the United States.

The peoples of a number of countries of the world have recently had totalitarian regimes forced upon them against their will. The Government of the United States has made frequent protests against coercion and intimidation, in violation of the Yalta agreement, in Poland, Rumania, and Bulgaria. I must also state that in a number of other countries there have been similar developments.

At the present moment in world history nearly every nation must choose between alternative ways of life. The choice is too often not a free one.

One way of life is based upon the will of the majority, and is distinguished by free institutions, representative government, free elections, guarantees of individual liberty, freedom of speech and religion, and freedom from political oppression.

The second way of life is based upon the will of a minority forcibly imposed upon the majority. It relies upon terror and oppression, a controlled press and radio, fixed elections, and the suppression of personal freedoms.

I believe that it must be the policy of the United States to support free peoples who are resisting attempted subjugation by armed minorities or by outside pressures.

lenge their authority; and even those who do are unable to make that challenge valid as against the organs of suppression of the state.

The Kremlin has also proved able to accomplish its purpose of building up in Russia, regardless of the interests of the inhabitants, an industrial foundation of heavy metallurgy, which is, to be sure, not yet complete but which is nevertheless continuing to grow and is approaching those of the other major industrial countries. All of this, however, both the maintenance of internal political security and the building of heavy industry, has been carried out at a terrible cost in human life and in human hopes and energies. It has necessitated the use of forced labor on a scale unprecedented in modern times under conditions of peace. It has involved the neglect or abuse of other phases of Soviet economic life, particularly agriculture, consumers' goods production, housing and transportation.

To all that, the war has added its tremendous toll of destruction, death and human exhaustion. In consequence of this, we have in Russia today a population which is physically and spiritually tired. The mass of the people are disillusioned, skeptical and no longer as accessible as they once were to the magical attraction which Soviet power still radiates to its followers abroad. The avidity with which people seized upon the slight respite accorded to the Church for tactical reasons during the war was eloquent testimony to the fact that their capacity for faith and devotion found little expression in the purposes of the régime.

In these circumstances, there are limits to the physical and nervous strength of people themselves. These limits are absolute ones, and are binding even for the cruelest dictatorship, because beyond them people cannot be driven. The forced labor camps and the other agencies of constraint provide temporary means of compelling people to work longer hours than their own volition or mere economic pressure would dictate; but if people survive them at all they become old before their time and must be considered as human casualties to the demands of dictatorship. In either case their best powers are no longer available to society and can no longer be enlisted in the service of the state. . . .

Meanwhile, a great uncertainty hangs over the political life of the Soviet Union. That is the uncertainty involved in the transfer of power from one individual or group of individuals to others. . . .

Thus the future of Soviet power may not be by any means as secure as Russian capacity for self-delusion would make it appear to the men in the Kremlin. That they can keep power themselves, they have demonstrated. That they can quietly and easily turn it over to others remains to be proved. Meanwhile, the hardships of their rule and the vicissitudes of international life have taken a heavy toll of the strength and hopes of the great people on whom their power rests. It is curious to note that the ideological power of Soviet authority is strongest today in areas beyond the frontiers of Russia, beyond the reach of its police power. This phenomenon brings to mind a comparison used by Thomas Mann in his great novel "Buddenbrooks." Observing that human institutions often show the greatest outward brilliance at a moment when inner decay is in reality farthest advanced, he compared the Buddenbrook family, in the days of its greatest glamour, to one of those stars whose light shines most brightly on this world when in reality it has long since ceased to exist. And who can say with assurance that the strong light still cast by the Kremlin on the dissatisfied peoples of the western world is not the powerful afterglow of a constellation which is in actuality on the wane? This cannot be proved. And it cannot be disproved. But the possibility remains (and in the opinion of this writer it is a strong one) that Soviet power, like the capitalist world of its conception, bears within it the seeds of its own decay, and that the sprouting of these seeds is well advanced.

The Rival

It is clear that the United States cannot expect in the foreseeable future to enjoy political intimacy with the Soviet régime. It must continue to regard the Soviet Union as a rival, not a partner, in the political arena. It must continue to expect that Soviet policies will reflect no abstract love of peace and stability, no real faith in the possibility of a permanent happy coexistence of the Socialist and capitalist worlds, but rather a cautious, persistent pressure toward the disruption and weakening of all rival influence and rival power.

Balanced against this are the facts that Russia, as opposed to the western world in general, is still by far the weaker party, that Soviet policy is highly flexible, and that Soviet society may well contain deficiencies which will eventually weaken its own total potential. This would of itself warrant the United States entering with reasonable confidence upon a policy of firm containment, designed to confront the Russians with unalterable counter-force at every point where they show signs of encroaching upon the interests of a peaceful and stable world.

But in actuality the possibilities for American policy are by no means limited to holding the line and hoping for the best. It is entirely possible for the United States to influence by its actions the internal developments, both within Russia and throughout the international Communist movement, by which Russian policy is largely determined. This is not only a question of the modest measure of informational activity which this government can conduct in the Soviet Union and elsewhere, although that, too, is important. It is rather a question of the degree to which the United States can create among the peoples of the world generally the impression of a country which knows what it wants, which is coping successfully with the problems of its internal life and with the responsibilities of a World Power, and which has a spiritual vitality capable of holding its own among the major ideological currents of the time. To the extent that such an impression can be created and maintained, the aims of Russian Communism must appear sterile and quixotic, the hopes and enthusiasm of Moscow's supporters must wane, and added strain must be imposed on the Kremlin's foreign policies. For the palsied decrepitude of the capitalist world is the keystone of Communist philosophy. Even the failure of the United States to experience the early economic depression which the ravens of the Red Square have been predicting with such complacent confidence since hostilities ceased would have deep and important repercussions throughout the Communist world. . . .

It would be an exaggeration to say that American behavior unassisted and alone could exercise a power of life and death over the Communist movement and bring about the early fall of Soviet power in Russia. But the United States has it in its power to increase enormously the strains under which Soviet policy must operate, to force upon the Kremlin a far greater degree of moderation and circumspection than it has had to observe in recent years, and in this way to promote tendencies which must eventually find their outlet in either the break-up or the gradual mellowing of Soviet power. For no mystical, Messianic movement—and particularly not that of the Kremlin—can face frustration indefinitely without eventually adjusting itself in one way or another to the logic of that state of affairs.

Thus the decision will really fall in large measure in this country itself. The issue of Soviet-American relations is in essence a test of the over-all worth of the United States as a nation among nations. To avoid destruction the United States need only measure up to its own best traditions and prove itself worthy of preservation as a great nation.

Surely, there was never a fairer test of national quality than this. In the light of these circumstances, the thoughtful observer of Russian-American relations will find no cause for complaint in the Kremlin's challenge to American society. He will rather experience a certain gratitude to a Providence which, by providing the American people with this implacable challenge, has made their entire security as a nation dependent on their pulling themselves together and accepting the responsibilities of moral and political leadership that history plainly intended them to bear.

VIEWPOINT 6

"American military power is peculiarly unsuited to a policy of containment which has to be enforced persistently and patiently for an indefinite period of time."

Containment of the Soviet Union Is Poor Policy

Walter Lippmann (1889-1974)

Walter Lippmann was a famous journalist and political philosopher. He wrote on politics, foreign affairs, and many other subjects in his "Today and Tomorrow" syndicated column, read by millions of people from 1931 to 1967.

Lippmann is credited by some historians with creating the phrase "cold war," which was the title of a book he wrote in 1947. *The Cold War* was a collection of related newspaper columns in which Lippmann criticized the ideas and recommendations expressed in an influential *Foreign Affairs* article by George F. Kennan, then director of planning at the U.S. State Department.

While Lippmann does not call for United States withdrawal from world affairs or appeasement of the Soviet Union, he criticizes Kennan's arguments for "containing" the Soviet Union on several grounds. He argues that the international behavior of the U.S.S.R. is better explained by reasons of history and physical security than by Marxism. He questions whether the United States can afford a policy of confronting and containing the Soviet Union throughout the globe, and he argues that such a policy would entangle the United States in many questionable alliances with other countries. Lippmann asserts that the primary threat to the United States is not worldwide Soviet expansionism or Communist ideology but the Soviet military occupation in Eastern Europe and its threat to Western Europe. He urges the United States to concentrate its diplomatic efforts on those issues.

An anonymous article on "The Sources of Soviet Conduct" appeared in the quarterly journal *Foreign Affairs* for July 1947 and shortly afterwards it was republished by *Life* magazine. By its quality alone it would have commanded wide attention. For it was manifestly the work of a man who had observed the Soviet regime closely with a trained eye and an educated mind, and had arrived at a theory as to why the conduct of the Soviet government reflects "no abstract love of peace and stability, no real faith in the possibility of a permanent happy co-existence of the socialist and capitalist worlds, but rather a continuous, persistent pressure towards the disruption and weakening of all rival influence and rival power."

A Statement of Policy

Almost immediately several of the leading correspondents in Washington identified the author, who signed himself "X," as being Mr. George F. Kennan who, after a tour of duty at the Embassy in Moscow, had recently been appointed by Secretary George C. Marshall to be the Director of the Policy Planning Staff of the Department of State. The attribution was not denied. After that Mr. X's article was no longer just one more report on the Soviet regime and what to do about it. It was an event, announcing that the Department of State had made up its mind, and was prepared to disclose to the American people, to the world at large, and of course also to the Kremlin the estimates, the calculations, and the conclusions on which the Department was basing its plans.

Mr. X's article is, therefore, not only an analytical interpretation of the sources of Soviet conduct. It is also a document of primary importance on the sources of American foreign policy—of at least that part of it which is known as the Truman Doctrine.

As such I am venturing to examine it critically in this essay. My criticism, I hasten to say at once, does not arise from any belief or hope that our conflict with the Soviet government is imaginary or that it can be avoided, or ignored, or easily disposed of. I agree entirely with Mr. X that the Soviet pressure cannot "be charmed or talked out of existence." I agree entirely that the Soviet power will expand unless it is prevented from expanding because it is confronted with power, primarily American power, that it must re-

Soviet Expansion in Europe, 1939-1948

Legend:
- ▬ ▬ Soviet border, 1939
- ——— Soviet border, 1947
- ■ Soviet gains in Western territory 1939-1947
- ▨ States under Soviet control by 1948
- ▦ Independent Communist State

Source: John Spanier, American Foreign Policy Since World War II, 12th ed. CQ Press, 1991.

spect. But I believe, and shall argue, that the strategical conception and plan which Mr. X recommends is fundamentally unsound, and that it cannot be made to work, and that the attempt to make it work will cause us to squander our substance and our prestige.

We must begin with the disturbing fact, which anyone who will reread the article can verify for himself, that Mr. X's conclusions depend upon the optimistic prediction that the "Soviet power . . . bears within itself the seeds of its own decay, and that the sprouting of these seeds is well advanced"; that if "anything were ever to occur to disrupt the unity and the efficacy of the Party as a political instrument, Soviet Russia might be changed overnight (*sic*) from one of the strongest to one of the weakest and most pitiable of national societies"; and "that Soviet society may well (*sic*) contain deficiencies which will eventually weaken its own total potential."

Of this optimistic prediction Mr. X himself says that it "cannot be proved. And it cannot be disproved." Nevertheless, he concludes that the United States should construct its policy on the assumption that the Soviet power is inherently weak and impermanent, and that this unproved assumption warrants our entering "with reasonable confidence upon a policy of firm containment, designed to confront the Russians with unalterable counterforce at every point where they show signs of encroaching upon the interests of a peaceful and a stable world."

I do not find much ground for reasonable confidence in a policy which can be successful only if the most optimistic prediction should prove to be true. Surely a sound policy must be addressed to the worst and hardest that may be judged to be probable, and not to the best and easiest that may be possible. . . .

In Mr. X's estimates there are no reserves for a rainy day. There is no margin of safety for bad luck, bad management, error and the unforeseen. He asks us to assume that the Soviet power is already decaying. He exhorts us to believe that our own highest hopes for ourselves will soon have been realized. Yet the policy he recommends is designed to deal effectively with the Soviet Union "as a rival, not a partner, in the political arena." Do we dare to assume, as we enter the arena and get set to run the race, that the Soviet Union will break its leg while the United States grows a pair of wings to speed it on its way?

Mr. X concludes his article on Soviet conduct and American policy by saying that "the thoughtful observer of Russian-American relations will . . . experience a certain gratitude to a Providence which, by providing the American people with this implacable challenge, has made their entire security as a nation dependent upon their pulling themselves together and accepting the responsibilities of moral and political leadership that history plainly intended them to bear." Perhaps. It may be that Mr. X has read the mind of Providence and that he knows what history plainly intended. But it is asking a good deal that the American people should stake their "entire security as a nation" upon a theory which, as he himself says, cannot be proved and cannot be disproved.

Surely it is by no means proved that the way to lead mankind is to spend the next ten or fifteen years, as Mr. X proposes we should, in reacting at "a series of constantly shifting geographical and political points, corresponding to the shifts and maneuvers of Soviet policy." For if history has indeed intended us to bear the responsibility of leadership, then it is not leadership to adapt ourselves to the shifts and maneuvers of Soviet policy at a series of constantly shifting geographical and political points. For that would mean for ten or fifteen years Moscow, not Washington,

65

would define the issues, would make the challenges, would select the ground where the conflict was to be waged, and would choose the weapons. And the best that Mr. X can say for his own proposal is that if for a long period of time we can prevent the Soviet power from winning, the Soviet power will eventually perish or "mellow" because it has been "frustrated."

A Dismal Conclusion

This is a dismal conclusion. Mr. X has, I believe, become bogged down in it because as he thought more and more about the conduct of the Soviet, he remembered less and less about the conduct of the other nations of the world. For while it may be true that the Soviet power would perish of frustration, if it were contained for ten or fifteen years, this conclusion is only half baked until he has answered the crucial question which remains: can the western world operate a policy of containment? Mr. X not only does not answer this question. He begs it, saying that it will be very discouraging to the Soviets, if the western world finds the strength and resourcefulness to contain the Soviet power over a period of ten or fifteen years.

Now the strength of the western world is great, and we may assume that its resourcefulness is considerable. Nevertheless, there are weighty reasons for thinking that the kind of strength we have and the kind of resourcefulness we are capable of showing are peculiarly unsuited to operating a policy of containment.

How, for example, under the Constitution of the United States is Mr. X going to work out an arrangement by which the Department of State has the money and the military power always available in sufficient amounts to apply "counterforce" at constantly shifting points all over the world? Is he going to ask Congress for a blank check on the Treasury and for a blank authorization to use the armed forces? Not if the American constitutional system is to be maintained. Or is he going to ask for an appropriation and for authority each time the Russians "show signs of encroaching upon the interests of a peaceful and stable world"? If that is his plan for dealing with the maneuvers of a dictatorship, he is going to arrive at the points of encroachment with too little and he is going to arrive too late. The Russians, if they intend to encroach, will have encroached while Congress is getting ready to hold hearings.

A policy of shifts and maneuvers may be suited to the Soviet system of government, which, as Mr. X tells us, is animated by patient persistence. It is not suited to the American system of government.

It is even more unsuited to the American economy which is unregimented and uncontrolled, and therefore cannot be administered according to a plan. Yet a policy of containment cannot be operated unless the Department of State can plan and direct exports and imports. For the policy demands that American goods be delivered or withheld at "constantly shifting geographical and political points corresponding to the shifts and maneuvers of Soviet policy." . . .

If then the Kremlin's challenge to American society is to be met by the policy which Mr. X proposes, we are committed to a contest, for ten or fifteen years, with the Soviet system which is planned and directed from Moscow. Mr. X is surely mistaken, it seems to me, if he thinks that a free and undirected economy like our own can be used by the diplomatic planners to wage a diplomatic war against a planned economy at a series of constantly shifting geographical and political points. He is proposing to meet the Soviet challenge on the ground which is most favorable to the Soviets, and with the very instruments, procedures, and weapons in which they have a manifest superiority. . . .

American Military Strength

American military power is peculiarly unsuited to a policy of containment which has to be enforced persistently and patiently for an indefinite period of time. If the Soviet Union were an island like Japan, such a policy could be enforced by American sea and air power. The United States could, without great difficulty, impose a blockade. But the Soviet Union has to be contained on land, and "holding the line" is therefore a form of trench warfare.

Yet the genius of American military power does not lie in holding positions indefinitely. That requires a massive patience by great hordes of docile people. American military power is distinguished by its mobility, its speed, its range and its offensive striking force. It is, therefore, not an efficient instrument for a diplomatic policy of containment. It can only be the instrument of a policy which has as its objective a decision and a settlement. It can and should be used to redress the balance of power which has been upset by the war. But it is not designed for, or adapted to, a strategy of containing, waiting, countering, blocking, with no more specific objective than the eventual "frustration" of the opponent.

The Americans would themselves probably be frustrated by Mr. X's policy long before the Russians were. . . .

The United States cannot by its own military power contain the expansive pressure of the Russians "at every point where they show signs of encroaching." The United States cannot have ready "unalterable counterforce" consisting of American troops. Therefore, the counterforces which Mr. X requires have to be composed of Chinese, Afghans, Iranians, Turks, Kurds, Arabs, Greeks, Italians, Austrians, of anti-Soviet Poles, Czechoslovaks, Bulgars, Yugoslavs, Albanians, Hungarians, Finns and Germans.

The policy can be implemented only by recruiting, subsidizing and supporting a heterogeneous array of satellites, clients, dependents and puppets. The instrument of the policy of containment is therefore a coalition of disorganized, disunited, feeble or disorderly nations, tribes and factions around the perimeter of the Soviet Union.

To organize a coalition among powerful modern states is, even in time of war and under dire necessity, an enormously difficult thing to do well. To organize a coalition of disunited, feeble and immature states, and to hold it together for a prolonged diplomatic siege, which might last for ten or fifteen years, is, I submit, impossibly difficult.

It would require, however much the real name for it were disavowed, continual and complicated intervention by the United States in the affairs of all the members of the coalition which we were proposing to organize, to protect, to lead and to use. Our diplomatic agents abroad would have to have an almost unerring capacity to judge correctly and quickly which men and which parties were reliable containers. Here at home Congress and the people would have to stand ready to back their judgments as to who should be nominated, who should be subsidized, who should be whitewashed, who should be seen through rose-colored spectacles, who should be made our clients and our allies.

Mr. X offers us the prospect of maintaining such a coalition indefinitely until—eventually—the Soviet power breaks up or mellows because it has been frustrated. It is not a good prospect. Even if we assume, which we ought not, that our diplomatic agents will know how to intervene shrewdly and skillfully all over Asia, the Middle East, and Europe, and even if we assume, which the Department of State cannot, that the American people will back them with a drawing account of blank checks both in money and in military power, still it is not a good prospect. For we must not forget that the Soviet Union, against which this coalition will be directed, will resist and react.

In the complicated contest over this great heterogeneous array of unstable states, the odds are heavily in favor of the Soviets. For if we are to succeed, we must organize our satellites as unified, orderly and reasonably contented nations. The Russians can defeat us by disorganizing states that are already disorganized, by disuniting peoples that are torn with civil strife, and by inciting their discontent which is already very great. . . .

There is still greater disadvantage in a policy which seeks to "contain" the Soviet Union by attempting to make "unassailable barriers" out of the surrounding border states. They are admittedly weak. Now a weak ally is not an asset. It is a liability. It requires the diversion of power, money, and prestige to support it and to maintain it. These weak states are vulnerable. Yet the effort to defend them brings us no nearer to a decision or to a settlement of the main conflict. Worst of all, the effort to develop such an unnatural alliance of backward states must alienate the natural allies of the United States.

The natural allies of the United States are the nations of the Atlantic community: that is to say, the nations of western Europe and of the Americas. The Atlantic Ocean and the Mediterranean Sea, which is an arm of the Atlantic Ocean, unite them in a common strategic, economic and cultural system. The chief components of the Atlantic community are the British Commonwealth of nations, the Latin states on both sides of the Atlantic, the Low Countries and Switzerland, Scandinavia and the United States. . . .

Now the policy of containment, as described by Mr. X, is an attempt to organize an anti-Soviet alliance composed in the first instance of peoples that are either on the shadowy extremity of the Atlantic community, or are altogether outside it. The active proponents of the policy have been concerned immediately with the anti-Soviet parties and factions of eastern Europe, with the Greeks, the Turks, the Iranians, the Arabs and Afghans, and with the Chinese Nationalists.

Instead of concentrating their attention and their efforts upon our old allies of the Atlantic community, the makers and the shapers of the policy of containment have for more than a year been reaching out for new allies on the perimeter of the Soviet Union. This new coalition, as we can see only too clearly in Greece, in Iran, in the Arab states and in China, cannot in fact be made to coalesce. Instead of becoming an unassailable barrier against the Soviet power, this borderland is a seething stew of civil strife. . . .

By concentrating our efforts on a diplomatic war in the borderlands of the Soviet Union, we have neglected—because we do not have unlimited power, resources, influence, and diplomatic brain power—the vital interests of our natural allies in western Europe, notably in reconstructing their economic life and in promoting a German settlement on which they can agree.

The failure of our diplomatic campaign in the borderlands, on which we have staked so much too much, has conjured up the specter of a Third World War. The threat of a Russian-American war, arising out of the conflict in the borderlands, is dissolving the natural alliance of the Atlantic community. For the British, the French, and all the other Europeans see that they are placed between the hammer and the anvil. They realize, even if we do not

realize it, that the policy of containment, in the hope that the Soviet power will collapse by frustration, cannot be enforced and
cannot be administered successfully, and that it must fail. Either
Russia will burst through the barriers which are supposed to contain her, and all of Europe will be at her mercy, or, at some point
and at some time, the diplomatic war will become a full scale
shooting war. In either event Europe is lost. Either Europe falls
under the domination of Russia, or Europe becomes the battlefield of a Russian-American war.

Stop Communism by Showing Capitalism Works Better

*The following editorial was published by the Value Line Investment
Survey, a New York corporation which provided services for investors.
It argued that instead of potentially costly military containment of the
Soviet Union, the United States should concentrate on demonstrating
the superiority of capitalism to communism.*

There is not such a vast gulf between the Russians and ourselves
that we could not live together in peace in our own parts of the
world. It is implicit in the Russian program to relax the present regi-
mentation of the individual's life. When that happens the difference
between us will be no greater than that between us and the socialist
state of Great Britain.

The contest of capitalism versus communism will then get down
to a question of which works better. That could be settled without
warfare. It would seem to be the part of wisdom for America to
strengthen capitalism by removing as many as possible of the controls that make it unworkable, such as tariffs, cartels, subsidized
prices, labor monopolies, and income taxes that prevent constructive enterprise. Nobody is going to stop the expansion of communism by sticking a $250,000,000 thorn into the side of Russia. Com-
munism will be stopped by something that works better. Russian
Communists are men. They have the same love of God and their fel-
lowmen that other people have. They can learn, but they will not be
taught at the point of a foreign gun.

Because the policy of containment offers these intolerable alternatives to our old allies, the real aim of every European nation,
including Great Britain, is to extricate itself from the Russian-
American conflict. While we have been devoting our energies to
lining up and bolstering up the Chinese Nationalists, the Iranians, the Turks, the Greek monarchists and conservatives, the anti-
Soviet Hungarians, Rumanians, Poles, the natural alignment of
the British, French, Belgians, Dutch, Swiss and Scandinavians has
been weakened. . . .

We may now ask why the official diagnosis of Soviet conduct, as disclosed by Mr. X's article, has led to such an unworkable policy for dealing with Russia. It is, I believe, because Mr. X has neglected even to mention the fact that the Soviet Union is the successor of the Russian Empire and that Stalin is not only the heir of Marx and of Lenin but of Peter the Great, and the Czars of all the Russias.

For reasons which I do not understand, Mr. X decided not to consider the men in the Kremlin as the rulers of the Russian State and Empire, and has limited his analysis to the interaction of "two forces": "the ideology inherited by the present Soviet leaders from the movement in which they had their political origin" and the "circumstances of the power which they have now exercised for nearly three decades in Russia."

Thus he dwells on the indubitable fact that they believe in the Marxian ideology and that "they have continued to be predominantly absorbed with the struggle to secure and make absolute the power which they seized in November 1917." But with these two observations alone he cannot, and does not, explain the conduct of the Soviet government in this postwar era—that is to say its aims and claims to territory and to the sphere of influence which it dominates. The Soviet government has been run by Marxian revolutionists for thirty years; what has to be explained by a planner of American foreign policy is why in 1945 the Soviet government expanded its frontiers and its orbit, and what was the plan and pattern of its expansion. That can be done only by remembering that the Soviet government is a Russian government and that this Russian government has emerged victorious over Germany and Japan.

Having omitted from his analysis the fact that we are dealing with a victorious Russia—having become exclusively preoccupied with the Marxian ideology, and with the communist revolution—it is no wonder that the outcome of Mr. X's analysis is nothing more definite, concrete and practical than that the Soviets will encroach and expand "at a series of constantly shifting geographical and political points." Mr. X's picture of the Soviet conduct has no pattern. It is amorphous. That is why his conclusions about how we should deal with the Soviets have no pattern, and are also amorphous. . . .

The westward expansion of the Russian frontier and of the Russian sphere of influence, though always a Russian aim, was accomplished when, as, and because the Red Army defeated the German army and advanced to the center of Europe. It was the mighty power of the Red Army, not the ideology of Karl Marx, which enabled the Russian government to expand its frontiers. It is the pressure of that army far beyond the new frontiers which makes the will of the Kremlin irresistible within the Russian

71

sphere of influence. It is the threat that the Red Army may advance still farther west—into Italy, into western Germany, into Scandinavia—that gives the Kremlin and the native communist parties of western Europe an abnormal and intolerable influence in the affairs of the European continent.

Therefore, the immediate and the decisive problem of our relations with the Soviet Union is whether, when, on what conditions the Red Army can be prevailed upon to evacuate Europe. . . .

I do not think there is any doubt in that the evacuation of Europe by the Red Army would alter the situation decisively. There would then be in the internal affairs of the European countries no alien and irresistible military force actually deciding or threatening to decide the internal issues of power and authority. . . .

Liberating Europe

The Kremlin will understand this, and we must expect it to exact the highest price it can obtain for what would be a deep reduction of its present power and influence in Europe, or, if it means to conquer Europe, to obstruct any settlement which meant that the Russian armies must evacuate Europe.

We shall in either case have clarified the real issue. Instead of seeking "to contain" the Soviet Union all over the Eurasian continent, we shall have the initiative and a definite and concrete objective; at the best we shall know the terms on which the main conflict can be settled; at the worst the Soviet Union will have shown its hand on an issue—the liberation of Europe from non-European armies—where there will be no doubt whatever that our cause is just, and that we are the champions of freedom, and that the great masses of the people of Europe will be with us because we stand for the very thing which only traitors can oppose.

We shall have written off the liabilities of the Truman Doctrine which must in practice mean inexorably an unending intervention in all the countries that are supposed to "contain" the Soviet Union. We shall be acting once more in the great American tradition which is to foster the independence of other countries, not to use other countries as the satellites of our own power, however beneficent, and as the instruments of our own policy, however well meant. Our aim will not be to organize an ideological crusade. It will not be to make Jeffersonian democrats out of the peasants of eastern Europe, the tribal chieftains, the feudal lords, the pashas, and the warlords of the Middle East and Asia, but to settle the war and to restore the independence of the nations of Europe by removing the alien armies—all of them, our own included.

CHAPTER 2

The Height of the Cold War

Chapter Preface

The decade following the establishment of the 1947 Truman Doctrine, in which President Harry S Truman declared a U.S. commitment to "support free peoples who are resisting attempted subjugation by armed minorities or by outside pressures," witnessed the expansion of the Cold War. The conflict evolved from a confrontation between two former World War II allies over the future of Europe into a global contest between two nuclear superpowers with rival ideologies. This evolution began with the Democratic presidency of Harry Truman and continued under the Republican presidency of Dwight Eisenhower. Much of the public and governmental debate over the Soviet-American Cold War rivalry concerned specific U.S. tactics and strategy in the contest rather than its fundamental necessity.

The years 1947 through 1949 were filled with significant Cold War developments in all areas of the world, including the United States. In 1947 the army, navy, and air force were unified under the new Department of Defense, and both the National Security Council and the Central Intelligence Agency were established. The creation of these new government departments under the president's administrative control greatly increased the president's power to create foreign policy. Also in 1947 Truman instituted loyalty programs designed to weed from government employment any person associated with communism.

Europe, in the meantime, was becoming divided into Eastern and Western segments, reflecting the rivalry between the Soviet Union and the Western powers. Consequently, to support its allies and combat the perceived spread of communism, the United States began moving ever further from its tradition of noninvolvement with European affairs. The Marshall Plan, announced in 1947, committed American economic aid to help rebuild Europe. The North Atlantic Treaty Organization, organized in 1949, committed the United States to come to the defense of Europe if it was attacked.

While the Truman administration was successful in its stated goals of containing communism and Soviet power in Europe, developments in Asia were more problematic. The biggest shock was in China, the world's most populous nation. In 1949 its leader, Chiang Kai-Shek, whom Americans had long supported, was driven out of China by Chinese communists led by Mao Zedong. When China and Russia signed an alliance in 1950, many observers foresaw the United States being threatened by a monolithic communist bloc of nations covering much of the world's area and population.

A further shock occurred when the Soviets exploded an atomic bomb in August 1949, ending America's monopoly on nuclear weapons. Soviet advances in this field led to a race to develop nuclear fusion bombs many times more powerful than those used on Japan in 1945. Soviet gains also led to charges and fears of espionage within the U.S. government, fears that seemed to be confirmed with the capture and trial of Julius and Ethel Rosenberg in 1950. Senator Joseph McCarthy of Wisconsin gained prominence through his communist "witchhunt" in which he accused people within the U.S. government of treason and betrayal to the communists. The furor over his charges epitomized the domestic turmoil caused by the Cold War.

America responded to what seemed to be a worsening situation in several ways. Within the U.S. government, a major review of the international situation resulted in NSC-68, a secret document prepared by the National Security Council, calling for the quadrupling of defense spending, the strengthening of alliance systems, and measures to convince the American public of the need to wage the costly Cold War. The report's picture of a vast communist enemy facing the United States seemed to be confirmed in the Korean War—the first direct military clash of the Cold War.

Despite these measures, the Truman administration came under attack by Republicans and others over the prosecution of the Cold War. While isolationism received a temporary boost from the unpopularity of the Korean War, most Republican criticism accused the Truman administration of not doing enough to fight communism. The 1952 Republican party platform charged that under the Democrats "more than 500 million non-Russian people of fifteen different countries have been absorbed into the power sphere of communist Russia, which proceeds confidently with its plans for world conquest." John Foster Dulles, soon to become secretary of state, campaigned for Eisenhower, arguing that merely containing the Soviet Union was not enough for the United States. Instead he advocated a policy of "boldness" and the "rollback" of Soviet gains in Eastern Europe. Some observers felt such declarations were dangerous at a time when the Soviet Union also possessed nuclear weapons.

Dulles's bold rhetoric continued during his tenure as secretary of state. He attempted to repeat the success of NATO in containing communist expansionism in Europe by establishing security alliances in the Middle East and Southeast Asia, and he backed up U.S. guarantees of protection with threats of "massive retaliation" against Soviet or Chinese aggression. Despite the warlike public posture of Dulles, the Eisenhower and Dulles years were a time of relative peace. The United States negotiated an armistice in Korea. When Soviet tanks entered Hungary in 1956 to quell dissent, the United States did not risk a military confrontation over the issue.

The United States did, however, increase its intervention in other countries, including covert operations by the Central Intelligence Agency. Covert operations assisted or even installed pro-American regimes in the Philippines, Guatemala, and Iran, but such activities did not break out into open warfare. Undoubtedly the increasing numbers of nuclear weapons possessed by both superpowers played a role in maintaining a tense peace.

VIEWPOINT 1

"It is quite clear from Soviet theory and practice that the Kremlin seeks to bring the free world under its dominion by the methods of the cold war."

The U.S. Should Increase Its Worldwide Efforts to Fight Communism

National Security Council

The National Security Council was created in 1947 to help coordinate U.S. foreign policy and defense. In 1950 President Truman directed the NSC to prepare a study analyzing the implications of three developments of the previous year: the Communist revolution in China, the successful Soviet development of an atomic bomb, and the United States' decision to develop hydrogen or thermonuclear bombs. A study group of high-ranking State and Defense Department officials headed by Paul Nitze, who had succeeded George F. Kennan as head of the U.S. State Department Policy Planning Staff, presented their seventy-page study to the president on April 7, 1950. The report, known as NSC 68, was one of the most comprehensive efforts by U.S. officials to analyze world events and plan a strategy for the Cold War.

NSC 68 paints an alarming picture of a world threatened by Soviet domination. It calls for the buildup of military strength of the

United States and argues that a growing U.S. economy can afford increases in its foreign commitments. In some respects, NSC 68 goes beyond the vision of containment expressed by Kennan, the State Department official in large part responsible for formulating early U.S. Cold War policy. Historians Thomas H. Etzold and John Lewis Gaddis write:

> NSC 68 assumed a view of the world in which gains for communism anywhere constituted, to an equivalent degree, losses for the United States and its allies. Kennan had never endorsed such a "zero sum game" view of the world; moreover, he had stressed the need to differentiate between international communism and Soviet expansionism, seeing in the former a possible instrument to be used in attempting to contain the latter. Kennan had also emphasized the need to define interests in terms of limited capabilities; NSC 68 took the approach that, because capabilities were not as limited as had been thought, interests need not be either.

Truman made the report's recommendations official U.S. policy on September 30, 1950, after the outbreak of the Korean War seemed to confirm many of its conclusions. The text remained classified until 1975.

Within the past thirty-five years the world has experienced two global wars of tremendous violence. It has witnessed two revolutions—the Russian and the Chinese—of extreme scope and intensity. It has also seen the collapse of five empires—the Ottoman, the Austro-Hungarian, German, Italian and Japanese—and the drastic decline of two major imperial systems, the British and the French. During the span of one generation, the international distribution of power has been fundamentally altered. For several centuries it had proved impossible for any one nation to gain such preponderant strength that a coalition of other nations could not in time face it with greater strength. The international scene was marked by recurring periods of violence and war, but a system of sovereign and independent states was maintained, over which no state was able to achieve hegemony.

Two complex sets of factors have now basically altered this historical distribution of power. First, the defeat of Germany and Japan and the decline of the British and French Empires have interacted with the development of the United States and the Soviet Union in such a way that power has increasingly gravitated to these two centers. Second, the Soviet Union, unlike previous aspirants to hegemony, is animated by a new fanatic faith, antithetical to our own, and seeks to impose its absolute authority over the rest of the world. Conflict has, therefore, become endemic and is waged, on the part of the Soviet Union, by violent or non-violent methods in accordance with the dictates of expediency. With the development of increasingly terrifying weapons of mass destruction, every individual faces the ever-present possibility of annihilation should the conflict enter the phase of total war.

On the one hand, the people of the world yearn for relief from the anxiety arising from the risk of atomic war. On the other hand, any substantial further extension of the area under the domination of the Kremlin would raise the possibility that no coalition adequate to confront the Kremlin with greater strength could be assembled. It is in this context that this Republic and its citizens in the ascendancy of their strength stand in their deepest peril. . . .

Three realities emerge as a consequence of this purpose: Our determination to maintain the essential elements of individual freedom, as set forth in the Constitution and Bill of Rights; our determination to create conditions under which our free and democratic system can live and prosper; and our determination to fight if necessary to defend our way of life, for which as in the Declaration of Independence, "with a firm reliance on the protection of Divine Providence, we mutually pledge to each other our lives, our Fortunes and our sacred Honor".

Fundamental Design of the Kremlin

The fundamental design of those who control the Soviet Union and the international communist movement is to retain and solidify their absolute power, first in the Soviet Union and second in the areas now under their control. In the mind of the Soviet leaders, however, achievement of this design requires the dynamic extension of their authority and the ultimate elimination of any effective opposition to their authority. . . .

The Kremlin regards the United States as the only major threat to the achievement of its fundamental design. There is a basic conflict between the idea of freedom under a government of laws, and the idea of slavery under the grim oligarchy of the Kremlin, which has come to a crisis with the polarization of power described [previously], and the exclusive possession of atomic weapons by the two protagonists. The idea of freedom, moreover, is peculiarly and intolerably subversive of the idea of slavery. But the converse is not true. The implacable purpose of the slave state to eliminate the challenge of freedom has placed the two great powers at opposite poles. It is this fact which gives the present polarization of power the quality of crisis. . . .

The Soviet Union is developing the military capacity to support its design for world domination. The Soviet Union actually possesses armed forces far in excess of those necessary to defend its national territory. These armed forces are probably not yet considered by the Soviet Union to be sufficient to initiate a war which would involve the United States. This excessive strength, coupled now with an atomic capability, provides the Soviet Union with great coercive power for use in time of peace in furtherance of its objectives and serves as a deterrent to the victims of its aggression from taking any action in opposition to its tactics which would risk war. . . .

At the time the Soviet Union has a substantial atomic stockpile and if it is assumed that it will strike a strong surprise blow and if it is assumed further that its atomic attacks will be met with no more effective defense opposition than the United States and its allies have programmed, results of those attacks could include:

a. Laying waste to the British Isles and thus depriving the Western Powers of their use as a base;

b. Destruction of the vital centers and of the communications of Western Europe, thus precluding effective defense by the Western Powers; and

c. Delivering devastating attacks on certain vital centers of the United States and Canada.

The possession by the Soviet Union of a thermonuclear capability in addition to this substantial atomic stockpile would result in tremendously increased damage. . . .

United States Policies

Our overall policy at the present time may be described as one designed to foster a world environment in which the American system can survive and flourish. It therefore rejects the concept of isolation and affirms the necessity of our positive participation in the world community.

This broad intention embraces two subsidiary policies. One is a policy which we would probably pursue even if there were no Soviet threat. It is a policy of attempting to develop a healthy international community. The other is the policy of "containing" the Soviet system. These two policies are closely interrelated and interact on one another. Nevertheless, the distinction between them is basically valid and contributes to a clearer understanding of what we are trying to do.

The policy of striving to develop a healthy international community is the long-term constructive effort which we are engaged in. It was this policy which gave rise to our vigorous sponsorship of the United Nations. It is of course the principal reason for our long continuing endeavors to create and now develop the Inter-American system. It, as much as containment, underlay our efforts to rehabilitate Western Europe. Most of our international economic activities can likewise be explained in terms of this policy. In a world of polarized power, the policies designed to develop a healthy international community are more than ever necessary to our own strength.

Cannot Trust the Soviets

Dean Acheson was secretary of state from 1949 to 1953 under President Harry S Truman. He played a key role in developing the Truman Doctrine, the Marshall Plan, and other early milestones of the Cold War. In this excerpt from a March 16, 1950, speech in Berkeley, California, he states that while the United States is willing to negotiate for peace, it cannot jeopardize its security by placing too much trust in the Soviet Union.

However much we may sympathize with the Soviet citizens who for reasons bedded deep in history are obliged to live under it, we are not attempting to change the governmental or social structure of the Soviet Union. The Soviet regime, however, has devoted a major portion of its energies and resources to the attempt to impose its system on other peoples. In this attempt it has shown itself prepared to resort to any method or stratagem including subversion, threats, and even military force. . . .

No one who has lived through these postwar years can be sanguine about reaching agreements in which reliance can be placed and which will be observed by the Soviet leaders in good faith. . . . We are always ready to discuss, to negotiate, to agree, but we are understandably loath to play the role of international sucker. We will take the initiative in the future as we have in the past in seeking agreement whenever there is any indication that this course would be a fruitful one. What is required is genuine evidence in conduct, not just in words, of an intention to solve the immediate problems and remove the tensions which divide us. I see no evidence that the Soviet leaders will change their conduct until the progress of the free world convinces them that they cannot profit from a continuation of these tensions.

As for the policy of "containment", it is one which seeks by all means short of war to (1) block further expansion of Soviet power, (2) expose the falsities of Soviet pretensions, (3) induce a retraction of the Kremlin's control and influence and (4) in general, so foster the seeds of destruction within the Soviet system that the Kremlin is brought at least to the point of modifying its behavior to conform to generally accepted international standards.

It was and continues to be cardinal in this policy that we possess superior overall power in ourselves or in dependable combination with other like-minded nations. One of the most important ingredients of power is military strength. In the concept of "containment", the maintenance of a strong military posture is deemed to be essential for two reasons: (1) as an ultimate guarantee of our national security and (2) as an indispensable backdrop to the conduct of the policy of "containment". Without superior aggregate military strength, in being and readily mobilizable, a policy of "containment"—which is in effect a policy of calculated and gradual coercion—is no more than a policy of bluff.

At the same time, it is essential to the successful conduct of a policy of "containment" that we always leave open the possibility of negotiation with the U.S.S.R. A diplomatic freeze—and we are in one now—tends to defeat the very purposes of "containment" because it raises tensions at the same time that it makes Soviet retractions and adjustments in the direction of moderated behavior more difficult. It also tends to inhibit our initiative and deprives us of opportunities for maintaining a moral ascendency in our struggle with the Soviet system.

In "containment" it is desirable to exert pressure in a fashion which will avoid so far as possible directly challenging Soviet prestige, to keep open the possibility for the U.S.S.R. to retreat before pressure with a minimum loss of face and to secure political advantage from the failure of the Kremlin to yield or take advantage of the openings we leave it.

We have failed to implement adequately these two fundamental aspects of "containment". In the face of obviously mounting Soviet military strength ours has declined relatively. Partly as a by-product of this, but also for other reasons, we now find ourselves at a diplomatic impasse with the Soviet Union, with the Kremlin growing bolder, with both of us holding on grimly to what we have and with ourselves facing difficult decisions. . . .

The U.S. Economy

In contrast to the war economy of the Soviet world, the American economy (and the economy of the free world as a whole) is at present directed to the provision of rising standards of living. The military budget of the United States represents 6 to 7 percent of its gross national product (as against 13.8 percent for the Soviet Union). Our North Atlantic Treaty allies devoted 4.8 percent of their national product to military purposes in 1949.

This difference in emphasis between the two economies means that the readiness of the free world to support a war effort is tending to decline relative to that of the Soviet Union. There is little direct investment in production facilities for military end-products and in dispersal. There are relatively few men receiving military training and a relatively low rate of production of weapons. However, given time to convert to a war effort, the capabilities of the United States economy and also of the Western European economy would be tremendous. In the light of Soviet military capabilities, a question which may be of decisive importance in the event of war is the question whether there will be time to mobilize our superior human and material resources for a war effort. . . .

The Soviet Union is now allocating nearly 40 percent of its gross available resources to military purposes and investment, much of which is in war-supporting industries. It is estimated that even in an emergency the Soviet Union could not increase this proportion to much more than 50 percent, or by one-fourth. The United States, on the other hand, is allocating only about 20 percent of its resources to defense and investment (or 22 percent including foreign assistance), and little of its investment outlays are directed to war-supporting industries. In an emergency the United States could allocate more than 50 percent of its resources to military purposes and foreign assistance, or five to six times as much as at present. . . .

An Expanding Economy

With a high level of economic activity, the United States could soon attain a gross national product of $300 billion per year, as was pointed out in the President's Economic Report (January 1950). Progress in this direction would permit, and might itself be aided by, a build-up of the economic and military strength of the United States and the free world; furthermore, if a dynamic expansion of the economy were achieved, the necessary build-up could be accomplished without a decrease in the national standard of living because the required resources could be obtained by siphoning off a part of the annual increment in the gross national product. These are facts of fundamental importance in considering the courses of action open to the United States. . . .

It is quite clear from Soviet theory and practice that the Kremlin seeks to bring the free world under its dominion by the methods of the cold war. The preferred technique is to subvert by infiltration and intimidation. Every institution of our society is an instrument which it is sought to stultify and turn against our purposes. Those that touch most closely our material and moral strength are obviously the prime targets, labor unions, civic enterprises, schools, churches, and all media for influencing opinion. The effort is not so much to make them serve obvious Soviet ends as to prevent them from serving our ends, and thus to make them sources of confusion in our economy, our culture, and our body politic. The doubts and diversities that in terms of our values are part of the merit of a free system, the weaknesses and the problems that are peculiar to it, the rights and privileges that free men enjoy, and the disorganization and destruction left in the wake of the last attack on our freedoms, all are but opportunities for the

Kremlin to do its evil work. Every advantage is taken of the fact that our means of prevention and retaliation are limited by these principles and scruples which are precisely the ones that give our freedom and democracy its meaning for us. None of our scruples deter those whose only code is, "morality is that which serves the revolution". . . .

Communism Must Be Destroyed

This excerpt from a speech by Missouri representative O.K. Armstrong, delivered February 22, 1952, is typical of the anticommunist feeling of that time.

Surely now we know there can be no collaboration with communism by the free world. It cannot be appeased. It cannot be contained. So long as this world-wide conspiracy exists, it will seek to destroy human liberties. There remains only one conclusion; communism must be defeated. It must be destroyed. Its virus must be eradicated. Its grip upon the people must be broken. Its victims must be liberated. Unless this is done, freedom will die, slowly but inevitably, all over the world.

At the same time the Soviet Union is seeking to create overwhelming military force, in order to back up infiltration with intimidation. In the only terms in which it understands strength, it is seeking to demonstrate to the free world that force and the will to use it are on the side of the Kremlin, that those who lack it are decadent and doomed. In local incidents it threatens and encroaches both for the sake of local gains and to increase anxiety and defeatism in all the free world.

The possession of atomic weapons at each of the opposite poles of power, and the inability (for different reasons) of either side to place any trust in the other, puts a premium on a surprise attack against us. It equally puts a premium on a more violent and ruthless prosecution of its design by cold war, especially if the Kremlin is sufficiently objective to realize the improbability of our prosecuting a preventive war. It also puts a premium on piecemeal aggression against others, counting on our unwillingness to engage in atomic war unless we are directly attacked. We run all these risks and the added risk of being confused and immobilized by our inability to weigh and choose, and pursue a firm course based on a rational assessment of each. . . .

Continuation of present trends . . . will lead progressively to the withdrawal of the United States from most of its present commitments in Europe and Asia and to our isolation in the Western Hemisphere and its approaches. This would result not from a conscious decision but from a failure to take the actions necessary to bring our capabilities into line with our commitments and thus to a withdrawal under pressure. This pressure might come from our present Allies, who will tend to seek other "solutions" unless they have confidence in our determination to accelerate our efforts to build a successfully functioning political and economic system in the free world.

There are some who advocate a deliberate decision to isolate ourselves. Superficially, this has some attractiveness as a course of action, for it appears to bring our commitments and capabilities into harmony by reducing the former and by concentrating our present, or perhaps even reduced military expenditures on the defense of the United States.

This argument overlooks the relativity of capabilities. With the United States in an isolated position, we would have to face the probability that the Soviet Union would quickly dominate most of Eurasia, probably without meeting armed resistance. It would thus acquire a potential far superior to our own, and would promptly proceed to develop this potential with the purpose of eliminating our power, which would, even in isolation, remain as a challenge to it and as an obstacle to the imposition of its kind of order in the world. There is no way to make ourselves inoffensive to the Kremlin except by complete submission to its will. Therefore isolation would in the end condemn us to capitulate or to fight alone and on the defensive, with drastically limited offensive and retaliatory capabilities in comparison with the Soviet Union. (These are the only possibilities, unless we are prepared to risk the future on the hazard that the Soviet Empire, because of over-extension or other reasons, will spontaneously destroy itself from within.)

The argument also overlooks the imponderable, but nevertheless drastic, effects on our belief in ourselves and in our way of life of a deliberate decision to isolate ourselves. As the Soviet Union came to dominate free countries, it is clear that many Americans would feel a deep sense of responsibility and guilt for having abandoned their former friends and allies. As the Soviet Union mobilized the resources of Eurasia, increased its relative military capabilities, and heightened its threat to our security, some would be tempted to accept "peace" on its terms, while many would seek to defend the United States by creating a regimented system which would permit the assignment of a tremendous part of our resources to defense. Under such a state of affairs our national morale would be corrupted and the integrity and vitality of our system subverted.

Under this course of action, there would be no negotiation, unless on the Kremlin's terms, for we would have given up everything of importance. . . .

A more rapid build-up of political, economic, and military strength and thereby of confidence in the free world than is now contemplated is the only course which is consistent with progress toward achieving our fundamental purpose. The frustration of the Kremlin design requires the free world to develop a successfully functioning political and economic system and a vigorous political offensive against the Soviet Union. These, in turn, require an adequate military shield under which they can develop. It is necessary to have the military power to deter, if possible, Soviet expansion, and to defeat, if necessary, aggressive Soviet or Soviet-directed actions of a limited or total character. The potential strength of the free world is great; its ability to develop these military capabilities and its will to resist Soviet expansion will be determined by the wisdom and will with which it undertakes to meet its political and economic problems. . . .

Our position as the center of power in the free world places a heavy responsibility upon the United States for leadership. We must organize and enlist the energies and resources of the free world in a positive program for peace which will frustrate the Kremlin design for world domination by creating a situation in the free world to which the Kremlin will be compelled to adjust. Without such a cooperative effort, led by the United States, we will have to make gradual withdrawals under pressure until we discover one day that we have sacrificed positions of vital interest.

It is imperative that this trend be reversed by a much more rapid and concerted build-up of the actual strength of both the United States and the other nations of the free world. The analysis shows that this will be costly and will involve significant domestic financial and economic adjustments. . . .

In summary, we must, by means of a rapid and sustained build-up of the political, economic, and military strength of the free world, and by means of an affirmative program intended to wrest the initiative from the Soviet Union, confront it with convincing evidence of the determination and ability of the free world to frustrate the Kremlin design of a world dominated by its will. Such evidence is the only means short of war which eventually may force the Kremlin to abandon its present course of action and to negotiate acceptable agreements on issues of major importance.

The whole success of the proposed program hangs ultimately on recognition by this Government, the American people, and all free peoples, that the cold war is in fact a real war in which the survival of the free world is at stake.

VIEWPOINT 2

"If portions of Europe or Asia wish to go Communistic . . . we cannot stop it. Instead we must make sure of our strength and be certain not to fritter it away in battles that could not be won."

The U.S. Should Not Embark on a Worldwide Effort to Fight Communism

Joseph P. Kennedy (1888-1969)

America's increasing involvement in world affairs in the early years of the Cold War was not without its critics. Many people opposed President Truman's policies, arguing that the United States should not become entangled in the affairs of other countries and that the United States was little affected by the threat of international communism.

A good example of "isolationist" thinking is featured in the following viewpoint, which is taken from a speech by Joseph P. Kennedy delivered December 12, 1950, and reprinted in the January 1951 issue of *Vital Speeches of the Day*. Kennedy, a wealthy businessman and father of future U.S. president John F. Kennedy, had served as U.S. ambassador to Great Britain from 1937 to 1940. During that time he had opposed U.S. intervention against Nazi Germany. In this speech given before the Law School Forum at the University of Virginia shortly after the outbreak of the Korean War, Kennedy argues that the military and economic aid the United States has poured into distant areas of the world has not benefited the United States. Kennedy states that rather than fight communism worldwide, the United States should strengthen its defenses closer to home. He cites the Korean War as an example of the costs and flaws of extensive American commitment to fight communism.

As far back as March 18, 1946, I set forth in *Life* magazine what I considered should be the fundamentals of American policy. The first and foremost of these was that we should make and keep ourselves strong. Fundamental to any successful dealing with the world, was the maintenance here in the United States of a high standard of living. Whatever concrete actions might be suggested, to bankrupt this nation in the pursuit of them would mean our self-destruction. . . .

I naturally opposed Communism but I said if portions of Europe or Asia wish to go Communistic or even have Communism thrust upon them, we cannot stop it. Instead we must make sure of our strength and be certain not to fritter it away in battles that could not be won.

But where are we now? Beginning with intervention in the Italian elections and financial and political aid to Greece and Turkey; we have expanded our political and financial programs on an almost unbelievably wide scale. Billions have been spent in the Marshall plan, further billions in the occupation of Berlin, Western Germany and Japan. Military aid has been poured into Greece, Turkey, Iran, the nations of the North Atlantic Pact, French Indo-China, and now in Korea we are fighting the fourth greatest war in our history.

Efforts Have Gained Little

What have we in return for this effort? Friends? We have far fewer friends than we had in 1945. In Europe they are still asking for our dollars but what kind of friendship have we bought there? Is Western Europe determined to preserve for itself those ideals of democracy that we have been preaching? Put to the test now as to whether she will arm herself effectively, even with our aid, to deal with the Russian threat, is she showing the kind of determination and the kind of will that amounts to anything? Plans for economic unification have fallen apart in the light of nationalistic differences. French military power is only a shadow of its former self, and a strong minority of Communist sympathizers keeps France in endless political turmoil. The military strength of Britain is one-fourth of what it was in 1946 and she shows every

Looming Economic Problems

U.S. foreign policy under Truman was frequently criticized for its economic costs. Herbert Hoover, a former U.S. president, argued in this December 20, 1950, national radio address that the costs of the foreign commitments the United States was taking on and the budget deficits they created could cause dire problems for America's economic future.

The 150,000,000 American people are already economically strained by government expenditures. It must not be forgotten that we are carrying huge burdens from previous wars including obligations to veterans and $260 billions of bond and currency issues from those wars. In the fiscal year 1952, federal and local expenditures are likely to exceed $90 billions. That is more than our total savings. We must finance huge deficits by further government issues. Inflation is already moving. The dollar has in six months fallen 15 or 20 percent in purchasing power. But we might with stern measures avoid the economic disintegration of such a load for a very few years. If we continued long on this road the one center of resistance in the world will collapse in economic disaster.

inclination to avoid the heavy burdens that would be involved in rebuilding it. West Germany, to date, has revealed no disposition to develop effective military strength. Italy is hopelessly ineffective and Greece can hardly police her own small territory. Where is there in all Europe any buffer against a massed Russian onslaught? Worse than this, where is there any determination to create such a buffer?

In the Middle East we have oil but no friends. Iran, Pakistan, even Egypt, seek neither our protection nor our influence. In Asia, China whose friendship with us seemed deep-seated and enduring, is now massed against us with men, powerful armies and new vengeful hatreds. Indonesia, Malay, Indo-China, are in revolt or heavy with discontent at the influences we represent. India is showing signs of succumbing to influences other than ours, more indigenous and more palatable to her desires. In Korea we are spending thousands of American lives to accomplish some unknown objective. Assume we stop the Reds somewhere across the belt of that peninsula, are we to continue fighting there indefinitely?

A Suicidal Policy

On the other side of the Iron Curtain are massed manpower and military strength of a type that the world has never seen. . . .

To engage these vast armies on the European or the Asian continent is foolhardy, but that is the direction towards which our policy has been tending.

That policy is suicidal. It has made us no foul weather friends. It has kept our armament scattered over the globe. It has picked one battlefield and threatens to pick others impossibly removed from our sources of supply. It has not contained Communism. By our methods of opposition it has solidified Communism, where otherwise Communism might have bred within itself internal dissensions. Our policy today is politically and morally a bankrupt policy.

I can see no alternative other than having the courage to wash up this policy and start with the fundamentals I urged more than five years ago. It is absurd to believe that the United Nations can lead us out of this situation. The veto power alone makes it a hopeless instrumentality for world peace. The unwillingness of half the world to want world peace makes impossible effective organization to impose any such peace. In short, our chief source of reliance must be ourselves and we cannot sacrifice ourselves to save those who do not seem to wish to save themselves.

A first step in the pursuit of this policy is to get out of Korea—indeed, to get out of every point in Asia which we do not plan realistically to hold in our own defense. Such a policy means that in the Pacific we will pick our own battlegrounds if we are forced to fight and not have them determined by political and ideological considerations that have no relationship to our own defense.

The next step in pursuit of this policy is to apply the same principle to Europe. Today it is idle to talk of being able to hold the line of the Elbe or the line of the Rhine. Why should we waste valuable resources in making such an attempt? If the weakened European nations wish to hold that line and demonstrate a determination to do so, it may be that we can afford them some help. But to put arms and men into a Quixotic military adventure makes no sense whatever. What have we gained by staying in Berlin? Everyone knows we can be pushed out the moment the Russians choose to push us out. Isn't it better to get out now and use the resources, that would otherwise be sacrificed, at a point that counts?

Defend Our Hemisphere

The billions that we have squandered on these enterprises could have been far more effectively used in this hemisphere and on the seas that surround it. Had we the defenses in Iceland today that one-hundredth of the money spent in Berlin could have built, we would have purchased safety with our money rather than added danger. We need defenses in this hemisphere, in Canada, in the Caribbean and in Latin America. After all, these are our neighbors whose security is inevitably tied up with our own. We have no reason to believe that cooperation on their part

Some Day They'll Come Crawling Back to Her

will not be forthcoming and we can, and should insist upon it.

People will say, however, that this policy will not contain Communism. Will our present policy do so? Can we possibly contain Communist Russia, if she chooses to march, by a far flung battle line in the middle of Europe? The truth is that our only real hope is to keep Russia, if she chooses to march, on the other side of the Atlantic and make Communism much too costly for her to try to cross the seas. It may be that Europe for a decade or a generation or more will turn Communistic. But in doing so, it may break of itself as a unified force. Communism still has to prove itself to its peoples as a government that will achieve for them a better way of living. The more people that it will have to govern, the more necessary it becomes for those who govern to justify themselves to those being governed. The more peoples that are under its yoke, the greater are the possibilities of revolt. Moreover, it seems certain that Communism spread over Europe will not rest content with being governed by a handful of men in the Kremlin. French or Italian Communists will soon develop splinter organizations that will destroy the singleness that today characterizes Russian Communism. Tito in Jugoslavia is already demonstrating this fact. Mao in China is not likely to take his orders too long from Stalin, especially when the only non-Asiatics left upon Asiatic soil to fight are the Russians.

Not Advocating Appeasement

This policy will, of course, be criticized as appeasement. No word is more mistakenly used. Is it appeasement to withdraw from unwise commitments, to arm yourself to the teeth and to make clear just exactly how and for what you will fight? If it is wise in our interest not to make commitments that endanger our security, and this is appeasement, then I am for appeasement. I can recall only too well the precious time bought by [Neville] Chamberlain at Munich. I applauded that purchase then; I would applaud it today. Today, however, while we have avoided a Munich we are coming perilously close to another Dunkirk. Personally, I should choose to escape the latter. . . .

An attitude of realism such as this is, I submit, in accord with our historic traditions. We have never wanted a part of other peoples' scrapes. Today we have them and just why, nobody quite seems to know. What business is it of ours to support French colonial policy in Indo-China or to achieve Mr. Syngman Rhee's concepts of democracy in Korea? Shall we now send the marines into the mountains of Tibet to keep the Dalai Lama on his throne? We can do well to mind our business and interfere only where somebody threatens our business and our homes. . . .

An Atlas, whose back is bowed and whose hands are busy holding up the world, has no arms to lift to deal with his own defense. Increase his burdens and you will crush him, or attack him from behind and he cannot turn. This is our present posture. It strangles our might. The suggestions I make would unleash our strength. They would, I am sure, give considerable pause to the strategists and planners of the Kremlin. They would—and I count this most—conserve American lives for American ends, not waste them in the freezing hills of Korea or on the battle-scarred plains of Western Germany.

VIEWPOINT 3

"In my opinion the State Department, which is one of the most important government departments, is thoroughly infested with Communists."

Communist Subversives Threaten America

Joseph McCarthy (1908-1957)

The Cold War had profound effects on America's domestic situation as well as its foreign policy. One of the most spectacular episodes of the era was the rise and fall of Joseph McCarthy, a senator from Wisconsin who gained notoriety for his obsessive hunts for communists within the U.S. government.

McCarthy was little known before gaining national attention with a speech in Wheeling, West Virginia, on February 12, 1950 (*Congressional Record*, 81st Congress, 2nd Session). In that address, excerpted here, McCarthy argues that the United States was denied the fruits of victory from World War II by treasonous subversives in the U.S. State Department. He especially blamed the 1949 Chinese communist takeover on treachery within the U.S. State Department. McCarthy was never able to provide supporting evidence for his accusations, including the one in this speech that fifty-seven communists were working in the State Department.

Despite this lack of proof, McCarthy gained widespread media attention and public support. In many respects the atmosphere of the United States was ripe for someone like McCarthy. China had undergone a communist revolution in 1949, prompting an intense debate over how America "lost" China. The Soviet Union exploded its own atomic bomb the same year, depriving the United

States of its nuclear monopoly and raising fears of Soviet espionage. Alger Hiss, a ranking American diplomat who had assisted Franklin Roosevelt in the 1945 Yalta summit, was charged with subversion and espionage, and in his second trial was found guilty, convincing many Americans of the possibility of treason in high places.

In addition to the general American unease and fear over internal subversion, Norman Graebner writes that part of the reason for McCarthy's popularity was that he provided a simple solution to America's foreign policy dilemmas, with no need for costly foreign commitments or tradeoffs. Graebner wrote:

> Pointing out that the nation, despite its magnificent efforts, had not won World War II, he explained the failure, not in terms of the power revolution in European and Asian politics, but in terms of treason in the Department of State. The speech thus conveyed an illusion of omnipotence, that the United States, under loyal leadership, could always have its way.

Five years after a world war has been won, men's hearts should anticipate a long peace, and men's minds should be free from the heavy weight that comes with war. But this is not such a period—for this is not a period of peace. This is a time of the "cold war." This is a time when all the world is split into two vast, increasingly hostile armed camps—a time of a great armaments race. . . .

Ladies and gentlemen, can there be anyone here tonight who is so blind as to say that the war is not on? Can there be anyone who fails to realize that the Communist world has said, "The time is now"—that this is the time for the show-down between the democratic Christian world and the Communist atheistic world?

Unless we face this fact, we shall pay the price that must be paid by those who wait too long.

Communist Gains

Six years ago, at the time of the first conference to map out the peace—Dumbarton Oaks—there was within the Soviet orbit 180,000,000 people. Lined up on the antitotalitarian side there were in the world at that time roughly 1,625,000,000 people. Today, only 6 years later, there are 800,000,000 people under the absolute domination of Soviet Russia—an increase of over 400 percent. On our side, the figure has shrunk to around 500,000,000. In other words, in less than 6 years the odds have changed from 9 to

1 in our favor to 8 to 5 against us. This indicates the swiftness of the tempo of Communist victories and American defeats in the cold war. As one of our outstanding historical figures once said, "When a great democracy is destroyed, it will not be because of enemies from without, but rather because of enemies from within."

McCarthy Was Right

Almost as controversial as Joseph McCarthy himself was his lawyer, Roy Cohn. Cohn first gained national attention by prosecuting the atomic espionage case of Julius and Ethel Rosenberg, who were convicted of passing secrets to the Soviet Union and sent to the electric chair. In 1968 Cohn wrote the book McCarthy, *telling of his work as McCarthy's counsel and defending McCarthy's character and methods.*

Looking back with whatever objectivity I can muster, I believe that even after all the excesses and mistakes are counted up, Senator McCarthy used the best methods available to him to fight a battle that needed to be fought. The methods were far from perfect, but they were not nearly as imperfect as uninformed critics suggest. . . . The "methods" attack on McCarthy suffers from a credibility gap because of the double standard of many critics, particularly the press, radio, and television. To them, anything McCarthy did was wrong, but the excesses and outrageous methods of those not investigating subversion are often overlooked or excused.

He may have been wrong in details, but he was right in essentials. Certainly few can deny that the Government of the United States had in it enough Communist sympathizers and pro-Soviet advisers to twist and pervert American foreign policy for close to two decades.

The truth of this statement is becoming terrifyingly clear as we see this country each day losing on every front.

At war's end we were physically the strongest nation on earth and, at least potentially, the most powerful intellectually and morally. Ours could have been the honor of being a beacon in the desert of destruction, a shining living proof that civilization was not yet ready to destroy itself. Unfortunately, we have failed miserably and tragically to arise to the opportunity.

The reason why we find ourselves in a position of impotency is not because our only powerful potential enemy has sent men to invade our shores, but rather because of the traitorous actions of those who have been treated so well by this Nation. It has not been the less fortunate or members of minority groups who have been selling this Nation out, but rather those who have had all the benefits that the wealthiest nation on earth has had to offer—the finest homes, the finest college education, and the finest jobs in Government we can give.

This is glaringly true in the State Department. There the bright young men who are born with silver spoons in their mouths are the ones who have been worst. . . .

In my opinion the State Department, which is one of the most important government departments, is thoroughly infested with Communists.

I have in my hand 57 cases of individuals who would appear to be either card carrying members or certainly loyal to the Communist Party, but who nevertheless are still helping to shape our foreign policy.

One thing to remember in discussing the Communists, in our Government is that we are not dealing with spies who get 30 pieces of silver to steal the blueprints of a new weapon. We are dealing with a far more sinister type of activity because it permits the enemy to guide and shape our policy. . . .

Alger Hiss

This brings us down to the case of one Alger Hiss who is important not as an individual any more, but rather because he is so representative of a group in the State Department. It is unnecessary to go over the sordid events showing how he sold out the Nation which had given him so much. Those are rather fresh in all of our minds.

However, it should be remembered that the facts in regard to his connection with this international Communist spy ring were made known to the then Under Secretary of State [Adolf] Berle 3 days after Hitler and Stalin signed the Russo-German alliance pact. At that time one Whittaker Chambers—who was also part of the spy ring—apparently decided that with Russia on Hitler's side, he could no longer betray our Nation to Russia. He gave Under Secretary of State Berle—and this is all a matter of record—practically all, if not more, of the facts upon which Hiss' conviction was based.

Under Secretary Berle promptly contacted Dean Acheson and received word in return that Acheson (and I quote) "could vouch for Hiss absolutely"—at which time the matter was dropped. And this, you understand, was at a time when Russia was an ally of Germany. This condition existed while Russia and Germany were invading and dismembering Poland, and while the Communist groups here were screaming "warmonger" at the United States for their support of the allied nations.

Again in 1943, the FBI had occasion to investigate the facts surrounding Hiss' contacts with the Russian spy ring. But even after that FBI report was submitted, nothing was done.

Then late in 1948—on August 5—when the Un-American Activities Committee called Alger Hiss to give an accounting, President Truman at once issued a Presidential directive ordering all Government agencies to refuse to turn over any information whatsoever in regard to the Communist activities of any Government employee to a congressional committee.

Senator Joseph McCarthy's accusations of communist subversion within the U.S. government, while never specifically proven, were believed by millions of Americans.

Incidentally, even after Hiss was convicted—it is interesting to note that the President still labeled the exposé of Hiss as a "red herring.". . .

As you hear this story of high treason, I know that you are saying to yourself, "Well, why doesn't the Congress do something about it?" Actually, ladies and gentlemen, one of the important reasons for the graft, the corruption, the dishonesty, the disloyalty, the treason in high Government positions—one of the most important reasons why this continues is a lack of moral uprising on the part of the 140,000,000 American people. In the light of history, however, this is not hard to explain.

It is the result of an emotional hang-over and a temporary moral lapse which follows every war. It is the apathy to evil which people who have been subjected to the tremendous evils of war feel. As the people of the world see mass murder, the destruction of defenseless and innocent people, and all of the crime and lack of morals which go with war, they become numb and apathetic. It has always been thus after war.

However, the morals of our people have not been destroyed. They still exist. This cloak of numbness and apathy has only needed a spark to rekindle them. Happily, this spark has finally been supplied.

Attacking Dean Acheson

As you know, very recently the Secretary of State proclaimed his loyalty to a man guilty of what has always been considered as the most abominable of all crimes—of being a traitor to the people who gave him a position of great trust. The Secretary of State in attempting to justify his continued devotion to the man who sold out the Christian world to the atheistic world, referred to Christ's Sermon on the Mount as a justification and reason therefor, and the reaction of the American people to this would have made the heart of Abraham Lincoln happy.

When this pompous diplomat in striped pants, with a phony British accent, proclaimed to the American people that Christ on the Mount endorsed communism, high treason, and betrayal of a sacred trust, the blasphemy was so great that it awakened the dormant indignation of the American people.

He has lighted the spark which is resulting in a moral uprising and will end only when the whole sorry mess of twisted, warped thinkers are swept from the national scene so that we may have a new birth of national honesty and decency in Government.

VIEWPOINT 4

"It is . . . apparent that the charges of Communist infiltration of and influence upon the State Department are false."

Communist Subversives Do Not Threaten America

The Tydings Committee

Senator Joseph McCarthy's charges of communist subversion in the U.S. State Department caused a national uproar. On March 8, 1950, a subcommittee of the Senate Foreign Relations Committee, headed by Senator Millard Tydings of Maryland, was established to investigate McCarthy's accusations. After testimony by McCarthy and those he had accused proved inconclusive (none of the nine people McCarthy specifically named were communists), the Committee decided to compare McCarthy's charges with internal State Department loyalty files.

These files had been kept since President Harry S Truman issued an executive order in 1947 requiring loyalty and background investigations of all government employees. The Federal Bureau of Investigation investigated thousands of people, not only for acts of espionage, but for any association with organizations or people considered "disloyal" or "subversive." Truman at first resisted the Tydings Committee's request to release the files, but eventually relented. McCarthy argued that the files, which failed to substantiate his charges, had been "raped" to remove derogatory material. The Tydings Committee disagreed, and in its concluding report, sharply criticized McCarthy for making false accusations and leading the country into hysteria. The report, excerpted here, is taken from *State Employee Loyalty Investigation, Report No. 2108*, July 20, 1950.

McCarthy responded to this report by actively campaigning against Tydings, and he is credited by many for preventing Tydings's reelection in 1952. McCarthy remained popular and powerful for another two years. In 1954 he charged the U.S. Army with coddling a communist sympathizer. The nationally televised hearings, in which McCarthy again failed to substantiate his charges, discredited him with much of the American public. In December 1954, he was officially censured by the U.S. Senate. Never to regain his former notoriety, he died in 1957.

Of the 81 alleged State Department employees, only 40 were found to be employed by the State Department at the time of the review. Seven of the so-called 81 were never employed by the State Department and the remaining 33 are no longer in the Department, having been separated either through resignation, termination, or reduction in force. Specifically, of the 33 former employees, 3 were separated in 1949; 16, in 1948; 12, in 1947; and 2, in 1946. . . .

. . . We have carefully and conscientiously reviewed each and every one of the loyalty files relative to the individuals charged by Senator McCarthy. In no instance was any one of them now employed in the State Department found to be a "card-carrying Communist," a member of the Communist Party, or "loyal to the Communist Party." Furthermore, in no instance have we found in our considered judgment that the decision to grant loyalty and security clearance has been erroneously or improperly made in the light of existing loyalty standards. Otherwise stated, we do not find basis in any instance for reversing the judgment of the State Department officials charged with responsibility for employee loyalty; or concluding that they have not conscientiously discharged their duties. . . .

What the State Department knows concerning an employee's loyalty is to be found in its loyalty and security files. These files contain all information bearing on loyalty, obtained from any and all sources, including, of course, the reports of full field investigations by the FBI. Interestingly, in this regard, no sooner had the President indicated that the files would be available for review by the subcommittee than Senator McCarthy charged they were being "raped," altered, or otherwise subjected to a "housecleaning." This charge was found to be utterly without foundation in fact.

100

The files were reviewed by representatives of the Department of Justice, and the Department has certified that all information bearing on the employee's loyalty as developed by the FBI appears in the files which were reviewed by the subcommittee. . . .

The Facts Behind the Charge of "Whitewash"

Seldom, if ever, in the history of congressional investigations has a committee been subjected to an organized campaign of vilification and abuse comparable to that with which we have been confronted throughout this inquiry. This campaign has been so acute and so obviously designed to confuse and confound the American people that an analysis of the factors responsible therefor is indicated.

America Needs Subversion

I.F. Stone was an investigative journalist based in Washington, D.C., and a longtime opponent of Joseph McCarthy. In March 1954, when government leaders were beginning to question and challenge McCarthy and his tactics, Stone attacked McCarthy's methods, arguing that the idea of rooting out "subversive" ideas is in itself detrimental to national security.

There are some charges which must be laughed off or brushed off. They cannot be disproved. If a man charges that he saw Eisenhower riding a broomstick over the White House, he will never be convinced to the contrary by sworn evidence that the President was in bed reading a Western at the time. Formal investigations . . . merely pander to paranoia and reward demagogy. What if McCarthy were next to attack the President and the Supreme Court? Are they, too, to be investigated? Is America to become a country in which any adventurer flanked by two ex-Communist screwballs will put any institution on the defensive? . . .

There must be renewed recognition that societies are kept stable and healthy by reform, not by thought police; this means that there must be free play for so-called "subversive" ideas—every idea "subverts" the old to make way for the new. To shut off "subversion" is to shut off peaceful progress and to invite revolution and war. American society has been healthy in the past because there has been a constant renovating "subversion" of this kind. Had we operated on the bogeyman theory of history, America would have destroyed itself long ago. It will destroy itself now unless and until a few men of stature have the nerve to speak again the traditional language of free society.

The first of these factors was the necessity of creating the impression that our inquiry was not thorough and sincere in order to camouflage the fact that the charges made by Senator McCarthy were groundless and that the Senate and the American people had been deceived. No sooner were hearings started than the cry of "whitewash" was raised along with the chant "investigate the charges and not McCarthy." This chant we have heard morning, noon, and night for almost 4 months from certain quarters for readily perceptible motives. Interestingly, had we elected to investigate Senator McCarthy, there would have been ample basis therefor, since we have been reliably informed that at the time he made the charges initially he had no information whatever to support them, and, furthermore, it early appeared that in securing Senate Resolution 231 a fraud had been perpetrated upon the Senate of the United States.

From the very outset of our inquiry, Senator McCarthy has sought to leave the impression that the subcommittee has been investigating him and not "disloyalty in the State Department." The reason for the Senator's concern is now apparent. He had no facts to support his wild and baseless charges, and lived in mortal fear that this situation would be exposed.

Few people, cognizant of the truth in even an elementary way, have, in the absence of political partisanship, placed any credence in the hit-and-run tactics of Senator McCarthy. He has stooped to a new low in his cavalier disregard of the facts.

The simple truth is that in making his speech at Wheeling, Senator McCarthy was talking of a subject and circumstances about which he knew nothing. His extreme and irresponsible statements called for emergency measures. As Senator Wherry told Emmanuel S. Larsen, "Oh, Mac has gone out on a limb and kind of made a fool of himself and we have to back him up now." Starting with nothing, Senator McCarthy plunged headlong forward, desperately seeking to develop some information, which colored with distortion and fanned by a blaze of bias, would forestall a day of reckoning.

Certain elements rallied to his support, particularly those who ostensibly fight communism by adopting the vile methods of the Communists themselves and in so doing actually hinder the fight of all right-minded people who detest and abhor communism in all its manifestations. We cannot, however, destroy one evil by the adoption of another. Senator McCarthy and McCarthyism have been exposed for what they are—and the sight is not a pretty one. . . .

The Big Lie

In concluding our report, we are constrained to make observations which we regard as fundamental.

It is, of course, clearly apparent that the charges of Communist infiltration of and influence upon the State Department are false. This knowledge is reassuring to all Americans whose faith has been temporarily shaken in the security of their Government by perhaps the most nefarious campaign of untruth in the history of our Republic.

We believe, however, that this knowledge and assurance, while important, will prove ultimately of secondary significance in contemplating the salutary aspects of our investigation. For, we believe that, inherent in the charges that have been made and the sinister campaign to give them ostensible verity, are lessons from which the American people will find inspiration for a rededication to the principles and ideals that have made this Nation great.

We have seen the technique of the "Big Lie," elsewhere employed by the totalitarian dictator with devastating success, utilized here for the first time on a sustained basis in our history. We have seen how, through repetition and shifting untruths, it is possible to delude great numbers of people.

We have seen the character of private citizens and of Government employees virtually destroyed by public condemnation on the basis of gossip, distortion, hearsay, and deliberate untruths. By the mere fact of their associations with a few persons of alleged questionable proclivities an effort has been made to place the stigma of disloyalty upon individuals, some of whom are little people whose only asset is their character and devotion to duty and country. This has been done without the slightest vestige of respect for even the most elementary rules of evidence or fair play or, indeed, common decency. Indeed, we have seen an effort not merely to establish guilt by association but guilt by accusation alone. The spectacle is one we would expect in a totalitarian nation where the rights of the individual are crushed beneath the juggernaut of statism and oppression; it has no place in America where government exists to serve our people, not to destroy them.

Creating Hysteria

We have seen an effort to inflame the American people with a wave of hysteria and fear on an unbelievable scale in this free Nation. Were this campaign founded in truth it would be questionable enough; where it is fraught with falsehood from beginning to end, its reprehensible and contemptible character defies adequate condemnation.

We sincerely believe that charges of the character which have been made in this case seriously impair the efforts of our agencies of Government to combat the problem of subversion. Furthermore, extravagant allegations, which cannot be proved and are not subject to proof, have the inevitable effect of dulling the awareness of all Americans to the true menace of communism. . . .

At a time when American blood is again being shed to preserve our dream of freedom, we are constrained fearlessly and frankly to call the charges, and the methods employed to give them ostensible validity, what they truly are: A fraud and a hoax perpetrated on the Senate of the United States and the American people. They represent perhaps the most nefarious campaign of half-truths and untruths in the history of this Republic. For the first time in our history, we have seen the totalitarian technique of the "big lie" employed on a sustained basis. The result has been to confuse and divide the American people, at a time when they should be strong in their unity, to a degree far beyond the hopes of the Communists themselves whose stock in trade is confusion and division. In such a disillusioning setting, we appreciate as never before our Bill of Rights, a free press, and the heritage of freedom that has made this Nation great.

VIEWPOINT 5

"By fighting a limited war in Korea, we have . . . [improved] the ability of the whole free world to resist Communist aggression."

The U.S. Campaign in Korea Is Justified

Harry S Truman (1884-1972)

The Korean War was the first extended armed conflict of the Cold War. The U.S. commitment to fight communism led to military intervention in this faraway Asian nation and to more than thirty-three thousand Americans being killed in action.

Korea, following its liberation from Japan in World War II, had been hastily divided between Soviet and American occupation zones. These zones ultimately became two separate countries: North Korea, which allied itself with the Soviet Union, and South Korea, which maintained close ties with the United States. Both countries claimed jurisdiction over the whole of Korea.

On June 25, 1950, forces from communist North Korea attacked South Korea. United States president Harry S Truman believed this attack was instigated by the Soviet Union and that the United States could not let the attack stand without a strong U.S. response. Action was necessary, he believed, in part to maintain U.S. credibility in its defense agreements with Europe and Japan. Truman's action was also affected by events the previous year in Korea's neighboring country, China. The U.S.-supported government of Chiang Kai-shek had been overthrown in 1949 by Chinese communists under the leadership of Mao Zedong, a development many Americans viewed with dismay because it seemed that the Soviet Union and China would successfully create a powerful communist bloc of 800 million people.

Truman secured UN resolutions condemning North Korea and authorizing the United States to command forces to respond. (The Soviet Union was unable to veto the actions because it was boycotting the meetings.) Truman dispatched U.S. soldiers under the direction of World War II hero General Douglas MacArthur. Under MacArthur's leadership, UN forces (relying largely on U.S. troops) successfully drove the North Koreans out of South Korea and pushed the invaders deep inside North Korea. However on November 25, 1950, as U.S. troops approached the Korean-Chinese border, China entered the war and turned the UN offensive into a massive retreat. The ultimate result was a bloody stalemate between two entrenched armies positioned approximately on North and South Korea's original borderline.

MacArthur advocated greater military steps against China, including bombing the country and using the forces of former Chinese leader Chiang Kai-shek, who was now leader of the island of Taiwan. Truman was determined to keep the war limited to Korea, fearing a wider war that could turn into World War III. He believed the Soviet Union, not China, should remain the primary focus of the Cold War. When MacArthur continued to express his views to journalists and legislators, Truman relieved him of command on April 11, 1951. The following viewpoint is taken from Truman's address to the United States explaining this unpopular firing. It is taken from the April 16, 1951 issue of the *Department of State Bulletin*. Truman defends U.S. policy in Korea, arguing that it was necessary to deter further communist aggression, and stating that the U.S. should continue to prevent a widening of the war.

The Korean conflict was one of many Cold War instances in which the United States intervened in the affairs of other nations in the name of thwarting communism.

The Communists in the Kremlin are engaged in a monstrous conspiracy to stamp out freedom all over the world. If they were to succeed, the United States would be numbered among their principal victims. It must be clear to everyone that the United States cannot—and will not—sit idly by and await foreign conquest. The only question is: When is the best time to meet the threat and how?

The best time to meet the threat is in the beginning. It is easier to put out a fire in the beginning when it is small than after it has become a roaring blaze.

And the best way to meet the threat of aggression is for the peace-loving nations to act together. If they don't act together, they are likely to be picked off, one by one. . . .

Lesson of History

If history has taught us anything, it is that aggression anywhere in the world is a threat to peace everywhere in the world. When that aggression is supported by the cruel and selfish rulers of a powerful nation who are bent on conquest, it becomes a clear and present danger to the security and independence of every free nation.

Risking World War III

Secretary of Defense George C. Marshall, a highly decorated U.S. Army general who had previously served as secretary of state and U.S. Army chief of staff, defended Truman's firing of MacArthur in Senate hearings in 1951.

Our efforts in Korea have given us some sorely needed time and impetus to accelerate the building of our defenses and those of our allies against the threatened onslaught of Soviet imperialism.

General MacArthur, on the other hand, would have us, on our own initiative, carry the conflict beyond Korea against the mainland of Communist China, both from the sea and from the air. He would have us accept the risk involvement not only in an extension of the war with Red China, but in an all-out war with the Soviet Union. He would have us do this even at the expense of losing our allies and wrecking the coalition of free peoples throughout the world. He would have us do this even though the effect of such action might expose Western Europe to attack by the millions of Soviet troops poised in Middle and Eastern Europe.

This is a lesson that most people in this country have learned thoroughly. This is the basic reason why we joined in creating the United Nations. And since the end of World War II we have been putting that lesson into practice—we have been working with other free nations to check the aggressive designs of the Soviet Union before they can result in a third world war. . . .

The aggression against Korea is the boldest and most dangerous move the Communists have yet made.

The attack on Korea was part of a greater plan for conquering all of Asia.

I would like to read to you from a secret intelligence report which came to us after the attack. It is a report of a speech a Communist army officer in North Korea gave to a group of spies and saboteurs last May, one month before South Korea was invaded.

The report shows in great detail how this invasion was part of a carefully prepared plot. Here is part of what the Communist officer, who had been trained in Moscow, told his men: "Our forces," he said, "are scheduled to attack South Korean forces about the middle of June. . . . The coming attack on South Korea marks the first step toward the liberation of Asia."

Notice that he used the word "liberation." That is Communist double-talk meaning "conquest."

I have another secret intelligence report here. This one tells what another Communist officer in the Far East told his men several months before the invasion of Korea. Here is what he said: "In order to successfully undertake the long awaited world revolution, we must first unify Asia. . . . Java, Indochina, Malaya, India, Tibet, Thailand, Philippines, and Japan are our ultimate targets. . . . The United States is the only obstacle on our road for the liberation of all countries in southeast Asia. In other words, we must unify the people of Asia and crush the United States."

That is what the Communist leaders are telling their people, and that is what they have been trying to do. . . .

A Limited War

The question we have had to face is whether the Communist plan of conquest can be stopped without general war. Our Government and other countries associated with us in the United Nations believe that the best chance of stopping it without general war is to meet the attack in Korea and defeat it there.

That is what we have been doing. It is a difficult and bitter task. But so far it has been successful.

So far, we have prevented World War III.

So far, by fighting a limited war in Korea, we have prevented aggression from succeeding and bringing on a general war. And the ability of the whole free world to resist Communist aggression has been greatly improved.

We have taught the enemy a lesson. He has found out that aggression is not cheap or easy. Moreover, men all over the world who want to remain free have been given new courage and new hope. They know now that the champions of freedom can stand up and fight and that they will stand up and fight.

Our resolute stand in Korea is helping the forces of freedom now fighting in Indochina and other countries in that part of the world. It has already slowed down the timetable of conquest.

In Korea itself, there are signs that the enemy is building up his ground forces for a new mass offensive. We also know that there have been large increases in the enemy's available air forces.

If a new attack comes, I feel confident it will be turned back. The United Nations fighting forces are tough and able and well

equipped. They are fighting for a just cause. They are proving to all the world that the principle of collective security will work. We are proud of all these forces for the magnificent job they have done against heavy odds. We pray that their efforts may succeed, for upon their success may hinge the peace of the world.

The Communist side must now choose its course of action. The Communist rulers may press the attack against us. They may take further action which will spread the conflict. They have that choice, and with it the awful responsibility for what may follow. The Communists also have the choice of a peaceful settlement which could lead to a general relaxation of tensions in the Far East. The decision is theirs, because the forces of the United Nations will strive to limit the conflict if possible.

We do not want to see the conflict in Korea extended. We are trying to prevent a world war—not to start one. The best way to do that is to make it plain that we and the other free countries will continue to resist the attack.

But you may ask: Why can't we take other steps to punish the aggressor? Why don't we bomb Manchuria and China itself?

109

Why don't we assist Chinese Nationalist troops to land on the mainland of China?

If we were to do these things we would be running a very grave risk of starting a general war. If that were to happen, we would have brought about the exact situation we are trying to prevent.

If we were to do these things, we would become entangled in a vast conflict on the continent of Asia and our task would become immeasurably more difficult all over the world.

What would suit the ambitions of the Kremlin better than for our military forces to be committed to a full-scale war with Red China?

It may well be that, in spite of our best efforts, the Communists may spread the war. But it would be wrong—tragically wrong—for us to take the initiative in extending the war.

The dangers are great. Make no mistake about it. Behind the North Koreans and Chinese Communists in the front lines stand additional millions of Chinese soldiers. And behind the Chinese stand the tanks, the planes, the submarines, the soldiers, and the scheming rulers of the Soviet Union.

Our aim is to avoid the spread of the conflict.

The course we have been following is the one best calculated to avoid an all-out war. It is the course consistent with our obligation to do all we can to maintain international peace and security. Our experience in Greece and Berlin shows that it is the most effective course of action we can follow.

First of all, it is clear that our efforts in Korea can blunt the will of the Chinese Communists to continue the struggle. The United Nations forces have put up a tremendous fight in Korea and have inflicted very heavy casualties on the enemy. Our forces are stronger now than they have been before. These are plain facts which may discourage the Chinese Communists from continuing their attack.

Second, the free world as a whole is growing in military strength every day. In the United States, in Western Europe, and throughout the world, free men are alert to the Soviet threat and are building their defenses. This may discourage the Communist rulers from continuing the war in Korea—and from undertaking new acts of aggression elsewhere.

If the Communist authorities realize that they cannot defeat us in Korea, if they realize it would be foolhardy to widen the hostilities beyond Korea, then they may recognize the folly of continuing their aggression. A peaceful settlement may then be possible. The door is always open.

Then we may achieve a settlement in Korea which will not compromise the principles and purposes of the United Nations.

I have thought long and hard about this question of extending the war in Asia. I have discussed it many times with the ablest military advisers in the country. I believe with all my heart that the course we are following is the best course.

I believe that we must try to limit the war to Korea for these vital reasons: to make sure that the precious lives of our fighting men are not wasted; to see that the security of our country and the free world is not needlessly jeopardized; and to prevent a third world war.

Firing MacArthur

A number of events have made it evident that General MacArthur did not agree with that policy. I have therefore considered it essential to relieve General MacArthur so that there would be no doubt or confusion as to the real purpose and aim of our policy.

It was with the deepest personal regret that I found myself compelled to take this action. General MacArthur is one of our greatest military commanders. But the cause of world peace is more important than an individual.

The change in commands in the Far East means no change whatever in the policy of the United States. We will carry on the fight in Korea with vigor and determination in an effort to bring the war to a speedy and successful conclusion. . . .

In the meantime, I want to be clear about our military objective. We are fighting to resist an outrageous aggression in Korea. We are trying to keep the Korean conflict from spreading to other areas. But at the same time we must conduct our military activities so as to insure the security of our forces. This is essential if they are to continue the fight until the enemy abandons its ruthless attempt to destroy the Republic of Korea.

That is our military objective—to repel attack and to restore peace.

In the hard fighting in Korea, we are proving that collective action among nations is not only a high principle but a workable means of resisting aggression. Defeat of aggression in Korea may be the turning point in the world's search for a practical way of achieving peace and security.

The struggle of the United Nations in Korea is a struggle for peace.

The free nations have united their strength in an effort to prevent a third world war.

That war can come if the Communist rulers want it to come. But this Nation and its allies will not be responsible for its coming.

We do not want to widen the conflict. We will use every effort to prevent that disaster. And in so doing we know that we are following the great principles of peace, freedom, and justice.

111

VIEWPOINT 6

"[O]nce war is forced upon us, there is no other alternative than to apply every available means to bring it to a swift end."

U.S. Policy in Korea Is Flawed

Douglas MacArthur (1880-1964)

Douglas MacArthur, one of the most famous and popular military leaders of World War II, commanded the Allied Forces in the Southwest Pacific and directed the postwar U.S. occupation of Japan. In 1950, President Harry S Truman named him commander of the UN military forces in their fight against the North Korean invaders of South Korea. MacArthur was able to repel the invaders and push them deep into North Korean territory. He was close to total victory in Korea when China, Korea's populous and newly communist neighbor, intervened on November 25, 1950, driving MacArthur's forces out of North Korea.

MacArthur became involved in a sharp policy dispute with Truman over strategy. He wished to bomb China directly and to "unleash" the forces of former Chinese leader Chiang Kai-shek, ruler of Formosa (Taiwan). Truman did not want to extend or widen the war. When MacArthur continued to make his disagreements with Truman public, Truman fired him on April 11, 1951.

MacArthur returned to the United States a hero. On April 19, 1951, he addressed a joint session of Congress. He defended his views on the Korean War. He argued that the security of Asia against communist aggression was vital for U.S. success in the Cold War, and that U.S. military policy in the area, especially in Korea, should strive for swift and total victory.

MacArthur's arguments on committing the United States to total victory were part of a recurring debate throughout the Cold War—what measures should the United States take to assure victory against communism and security for democracy?

I do not stand here as advocate for any partisan cause, for the issues are fundamental and reach quite beyond the realm of partisan consideration. They must be resolved on the highest plane of national interest if our course is to prove sound and our future protected. I trust, therefore, that you will do me the justice of receiving that which I have to say as solely expressing the considered viewpoint of a fellow American. I address you with neither rancor nor bitterness in the fading twilight of life with but one purpose in mind, to serve my country.

The issues are global and so interlocked that to consider the problems of one sector oblivious to those of another is but to court disaster for the whole.

The Importance of Asia

While Asia is commonly referred to as the gateway to Europe, it is no less true that Europe is the gateway to Asia, and the broad influence of the one cannot fail to have its impact upon the other.

There are those who claim our strength is inadequate to protect on both fronts, that we cannot divide our effort. I can think of no greater expression of defeatism. If a potential enemy can divide his strength on two fronts, it is for us to counter his effort.

The Communist threat is a global one. Its successful advance in one sector threatens the destruction of every other sector. You cannot appease or otherwise surrender to communism in Asia without simultaneously undermining our efforts to halt its advance in Europe.

Beyond pointing out these general truisms, I shall confine my discussion to the general areas of Asia. Before one may objectively assess the situation now existing there, he must comprehend something of Asia's past and the revolutionary changes which have marked her course up to the present. Long exploited by the so-called colonial powers, with little opportunity to achieve any degree of social justice, individual dignity, or a higher standard of life such as guided our own noble administration of the Philippines, the peoples of Asia found their opportunity in the war just past to throw off the shackles of colonialism and now see the dawn of new opportunity and heretofore unfelt dignity and the self-respect of political freedom.

Mustering half of the earth's population and 60 percent of its natural resources these peoples are rapidly consolidating a new force, both moral and material, with which to raise the living standard and erect adaptations of the design of modern progress to their own distinct cultural environments. Whether one adheres to the concept of colonization or not, this is the direction of

113

Failure in Korea

The 1952 Republican Party platform, excerpted here, sharply criticized President Truman's foreign policy, including his handling of the Korean War. Faced with growing unpopularity, Truman decided not to run for reelection. Dwight Eisenhower, like MacArthur, a general and World War II hero, won the Republican nomination for president and the general election. Eisenhower, like Truman, did not want a wider war and signed an armistice with North Korea in 1953.

In South Korea, they [the Truman administration] withdrew our occupation troops in the face of the aggressive, poised for action, Communist military strength on its northern border. They publicly announced that Korea was of no concern to us. Then when the Communist forces acted to take what seemed to have been invited, they committed this nation to fight back under the most unfavorable conditions. Already the tragic cost is over 110,000 American casualties.

With foresight, the Korean War would never have happened.

In going back into Korea, they evoked the patriotic and sacrificial support of the American people. But by their hampering orders they produced stalemates and ignominious bartering with our enemies, and they offer no hope of victory.

Asian progress and it may not be stopped. It is a corollary to the shift of the world economic frontiers, as the whole epi-center of world affairs rotates back toward the area whence it started. In this situation it becomes vital that our own country orient its policies in consonance with this basic evolutionary condition rather than pursue a course blind to the reality that the colonial era is now past and the Asian peoples covet the right to shape their own free destiny. What they seek now is friendly guidance, understanding, and support, not imperious direction; the dignity of equality, not the shame of subjugation. Their prewar standard of life, pitifully low, is infinitely lower now in the devastation left in war's wake. World ideologies play little part in Asian thinking and are little understood. What the peoples strive for is the opportunity for a little more food in their stomachs, a little better clothing on their backs, a little firmer roof over their heads, and the realization of a normal nationalist urge for political freedom. These political-social conditions have but an indirect bearing upon our own national security, but do form a backdrop to contemporary planning which must be thoughtfully considered if we are to avoid the pitfalls of unrealism.

Of more direct and immediate bearing upon our national security are the changes wrought in the strategic potential of the Pacific Ocean in the course of the past war. Prior thereto, the western strategic frontier of the United States lay on the littoral line of the Americas with an exposed island salient extending out through Hawaii, Midway, and Guam to the Philippines. That salient proved not an outpost of strength but an avenue of weakness along which the enemy could and did attack. The Pacific was a potential area of advance for any predatory force intent upon striking at the bordering land areas.

America's Strategic Defense

All this was changed by our Pacific victory. Our strategic frontier then shifted to embrace the entire Pacific Ocean which became a vast moat to protect us as long as we held it. Indeed, it acts as a protective shield for all of the Americas and all free lands of the Pacific Ocean area. We control it to the shores of Asia by a chain of islands extending in an arc from the Aleutians to the Marianas held by us and our free allies.

From this island chain we can dominate with sea and air power every Asiatic port from Vladivostok to Singapore and prevent any hostile movement into the Pacific. Any predatory attack from Asia must be an amphibious effort. No amphibious force can be successful without control of the sea lanes and the air over those lanes in its avenue of advance. With naval and air supremacy and modest ground elements to defend bases, any major attack from continental Asia toward us or our friends of the Pacific would be doomed to failure. Under such conditions the Pacific no longer represents menacing avenues of approach for a prospective invader—it assumes instead the friendly aspect of a peaceful lake. Our line of defense is a natural one and can be maintained with a minimum of military effort and expense. It envisions no attack against anyone nor does it provide the bastions essential for offensive operations, but properly maintained would be invincible defense against aggression.

The holding of this littoral defense line in the western Pacific is entirely dependent upon holding all segments thereof, for any major breach of that line by an unfriendly power would render vulnerable to determined attack every other major segment. This is a military estimate as to which I have yet to find a military leader who will take exception.

For that reason I have strongly recommended in the past as a matter of military urgency that under no circumstances must Formosa fall under Communist control.

Such an eventuality would at once threaten the freedom of the Philippines and the loss of Japan, and might well force our western frontier back to the coasts of California, Oregon, and Washington. . . .

On Formosa, the Government of the Republic of China has had the opportunity to refute by action much of the malicious gossip

115

Hemmed In

Reg Manning. Reprinted with permission.

which so undermined the strength of its leadership on the Chinese mainland.

The Formosan people are receiving a just and enlightened administration with majority representation on the organs of government; and politically, economically, and socially appear to be advancing along sound and constructive lines.

The Korean War

With this brief insight into the surrounding areas I now turn to the Korean conflict. While I was not consulted prior to the President's decision to intervene in the support of the Republic of Korea, that decision from a military standpoint proved a sound one. As I say, a brief and sound one as we hurled back the invaders and decimated his forces. Our victory was complete and our objectives within reach when Red China intervened with numerically superior ground forces. This created a new war and an entirely new situation, a situation not contemplated when our forces were committed against the North Korean invaders, a situation which called for new decisions in the diplomatic sphere to permit the realistic adjustment of military strategy. Such decisions have not been forthcoming.

While no man in his right mind would advocate sending our ground forces into continental China—and such was never given a thought—the new situation did urgently demand a drastic revision of strategic planning if our political aim was to defeat this new enemy as we had defeated the old.

Apart from the military need as I saw it to neutralize sanctuary, protection given to the enemy north of the Yalu, I felt that military necessity in the conduct of the war made necessary:

First, the intensification of our economic blockade against China.

Second, the imposition of a naval blockade against the China coast.

Third, removal of restrictions on air reconnaissance of China's coastal areas and of Manchuria.

Fourth, removal of restrictions on the forces of the Republic of China on Formosa with logistical support to contribute to their effective operation against the Chinese mainland.

For entertaining these views all professionally designed to support our forces committed to Korea and bring hostilities to an end with the least possible delay and at a saving of countless American and Allied lives. I have been severely criticized in lay circles, principally abroad, despite my understanding that from a military standpoint the above views have been fully shared in the past by practically every military leader concerned with the Korean campaign, including our own Joint Chiefs of Staff.

I called for reinforcements, but was informed that reinforcements were not available. I made clear that if not permitted to utilize the friendly Chinese force of some 600,000 men on Formosa; if not permitted to blockade the China coast to prevent the Chinese Reds from getting succor from without; and if there were to be no hope of major reinforcements, the position of the command from the military standpoint forbade victory. We could hold in Korea by constant maneuver and at an approximate area where our supply advantages were in balance with the supply line disadvantages of the enemy, but we could hope at best for only an indecisive campaign, with its terrible and constant attrition upon our forces if the enemy utilized his full military potential. I have constantly called for the new political decisions essential to a solution. Efforts have been made to distort my position. It has been said in effect that I was a warmonger. Nothing could be further from the truth. I know war as few other men now living know it, and nothing to me is more revolting. . . .

No Substitute for Victory

But once war is forced upon us, there is no other alternative than to apply every available means to bring it to a swift end. War's very object is victory—not prolonged indecision. In war, indeed, there can be no substitute for victory.

There are some who for varying reasons would appease Red China. They are blind to history's clear lesson. For history teaches with unmistakable emphasis that appeasement but begets new and bloodier war. It points to no single instance where the end has justified that means—where appeasement has led to more than a sham peace. Like blackmail, it lays the basis for new and successively greater demands, until, as in blackmail, violence becomes the only other alternative. Why, my soldiers asked of me, surrender military advantages to an enemy in the field? I could not answer. Some may say to avoid spread of the conflict into an all-out war with China; others, to avoid Soviet intervention. Neither explanation seems valid. For China is already engaging with the maximum power it can commit and the Soviet will not necessarily mesh its actions with our moves. Like a cobra, any new enemy will more likely strike whenever it feels that the relativity in military or other potential is in its favor on a world-wide basis.

The tragedy of Korea is further heightened by the fact that as military action is confined to its territorial limits, it condemns that nation, which it is our purpose to save, to suffer the devastating impact of full naval and air bombardment, while the enemy's sanctuaries are fully protected from such attack and devastation. Of the nations of the world, Korea alone, up to now, is the sole one which has risked its all against communism. The magnificence of the courage and fortitude of the Korean people defies description. They have chosen to risk death rather than slavery. Their last words to me were "Don't scuttle the Pacific."

I have just left your fighting sons in Korea. They have met all tests there and I can report to you without reservation they are splendid in every way. It was my constant effort to preserve them and end this savage conflict honorably and with the least loss of time and a minimum sacrifice of life. Its growing bloodshed has caused me the deepest anguish and anxiety. Those gallant men will remain often in my thoughts and in my prayers always.

VIEWPOINT 7

"Local defenses must be reinforced by the further deterrent of massive retaliatory power."

The U.S. Should Use Atomic Threats to Deter Communism

John Foster Dulles (1888-1959)

John Foster Dulles served as secretary of state under President Dwight Eisenhower from 1953 to 1959. Along with his brother Allen Dulles, Eisenhower's director of the Central Intelligence Agency, he played a key role in the Cold War in the 1950s.

The following viewpoint is taken from a controversial speech Dulles presented on January 12, 1954. The speech was excerpted in *American Foreign Policy, 1950-1955*. (Washington, DC: Department of State, 1957). Dulles criticized the Cold War policies of the previous (Truman) administration by arguing that they allowed America's foes, China and the Soviet Union, to hold the initiative for action and that they were too costly in both money and military reserves. Dulles proposed instead a greater reliance on America's nuclear weapons as threats against any development from China and the Soviet Union the United States deemed counter to its interests. By relying on such nuclear threats, Dulles argues, the United States can avoid being bogged down in land wars such as the one in Korea.

Dulles concludes with expressions of the moral superiority of freedom over communism and the belief that the ideals of freedom will ultimately undermine the communist powers.

It is now nearly a year since the Eisenhower Administration took office. During that year I have often spoken of various parts of our foreign policies. Tonight I should like to present an overall view of those policies which relate to our security.

First of all, let us recognize that many of the preceding foreign policies were good. Aid to Greece and Turkey had checked the Communist drive to the Mediterranean. The European Recovery Program had helped the peoples of Western Europe to pull out of the post-war morass. The Western powers were steadfast in Berlin and overcame the blockade with their airlift. As a loyal member of the United Nations, we had reached with force to repel the Communist attack in Korea. When that effort exposed our military weakness, we rebuilt rapidly our military establishment. We also sought a quick buildup of armed strength in Western Europe.

These were the acts of a nation which saw the danger of Soviet Communism; which realized that its own safety was tied up with that of others; which was capable of responding boldly and promptly to emergencies. These are precious values to be acclaimed. Also, we can pay tribute to Congressional bi-partisanship which puts the nation above politics.

Reflex Actions

But we need to recall that what we did was in the main emergency action, imposed on us by our enemies.

Let me illustrate.

1. We did not send our army into Korea because we judged, in advance, that it was sound military strategy to commit our army to fight land battles in Asia. Our decision had been to pull out of Korea. It was Soviet-inspired action that pulled us back.

2. We did not decide in advance that it was wise to grant billions annually as foreign economic aid. We adopted that policy in response to the Communist efforts to sabotage the free economies of Western Europe.

3. We did not build up our military establishment at a rate which involved huge budget deficits, a depreciating currency and a feverish economy, because this seemed, in advance, a good policy. Indeed, we decided otherwise until the Soviet military threat was clearly revealed.

We live in a world where emergencies are always possible and our survival may depend upon our capacity to meet emergencies. Let us pray that we shall always have that capacity. But, having said that, it is necessary also to say that emergency measures—however good for the emergency—do not necessarily make good permanent policies. Emergency measures are costly, they are superficial and they imply that the enemy has the initiative. They cannot be depended on to serve our long-time interests.

The United States Should Develop the Hydrogen Bomb

On January 13, 1950, the Joint Chiefs of Staff of the U.S. armed forces issued a top secret report to the Atomic Energy Commission, excerpted here. It advocated the development of the hydrogen bomb, a "super bomb" many times more powerful than the atomic weapons dropped on Hiroshima and Nagasaki. The report argued that this weapon could have a decisive impact as a retaliatory threat on the Soviet Union. The United States exploded its first hydrogen bomb in 1952; the Soviets developed them by 1953.

The Joint Chiefs of Staff realize that a balance between the defensive and the offensive aspects of warfare is essential if the United States is so to mobilize its strategic resources that it can develop its full capabilities against an enemy. The nature of modern war is such that defense alone cannot bring about a favorable decision. They believe that the truism, "the best defense is a good offense", is still valid. Hence, they are convinced that it is necessary to have within the arsenal of the United States a weapon of the greatest capability, in this case the super bomb. Such a weapon would improve our defense in its broadest sense, as a potential offensive weapon, a possible deterrent to war, a potential retaliatory weapon, as well as a defensive weapon against enemy forces.

This "long time" factor is of critical importance. The Soviet Communists are planning for what they call "an entire historical era," and we should do the same. They seek, through many types of maneuvers, gradually to divide and weaken the free nations by overextending them in efforts which, as Lenin put it, are "beyond their strength, so that they come to practical bankruptcy." Then, said Lenin, "our victory is assured." Then, said Stalin, will be "the moment for the decisive blow."

In the face of this strategy, measures cannot be judged adequate merely because they ward off an immediate danger. It is essential to do this, but it is also essential to do so without exhausting ourselves.

Changes Needed

When the Eisenhower Administration applied this test, we felt that some transformations were needed.

It is not sound military strategy permanently to commit U.S. land forces to Asia to a degree that leaves us no strategic reserves.

121

It is not sound economics, or good foreign policy, to support permanently other countries; for in the long run, that creates as much ill will as good will.

Also, it is not sound to become permanently committed to military expenditures so vast that they lead to "practical bankruptcy."

Change was imperative to assure the stamina needed for permanent security. But it was equally imperative that change should be accompanied by understanding of our true purposes. Sudden and spectacular change had to be avoided. Otherwise, there might have been a panic among our friends, and miscalculated aggression by our enemies. We can, I believe, make a good report in these respects.

We need allies and collective security. Our purpose is to make these relations more effective, less costly. This can be done by placing more reliance on deterrent power, and less dependence on local defensive power.

This is accepted practice so far as local communities are concerned. We keep locks on our doors; but we do not have an armed guard in every home. We rely principally on a community security system so well equipped to punish any who break in and steal that, in fact, would-be aggressors are generally deterred. That is the modern way of getting maximum protection at a bearable cost.

A Maximum Deterrent

What the Eisenhower Administration seeks is a similar international security system. We want, for ourselves and the other free nations, a maximum deterrent at a bearable cost.

Local defense will always be important. But there is no local defense which alone will contain the mighty land power of the Communist world. Local defenses must be reinforced by the further deterrent of massive retaliatory power. A potential aggressor must know that he cannot always prescribe battle conditions that suit him. Otherwise, for example, a potential aggressor, who is glutted with manpower, might be tempted to attack in confidence that resistance would be confined to manpower. He might be tempted to attack in places where his superiority was decisive.

The way to deter aggression is for the free community to be willing and able to respond vigorously at places and with means of its own choosing.

So long as our basic policy concepts were unclear, our military leaders could not be selective in building our military power. If an enemy could pick his time and place and method of warfare—and if our policy was to remain the traditional one of meeting aggression by direct and local opposition—then we needed to be ready to fight in the arctic and in the tropics; in Asia, the Near East and in Europe; by sea, by land and by air; with old weapons and with new weapons.

The total cost of our security efforts, at home and abroad, was over $50,000,000,000 per annum, and involved, for 1953, a projected budgetary deficit of $9,000,000,000; and $11,000,000,000 for 1954. This was on top of taxes comparable to war-time taxes; and the dollar was depreciating in effective value. Our allies were similarly weighed down. This could not be continued for long without grave budgetary, economic and social consequences.

But before military planning could be changed, the President and his advisers, as represented by the National Security Council, had to take some basic policy decisions. This has been done. The basic decision was to depend primarily upon a great capacity to retaliate, instantly, by means and at places of our choosing. Now the Department of Defense and the Joint Chiefs of Staff can shape our military establishment to fit what is our policy, instead of having to try to be ready to meet the enemy's many choices. That permits of a selection of military means instead of a multiplication of means. As a result, it is now possible to get, and share, more basic security at less cost. . . .

We do not, of course, claim to have found some magic formula that ensures against all forms of Communist successes. It is normal that at some times and at some places there may be setbacks to the cause of freedom. What we do expect to ensure is that any setbacks will have only temporary and local significance because they will leave unimpaired those free world assets which in the long run will prevail.

If we can deter such aggression as would mean general war, and that is our confident resolve, then we can let time and fundamentals work for us. We do not need self-imposed policies which sap our strength.

The fundamental, on our side, is the richness—spiritual, intellectual and material—that freedom can produce and the irresistible attraction it then sets up. That is why we do not plan ourselves to shackle freedom to preserve freedom. We intend that our conduct and example shall continue, as in the past, to show all men how good can be the fruits of freedom.

If we rely on freedom, then it follows that we must abstain from diplomatic moves which would seem to endorse captivity. That would, in effect, be a conspiracy against freedom. I can assure you that we shall never seek security for ourselves by such a "deal."

Negotiating with the USSR

We do negotiate about specific matters but only to advance the cause of human welfare.

President Eisenhower electrified the world with his proposal to lift a great weight of fear by turning atomic energy from a means of death into a source of life. Yesterday, I started procedural talks with the Soviet Government on that topic.

We have persisted, with our Allies, in seeking the unification of Germany and the liberation of Austria. Now the Soviet rulers have agreed to discuss these questions. We expect to meet them soon in Berlin. I hope they will come with a sincerity which will equal our own.

We have sought a conference to unify Korea and relieve it of foreign troops. So far, our persistence is unrewarded; but we have not given up.

These efforts at negotiation are normal initiatives that breathe the spirit of freedom. They involve no plan for a partnership division of world power with those who suppress freedom.

If we persist in the courses I outline we shall confront dictatorship with a task that is, in the long run, beyond its strength. For unless it changes, it must suppress the human desires that freedom satisfies—as we shall be demonstrating.

If the dictators persist in their present course then it is they who will be limited to superficial successes, while their foundation crumbles under the tread of their iron boots. . . .

We can be sure that there is going on, even within Russia, a silent test of strength between the powerful rulers and the multitudes of human beings. Each individual no doubt seems by himself to be helpless in this struggle. But their aspirations in the aggregate make up a mighty force.

There are signs that the rulers are bending to some of the human desires of their people. There are promises of more food, more household goods, more economic freedom.

That does not prove that the Soviet rulers have themselves been converted. It is rather that they may be dimly perceiving a basic fact, that is that there are limits to the power of any rulers indefinitely to suppress the human spirit.

In that God-given fact lies our greatest hope. It is a hope that can sustain us. For even if the path ahead be long and hard, it need not be a warlike path; and we can know that at the end may be found the blessedness of peace.

VIEWPOINT 8

"Atomic retaliation can only be an answer to open military aggression. . . . The crucial problem of national and social revolutions, that Moscow . . . exploits, Mr. Dulles fails to face."

The U.S. Should Not Use Atomic Threats to Deter Communism

Hans J. Morgenthau (1904-1980)

Hans J. Morgenthau was a professor of political science and director of the Center for the Study of American Foreign and Military Policy at the University of Chicago. He was a frequent commentator and critic on U.S. foreign policy. His many writings include *Politics Among Nations*, the standard textbook for many students of international relations.

In the following viewpoint Morgenthau criticizes the strategy of "instant retaliation" propounded by U.S. secretary of state John F. Dulles in a January 12, 1954, speech. Morgenthau questions whether threats of nuclear retaliation can be credible given the fact that the Soviet Union also possessed nuclear weapons. In addition, he argues that threats of retaliation would be of little use in responding to the many social and political revolutions then sweeping Asia, Africa, and other parts of the world, and that Dulles's policy may increase the chances of a nuclear war.

The "Instant Retaliation" speech of Secretary Dulles, delivered on January 12, [1954], was presented as a major redefinition of United States policy for the decade to come. Its importance, if not its meaning, was confirmed by the debate it has provoked. Lester Pearson has questioned it; Adlai Stevenson has criticized it; Vice President Nixon has defended it; Sir John Slessor has amplified it; Secretary Wilson has minimized it; Admiral Radford and his colleagues have set out to "explain" it and ended by explaining it away; President Eisenhower has stated that the new doctrine is not a new doctrine at all; Secretary Dulles has reaffirmed its newness in a somewhat more modest form.

Through the confusion of these conflicting statements certain clear lines of argument can be seen. Congress and our allies have asked who will decide on "instant retaliation" and have been assured that their "consent and acquiescence" is necessary. Army and Navy spokesmen have stressed that conventional weapons are still needed and this also is conceded. Objections have been advanced to the rigidity of the Dulles formula and in turn the Secretary of State acknowledges that its application in any given situation will turn on the facts. For all these modifications and qualifications, however, the doctrine itself has not been questioned by those in power. The January 12 speech stands in its essentials, as the expression of a major step by the National Security Council. It outlines a fundamental change that has taken place in United States strategy, and that is affirmed day by day, in important decisions such as those to eliminate three active Army divisions, to reduce naval personnel by 100,000 men, to extend the use of atomic weapons, and at the same time to warn our opponents that, in the event of new aggression in Korea, our counter-action will not stop short at that nation's Northern frontier.

With this in mind let us start over by re-examining the January 12 address, setting aside interpretations of Secretary Dulles' address by his colleagues, and assuming that he meant precisely what he said.

Five Points

Mr. Dulles makes essentially five points which serve as the keystones of the new policy.

First, "emergency action, imposed on us by our enemies" and exemplified by the Korean War and the Marshall Plan, must be replaced by a long-term plan which provides "a maximum deterrent at a bearable cost."

Second, we shall—and this is "the basic decision" made by the President and the National Security Council—"depend primarily

126

upon a great capacity to retaliate, instantly, by means and at places of our choosing."

Third, as a corollary to "placing more reliance on deterrent power," we shall depend less on "local defensive power."

Fourth, "broadly speaking, foreign budgetary aid is being limited to situations where it clearly contributes to military strength."

Fifth, "if we can deter such aggression as would mean general war . . . then we can let time and fundamentals work for us. . . . The fundamental, on our side, is the richness—spiritual, intellectual and material—that freedom can produce and the irresistible attraction it then sets up." Thus "we shall confront dictatorship with a task that is, in the long run, beyond its strength.". . .

U.S. Policies May Lead to World Destruction

Lewis Mumford was a noted writer, architect, and social critic. On March 28, 1954, he wrote a letter to the editor of the New York Times *commenting on the development of the hydrogen bomb and on the policies of the Eisenhower administration concerning nuclear weapons. He argues that those policies risk a nuclear war with worldwide destruction.*

There are many alternative courses to the policy to which we have committed ourselves, practically without debate. The worst of all these alternatives, submission to Communist totalitarianism, would still be far wiser than the final destruction of civilization.

As for the best of these alternatives, a policy of working firmly toward justice and cooperation, and free intercourse with all other peoples, in the faith that love begets love as surely as hatred begets hatred—would, in all probability, be the one instrument capable of piercing the strong political armor of our present enemies.

Once the facts of our policy of total extermination are publicly canvassed, and the final outcome, mass suicide, is faced, I believe that the American people are still sane enough to come to a wiser decision than our Government has yet made. They will realize that retaliation is not protection; that total extermination of both sides is not victory; that a constant state of morbid fear, suspicion and hatred is not security; that, in short, what seems like unlimited power has become impotence.

The new policy assumes that the threat to the US will take the form of open military aggression to be prevented by the threat, or answered by the reality, of atomic retaliation. With this assumption the new policy reverts to the pattern of the 40's when the American monopoly of the atomic bomb or at least of a stockpile of atomic bombs sufficient to wage successful atomic war stabilized the line of demarcation of 1945 between East and West. The virtual certainty that any step taken by the Soviet Union beyond that line would lead to the outbreak of a third world war, fought only by the US with atomic weapons, may have prevented such a step from being taken. It may seem trite, but in view of the somnambulistic quality of much official argumentation it is not superfluous, to point out that a policy of atomic retaliation is a sure deterrent only if the retaliatory power has a monopoly or at least a vast superiority in the retaliatory weapon. But what if the power to be retaliated against is in a position to retaliate against the retaliation or to make retaliation impossible by prevention?

Local Aggression

The new policy is intended in future to make local aggression, Korea-style, impossible; for no government in its senses will embark upon local aggression in the knowledge that its industrial and population centers will be reduced to rubble in retaliation. In other words, the policy of atomic retaliation, by the very fact of its announcement, removes the need for its implementation. However, this is not the end of the story. It is easy to imagine situations where local aggression will not be deterred by the threat of atomic retaliation but will be regarded by the aggressor nation of such vital importance to itself that it must be undertaken in spite of the risk of an atomic war. One can well imagine a situation arising in Central Europe which will induce the Soviet Union to take military measures which come under the heading of local aggression. . . .

The new policy shifts the emphasis from the conventional weapons to the new instruments of atomic power. By doing so, it recognizes what, at least in theory, has not always been recognized before, namely, that the United States has not the resources to oppose more than one local aggression at a time by local means. The United States would not have been able to fight two Korean Wars at the same time. By recognizing these limits of American strength, the new policy also recognizes that there may be local aggressions to which we have no answer at all, *e.g.* Indo-China, or against which our only answer is the atomic bomb. The shift from the traditional weapons of local defense to atomic weapons, then, on the one hand, limits our ability to meet local aggression by local means, as we did in Korea, and, on the other, increases the temptation to use the atomic bomb against local aggression where under the old strategy we might have used traditional weapons. In other words, the new policy tends to limit our choices. Formerly we could have met local aggression by doing nothing, by resisting it locally, or by striking at its source with atomic bombs. The new policy contracts the sphere within which the second alternative can operate. Confronted with a choice between doing nothing at all or dropping an atomic bomb, the new policy increases the incentive for doing the latter. In the words of William Graham Sumner, "For what we prepare for is what we shall get."

Third World Revolutions

Yet the chances that any of these contingencies will actually come to pass may well be small. For the immediate threat to the security of the West arises not from local aggression, Soviet inspired or otherwise, nor from atomic war deliberately embarked upon by the Soviet Union, but from the revolutionary fire which is sweeping through much of Asia, Africa, Western Europe and Latin America. Atomic retaliation can only be an answer to open military aggression. It stands to reason that to drop atomic bombs on Moscow or Peking is no answer to the threat of Communist revolution in Italy or Indo-China. The crucial problem of national and social revolutions, that Moscow did not create but which it exploits, Mr. Dulles fails to face. The generalities of freedom are offered, of course; it is the specifics of freedom that concern the nations whose futures are now in doubt. . . .

A Matter of Saving Money

Perhaps, however, the key to the new policy is to be sought not in such considerations of high political and military policy, but in the fact that in a speech of about 3,500 words there are no less than 15 references to the comparative cost of alternative policies and to the cheapness of the new one. Perhaps it is all a matter of saving money. Perhaps the *London Times* is right in saying: "It is indeed hard to see where and how the great strategic change has taken place, though it is not hard to recognize the economic reason why it has become politically desirable to assume that it has done so."

If the economic interpretation of the new policy is correct, and much in the recent statements of the President and of Mr. Dulles point to its correctness, it may again seem trite, but it is not superfluous, to remind the money savers that a Korean War, even one fought in perpetuity, is cheaper in every respect than an atomic war.

CHAPTER 3

Coexistence and Conflict

Chapter Preface

Much as Dwight Eisenhower had done eight years before, John F. Kennedy succeeded in capturing the presidency in 1960 by attacking the incumbent administration for failing to lead the United States toward victory in the Cold War. He attacked Eisenhower's resistance against increased U.S. defense spending. He argued that the United States needed a better response to the proliferation of new nations breaking away from European colonial empires, especially given Soviet leader Nikita Khrushchev's announced intent of supporting "wars of liberation" in the Third World. He capitalized on American fears dating from the 1957 Soviet launching of the Sputnik space satellite by arguing that a dangerous "missile gap" between the Soviet Union and the United States threatened U.S. security. (No such gap existed, as Kennedy found out when he attained office.) Kennedy's 1961 inaugural address promised that America would "bear any burden, . . . oppose any foe to assure the survival and success of liberty."

However, events in two countries were soon to have profound effects on the debate over the Cold War. The two countries that so affected the United States were Cuba and Vietnam.

In 1959, Cuba, an island nation ninety miles south of Florida, had become the only communist state and Soviet ally in the Western Hemisphere. The United States, under the leadership of both Eisenhower and his successor, John Kennedy, tried to repeat the successes of covert intervention in Guatemala and Iran by training Cuban exiles in a plan to invade Cuba. In April 1961, about fifteen hundred Cuban exiles armed and trained by the United States in Guatemala carried out an amphibious assault at the Bay of Pigs. The operation failed miserably and many nations around the world condemned the United States for supporting it.

In October 1962, a U.S. spy plane discovered Soviet missile bases under construction in Cuba. President Kennedy demanded withdrawal of Soviet missiles and ordered a naval blockade of Cuba. For the next few days, until Soviet premier Khrushchev agreed to withdraw the Soviet missiles, the two superpowers teetered on the brink of a nuclear war. Khrushchev's decision to back down reflected U.S. superiority in military and nuclear force and probably led to his ouster as Soviet leader in 1964.

The Cuban missile crisis had sobering effects on both adversaries in the Cold War and led to renewed efforts at negotiations. In October 1963, the two countries signed the Nuclear Test Ban Treaty. However, the Soviet Union simultaneously began a large military buildup to prevent being in an inferior position in the event of a future confrontation with the United States.

While direct U.S.-Soviet conflict faded into the background, the United States became increasingly embroiled in a debate over Vietnam, a former French colony whose independence movement was led by communist nationalist leader Ho Chi Minh. Following French defeat in 1954 the country was divided into North Vietnam under communist leadership and South Vietnam under an anticommunist regime supported by the United States. Concerned that Vietnam would become wholly communist and would precipitate a "domino effect," spreading communism throughout the region, the United States under presidents Eisenhower and Kennedy sought to contain communism in Southeast Asia much as it had previously attempted to contain communism in Europe. U.S. involvement gradually escalated until, by the time Kennedy was assassinated in November 1963, more than sixteen thousand Americans were advising and assisting the South Vietnamese in their civil war with North Vietnam.

Kennedy's successor, Lyndon Johnson, greatly increased U.S. involvement in Vietnam. At its peak, over a half-million soldiers were deployed in that conflict. However, as the war dragged on with no end in sight, an increasing number of Americans questioned America's role and further questioned the Cold War precepts that guided it. Former diplomats such as George Kennan asserted that Vietnam was of little importance to America's security. Arkansas senator J. William Fulbright argued that America could not win against the nationalistic Vietnamese communists. Radical antiwar activists went further in questioning the whole basis of the Cold War. They argued that U.S. motivation was not to contain communism, but to increase the power of the United States over the Third World. Historian Robert Kelley writes:

> What, then, were the real reasons why America was in Vietnam? Not for noble purposes, said the antiwar activists, but because a war was what America's military-industrial complex wanted. . . . The United States had sent a huge army, navy, and air force to wage war in Vietnam, such people insisted, because of a corruption deep within American society itself . . . spawned by the domination of powerful corporations whose aim was to exploit the whole world.

In Vietnam, America reached the limits of its global anticommunist policy. Vietnam was largely responsible for the withdrawal of Lyndon Johnson from the 1968 presidential race and for the eventual victory of Richard Nixon. Nixon's inaugural address, in which he spoke of a country divided, tired of war, and having a "crisis of the spirit" was far different in tone than the proud message delivered by John F. Kennedy eight years earlier.

VIEWPOINT 1

"Both the United States . . . and the Soviet Union . . . have a mutually deep interest in a just and genuine peace and in halting the arms race."

The U.S. Should Seek Peaceful Coexistence with the Soviet Union

John F. Kennedy (1917-1963)

John F. Kennedy was president of the United States from 1961 to 1963. His presidency was dominated by U.S.-Soviet relations, including perhaps the most tense incident of the Cold War—the Cuban missile crisis.

In October 1962, the United States discovered Soviet missile sites in Cuba, an island nation ninety miles off the Florida coast which had undergone a communist revolution in 1959 and had aligned itself with the Soviet Union. Kennedy imposed a naval blockade and demanded withdrawal of the missiles. For six tense days the world teetered on the brink of nuclear war. The crisis ended as suddenly as it began when Soviet leader Nikita Khrushchev backed down and agreed to withdraw the missiles in exchange for a U.S. pledge of nonintervention in Cuba, a proposal to which Kennedy agreed.

The following viewpoint is taken from a commencement address Kennedy gave at American University on June 10, 1963, about half a year after the crisis. It is taken from the July 1, 1963 issue of the *Department of State Bulletin*. Historian Henry Steele Commager writes:

Both the USSR and the United States emerged somewhat sobered and chastened from the near-disaster of the Cuban missile crisis. In the spring of 1963, they initiated a series of quiet diplomatic conversations about disarmament and the general reduction of tensions; and whereas in the past disarmament negotiations had always degenerated into propaganda contests, this time both sides showed a serious interest in reducing the risk of nuclear confrontation like the one which they had so recently passed. Kennedy's commencement address at American University gave public notice that he had been reconsidering the whole question of Soviet-American relations and had come to the conclusion that it was time, in effect, to liquidate the Cold War in Europe. . . . For the first time, it became politically respectable to discuss foreign affairs without resorting automatically to the rhetoric of the Cold War.

The nuclear negotiations Kennedy mentions in his address culminated in the successful ratification of the Nuclear Test Ban Treaty in September 1963, two months before Kennedy was assassinated.

"There are few earthly things more beautiful than a University," wrote John Masefield, in his tribute to the English universities—and his words are equally true here. He did not refer to spires and towers, to campus greens and ivied walls. He admired the splendid beauty of the university, he said, because it was "a place where those who hate ignorance may strive to know, where those who perceive truth may strive to make others see."

I have, therefore, chosen this time and this place to discuss a topic on which ignorance too often abounds and the truth is too rarely perceived—yet it is the most important topic on earth: world peace.

What kind of peace do I mean? What kind of peace do we seek? Not a Pax Americana enforced on the world by American weapons of war. Not the peace of the grave or the security of the slave. I am talking about genuine peace, the kind of peace that makes life on earth worth living, the kind that enables men and nations to grow and to hope and to build a better life for their children—not merely peace for Americans but peace for all men and women, not merely peace in our time but peace for all time.

I speak of peace because of the new face of war. Total war makes no sense in an age when great powers can maintain large and relatively invulnerable nuclear forces and refuse to surrender without resort to those forces. It makes no sense in an age when a single nuclear weapon contains almost 10 times the explosive force delivered by all of the Allied air forces in the Second World War. It makes no sense in an age when the deadly poisons produced by a nuclear exchange would be carried by the wind and water and soil and seed to the far corners of the globe and to generations yet unborn.

The Military-Industrial Complex

On January 17, 1961, three days before he left office, President Dwight D. Eisenhower delivered his farewell address to the nation. While noting that the United States must keep its defenses strong, Eisenhower warned that the Cold War defense buildup had strengthened the nation's armed forces and defense industries enough for them to form a powerful "military-industrial complex." This rise of a national security establishment, he noted, could endanger the American way of life as much as any outside threat.

Until the latest of our world conflicts, the United States had no armaments industry. American makers of plowshares could, with time and as required, make swords as well. But now we can no longer risk emergency improvisation of national defense; we have been compelled to create a permanent armaments industry of vast proportions. Added to this, three and a half million men and women are directly engaged in the defense establishment. We annually spend on military security more than the net income of all United States corporations.

This conjunction of an immense military establishment and a large arms industry is new in the American experience. The total influence—economic, political, even spiritual—is felt in every city, every statehouse, every office of the federal government. We recognize the imperative need for this development. Yet we must not fail to comprehend its grave implications. Our toil, resources, and livelihood are all involved; so is the very structure of our society.

In the councils of government, we must guard against the acquisition of unwarranted influence, whether sought or unsought, by the military-industrial complex. The potential for the disastrous rise of misplaced power exists and will persist.

Today the expenditure of billions of dollars every year on weapons acquired for the purpose of making sure we never need to use them is essential to keeping the peace. But surely the acquisition of such idle stockpiles—which can only destroy and never create—is not the only, much less the most efficient, means of assuring peace.

I speak of peace, therefore, as the necessary rational end of rational men. I realize that the pursuit of peace is not as dramatic as the pursuit of war, and frequently the words of the pursuer fall on deaf ears. But we have no more urgent task.

Some say that it is useless to speak of world peace or world law or world disarmament—and that it will be useless until the leaders of the Soviet Union adopt a more enlightened attitude. I hope they do. I believe we can help them do it. But I also believe that we must reexamine our own attitude, as individuals and as a nation, for our attitude is as essential as theirs. And every graduate of this school, every thoughtful citizen who despairs of war and wishes to bring peace, should begin by looking inward—by examining his own attitude toward the possibilities of peace, toward the Soviet Union, toward the course of the cold war, and toward freedom and peace here at home.

The Possibilities of Peace

First: Let us examine our attitude toward peace itself. Too many of us think it is impossible. Too many think it unreal. But that is a dangerous, defeatist belief. It leads to the conclusion that war is inevitable, that mankind is doomed, that we are gripped by forces we cannot control.

We need not accept that view. Our problems are manmade; therefore they can be solved by man. And man can be as big as he wants. No problem of human destiny is beyond human beings. Man's reason and spirit have often solved the seemingly unsolvable, and we believe they can do it again.

I am not referring to the absolute, infinite concept of universal peace and good will of which some fantasies and fanatics dream. I do not deny the values of hopes and dreams, but we merely invite discouragement and incredulity by making that our only and immediate goal.

Let us focus instead on a more practical, more attainable peace, based not on a sudden revolution in human nature but on a gradual evolution in human institutions—on a series of concrete actions and effective agreements which are in the interest of all concerned. There is no single, simple key to this peace, no grand or magic formula to be adopted by one or two powers. Genuine peace must be the product of many nations, the sum of many acts. It must be dynamic, not static, changing to meet the challenge of each new generation. For peace is a process, a way of solving problems.

With such a peace there will still be quarrels and conflicting interests, as there are within families and nations. World peace, like community peace, does not require that each man love his neighbor; it requires only that they live together in mutual tolerance, submitting their disputes to a just and peaceful settlement. And history teaches us that enmities between nations, as between individuals, do not last forever. However fixed our likes and dislikes may seem, the tide of time and events will often bring surprising changes in the relations between nations and neighbors.

136

So let us persevere. Peace need not be impracticable, and war need not be inevitable. By defining our goal more clearly, by making it seem more manageable and less remote, we can help all peoples to see it, to draw hope from it, and to move irresistibly toward it.

Common Interests with the Soviet Union

Second: Let us reexamine our attitude toward the Soviet Union. It is discouraging to think that their leaders may actually believe what their propagandists write. It is discouraging to read a recent authoritative Soviet text on military strategy and find, on page after page, wholly baseless and incredible claims—such as the allegation that "American imperialist circles are preparing to unleash different types of wars . . . that there is a very real threat of a preventative war being unleashed by American imperialists against the Soviet Union . . . [and that] the political aims of the American imperialists are to enslave economically and politically the European and other capitalist countries . . . [and] to achieve world domination . . . by means of aggressive wars."

Truly as it was written long ago: "The wicked flee when no man pursueth." Yet it is sad to read these Soviet statements—to realize the extent of the gulf between us. But it is also a warning—a warning to the American people not to fall into the same trap as the Soviets, not to see only a distorted and desperate view of the other side, not to see conflict as inevitable, accommodation as impossible, and communication as nothing more than an exchange of threats.

No government or social system is so evil that its people must be considered as lacking in virtue. As Americans we find communism profoundly repugnant as a negation of personal freedom and dignity. But we can still hail the Russian people for their many achievements—in science and space, in economic and industrial growth, in culture and in acts of courage.

Among the many traits the peoples of our two countries have in common, none is stronger than our mutual abhorrence of war. Almost unique among the major world powers, we have never been at war with each other. And no nation in the history of battle ever suffered more than the Soviet Union suffered in the course of the Second World War. At least 20 million lost their lives. Countless millions of homes and farms were burned or sacked. A third of the nation's territory, including nearly two-thirds of its industrial base, was turned into a wasteland—a loss equivalent to the devastation of this country east of Chicago.

Today, should total war ever break out again—no matter how—our two countries would become the primary targets. It is an ironical but accurate fact that the two strongest powers are the two in the most danger of devastation. All we have built, all we have worked for, would be destroyed in the first 24 hours. And even in the cold war, which brings burdens and dangers to so many countries—including this nation's closest allies—our two countries bear the heaviest burdens. For we are both devoting massive sums of money to weapons that could be better devoted to combating ignorance, poverty, and disease. We are both caught up in a vicious and dangerous cycle in which suspicion on one side breeds suspicion on the other and new weapons beget counterweapons.

In short, both the United States and its allies, and the Soviet Union and its allies, have a mutually deep interest in a just and genuine peace and in halting the arms race. Agreements to this end are in the interests of the Soviet Union as well as ours, and even the most hostile nations can be relied upon to accept and keep those treaty obligations, and only those treaty obligations, which are in their own interest.

So let us not be blind to our differences, but let us also direct attention to our common interests and to the means by which those differences can be resolved. And if we cannot end now our differences, at least we can help make the world safe for diversity. For in the final analysis our most basic common link is that we all inhabit this planet. We all breathe the same air. We all cherish our children's future. And we are all mortal.

The Pursuit of Peace

Third: Let us reexamine our attitude toward the cold war, remembering that we are not engaged in a debate, seeking to pile up debating points. We are not here distributing blame or pointing the finger of judgment. We must deal with the world as it is and not as it might have been had the history of the last 18 years been different.

We must, therefore, persevere in the search for peace in the hope that constructive changes within the Communist bloc might bring within reach solutions which now seem beyond us. We must conduct our affairs in such a way that it becomes in the Communists' interest to agree on a genuine peace. Above all, while defending our own vital interests, nuclear powers must avert those confrontations which bring an adversary to a choice of either a humiliating retreat or a nuclear war. To adopt that kind of course in the nuclear age would be evidence only of the bankruptcy of our policy—or of a collective death wish for the world.

To secure these ends, America's weapons are nonprovocative, carefully controlled, designed to deter, and capable of selective use. Our military forces are committed to peace and disciplined in self-restraint. Our diplomats are instructed to avoid unneces-

Soviet premier Nikita S. Khrushchev and U.S. president John F. Kennedy meet in Vienna, Austria, on June 4, 1961. Tense and confrontational, the meetings were followed by military buildups in both countries.

sary irritants and purely rhetorical hostility.

For we can seek a relaxation of tensions without relaxing our guard. And, for our part, we do not need to use threats to prove that we are resolute. We do not need to jam foreign broadcasts out of fear our faith will be eroded. We are unwilling to impose our system on any unwilling people, but we are willing and able to engage in peaceful competition with any people on earth.

Meanwhile we seek to strengthen the United Nations, to help solve its financial problems, to make it a more effective instrument of peace, to develop it into a genuine world security system—a system capable of resolving disputes on the basis of law, of insuring the security of the large and the small, and of creating conditions under which arms can finally be abolished.

At the same time we seek to keep peace inside the non-Communist world, where many nations, all of them our friends, are divided over issues which weaken Western unity, which invite Communist intervention, or which threaten to erupt into war.

Our efforts in West New Guinea, in the Congo, in the Middle East, and in the Indian subcontinent have been persistent and patient despite criticism from both sides. We have also tried to set an example for others—by seeking to adjust small but significant differences with our own closest neighbors in Mexico and in Canada.

Alliances

Speaking of other nations, I wish to make one point clear. We are bound to many nations by alliances. Those alliances exist because our concern and theirs substantially overlap. Our commitment to defend Western Europe and West Berlin, for example, stands undiminished because of the identity of our vital interests. The United States will make no deal with the Soviet Union at the expense of other nations and other peoples, not merely because they are our partners but also because their interests and ours converge.

Our interests converge, however, not only in defending the frontiers of freedom but in pursuing the paths of peace. It is our hope—and the purpose of Allied policies—to convince the Soviet Union that she, too, should let each nation choose its own future, so long as that choice does not interfere with the choices of others. The Communist drive to impose their political and economic system on others is the primary cause of world tension today. For there can be no doubt that, if all nations could refrain from interfering in the self-determination of others, the peace would be much more assured.

This will require a new effort to achieve world law, a new context for world discussions. It will require increased understanding between the Soviets and ourselves. And increased understanding will require increased contact and communication. One step in this direction is the proposed arrangement for a direct line between Moscow and Washington, to avoid on each side the dangerous delays, misunderstandings, and misreadings of the other's actions which might occur at a time of crisis.

We have also been talking in Geneva about other first-step measures of arms control, designed to limit the intensity of the arms race and to reduce the risks of accidental war. Our primary long-range interest in Geneva, however, is general and complete disarmament, designed to take place by stages, permitting parallel political developments to build the new institutions of peace which would take the place of arms. The pursuit of disarmament has been an effort of this Government since the 1920's. It has been urgently sought by the past three administrations. And however dim the prospects may be today, we intend to continue this effort—to continue it in order that all countries, including our own, can better grasp what the problems and possibilities of disarmament are.

The one major area of these negotiations where the end is in sight, yet where a fresh start is badly needed, is in a treaty to outlaw nuclear tests. The conclusion of such a treaty—so near and yet so far—would check the spiraling arms race in one of its most dangerous areas. It would place the nuclear powers in a position to deal more effectively with one of the greatest hazards which man faces in 1963, the further spread of nuclear arms. It would increase our security; it would decrease the prospects of war. Surely this goal is sufficiently important to require our steady pursuit, yielding neither to the temptation to give up the whole effort nor the temptation to give up our insistence on vital and responsible safeguards.

Two Decisions

I am taking this opportunity, therefore, to announce two important decisions in this regard.

First: Chairman Khrushchev, Prime Minister Macmillan, and I have agreed that high-level discussions will shortly begin in Moscow looking toward early agreement on a comprehensive test ban treaty. Our hopes must be tempered with the caution of history, but with our hopes go the hopes of all mankind.

Second: To make clear our good faith and solemn convictions on the matter, I now declare that the United States does not propose to conduct nuclear tests in the atmosphere so long as other states do not do so. We will not be the first to resume. Such a declaration is no substitute for a formal binding treaty, but I hope it will help us achieve one. Nor would such a treaty be a substitute for disarmament, but I hope it will help us achieve it. . . .

The United States, as the world knows, will never start a war. We do not want a war. We do not now expect a war. This generation of Americans has already had enough—more than enough—of war and hate and oppression. We shall be prepared if others wish it. We shall be alert to try to stop it. But we shall also do our part to build a world of peace where the weak are safe and the strong are just. We are not helpless before that task or hopeless of its success. Confident and unafraid, we labor on—not toward a strategy of annihilation but toward a strategy of peace.

VIEWPOINT 2

"It is clear that when Communists employ the language of 'peace,' they do so to mask their true strategic purpose: the isolation, encirclement, weakening, and final destruction of the free world and its way of life."

The U.S. Should Not Seek Peaceful Coexistence with the Soviet Union

Richard V. Allen (1936-)

The dynamics of U.S.-Soviet relations changed when longtime Soviet dictator Joseph Stalin died. His eventual replacement, Nikita Khrushchev, attacked many of Stalin's policies and sought reforms in both domestic and foreign policy. One of the points he stressed in many speeches was the necessity of "peaceful coexistence" with the United States, especially since war between the two nations threatened nuclear destruction on a gigantic scale. In a 1959 speech to the USSR Supreme Soviet Khrushchev stated:

> With the present balance of forces on the world scene, with the level attained by military technology, no one except those who are entirely out of touch with reality can suggest any other road of development of relations between states with different social systems than the road of peaceful coexistence. . . .
>
> Capitalists do not approve of the socialist social system. Our ideology, our world outlook, are alien to them. We citizens of

the socialist states equally disapprove of the capitalist order and the bourgeois ideology. But we must live peacefully, resolving international problems that arise by peaceful means only. Hence the need for reciprocal concessions.

Opinions within the United States differed as to whether "peaceful coexistence" could be a first step toward the end of the Cold War or whether it was merely a tactic designed to keep the United States and its allies off their guard. Among the people that took the latter view was Richard V. Allen, who in 1964 wrote *Peaceful Coexistence: A Communist Blueprint for Victory*, excerpted here. Allen notes that the Soviet Union maintained its belief in the inevitability of worldwide communist revolution, and that it was providing support to insurgent revolutions in Asia, Africa, and Latin America. He concludes that the United States should be wary of peaceful overtures from the Soviet Union and that communism remains a serious threat to the United States. At the time of this writing Allen was an analyst for the Center for Strategic Studies at Georgetown University. He later served as a presidential assistant to Richard Nixon and as national security adviser to President Ronald Reagan in 1981-82.

Traditionally, Communists have always given the greatest care to defining carefully the strategic course of action to be followed over a given period of time. Tactics may vary within the period of time in which the strategy operates, but the latter will remain constant until officially changed and until that change has been proclaimed to the world movement. . . .

Strategy or Tactic?

Is "peaceful coexistence" a strategy or a tactic?

> The Marxist-Leninists do not understand the policy of peaceful coexistence as a tactical maneuver designed for some limited span of time, but as the strategic line designed for the whole period of the transition from capitalism to socialism on a world scale.
>
> (*Pravda*, December 6, 1963)

Peaceful coexistence is therefore the strategy which will carry forth the Communist revolution to the final overthrow of the free world and the establishment of worldwide Communist rule. To take it as something less important than the "strategic line," or to dismiss it as a "semantic phrase" would be to ignore the fundamental statement of the plan to accomplish the final phase of the attack against the non-Communist world.

"See How Many are Staying on Our Side."

BERLIN WALL
ERECTED
AUG. 13, 1961

As the principle "strategic line" of the majority of the Communist movement, peaceful coexistence is quite young. It received its initial, cautious formulation and blessing by Khrushchev at the Twentieth Party Congress in 1956, but escaped widespread attention in the West because of the sensational nature of the "de-Stalinization" pronouncements made at that time. It was Stalin, however, who first affirmed that "coexistence" was a temporary possibility designed to buy time. Speaking at the Fifteenth Congress of the Communist Party of the Soviet Union in 1927, he said that

> The period of "peaceful coexistence" is receding into the past, giving way to a period of imperialist attacks. . . . Hence our task is to pay attention to contradictions in the capitalist camp, to delay war by "buying off" the capitalists and to take all measures to maintain peaceful relations. . . . Our relations with the capitalist countries are based on the assumption that the coexistence of the two opposing systems is possible. Practice has fully confirmed this.

Still earlier references to coexistence may be found in Trotsky and Lenin, but until recent years it has been a descriptive slogan; i.e., it described a condition to which, however unfortunate for the Communists, they had to adapt.

Under conditions of obvious inferiority to the "capitalist world," until 1956 the Communists described their position as one of "capitalist encirclement." The major task under those conditions, according to Stalin, was to strike incessantly at the "weakest link" of the capitalist chain in an effort to break out of the "encirclement." At the Twentieth Party Congress the declaration was made that the chain had been broken, and that the worldwide revolution had begun to enter the final phase of human history, the "transition from capitalism to socialism on a worldwide scale." It is in this phase that the Communists relinquish the defensive position assumed under the previous conditions of peaceful coexistence, and go over to the strategic offensive under a new and enriched kind of peaceful coexistence.

While the phraseology has undergone no change—i.e., "peaceful coexistence" is still used to describe Communist policy objectives—the content of the slogan has changed radically to accommodate the new period of the offensive. Thus it is that the period of peaceful coexistence contains such nonpeaceful events as the construction of the Berlin Wall and the Cuban missile buildup.

A Form of Class Struggle

As to its specific content Nikita Khrushchev has said that

> the policy of peaceful coexistence, as regards its social content, is a form of intense economic, political, and ideological struggle of the proletariat against the aggressive forces of imperialism in the international arena.

From this definition, it would appear that peaceful coexistence, inasmuch as it prescribes "intense struggle," does not accord with the meaning of the word "peaceful." But the *Statement of the 81 Communist and Workers Parties* of December 1960, a major policy declaration, goes into greater detail:

> The policy of peaceful coexistence is a policy of mobilizing the masses and launching vigorous action against the enemies of

peace. Peaceful coexistence of states does not imply renunciation of the class struggle. . . . The coexistence of states with different social systems is a form of class struggle between socialism and capitalism. In conditions of peaceful coexistence favorable opportunities are provided for the development of the
class struggle in the capitalist countries and the national-liberation movement of the peoples of the colonial and dependent
countries. In their turn, the successes of the revolutionary class
and national-liberation struggle promote peaceful coexistence.
The Communists consider it their duty to fortify the faith of the
people in the possibility of furthering peaceful coexistence, their
determination to prevent world war. They will do their utmost
for the people to weaken imperialism and limit its sphere of action by an active struggle for peace, democracy, and national
liberation.

It should be noted that Communists consider peaceful coexistence and the "national liberation movement," the revolutionary
movement in the underdeveloped countries, to be mutually rein-
forcing. The principal impact of this mutual reinforcement is the
ability to "limit the sphere of action" of "imperialism." Accurately translated, this means that the successes of the Communists can be turned into an advantage by restricting the freedom
of action of the Western countries, chiefly the United States. . . .

It is fairly safe to assume that the Communists do not desire a
general war at this time. They fully realize that whatever benefits
would accrue to them as the result of a war would be outweighed
by the damage which they would suffer. Khrushchev, speaking
on August 19, 1963, stressed that "we Communists want to win
this struggle with the least losses."

However, it is quite a different matter to assume that, because
the Communists do not view war as a realistic instrument of policy at the present time, they will never employ it. It is also necessary to point out that the Communists have differentiated between the various types of wars, and have clearly delineated
those which *are* acceptable and are to be *encouraged and assisted.* . . .

Communists Seek Victory

While it has become fashionable in the West to speak of "victory" in the cold war as "meaningless," the Communists persist
in employing it as an official goal. Needless to say, they have a
very real appreciation that "victory" by means of nuclear war
would very probably be a victory in the true sense for no one; but
to exclude a single method of achieving victory as an unrealistic
instrument of policy does not signify that the entire concept of
victory has been relinquished.

That Communists envision a genuine "victory" is demonstrated by the remarks of Khrushchev in July 1963 following the signing of the Nuclear Test Ban Treaty:

> Today the imperialists pretend to be brave, but only in words, whereas in reality they tremble before the world of growing and strengthening socialism. And let them tremble. So much the better for us.
>
> If everyone acted and thought in the Communist way then there would be no antagonistic classes and Communism would already be victorious everywhere. However, while there are still two systems, socialist and capitalist, each system has its own policy, its own course, and we cannot but take into account the fact that two systems exist. *A fight is in progress between these two systems, a life and death combat. But we Communists want to win this struggle with the least losses and there is no doubt whatsoever that we shall win.*

The recognition that two systems do *in fact* exist in the same world is given only grudgingly; and because there does exist in the world an alternative system to that of the Communists, the contest between them assumes, in Khrushchev's own words, the form of "a life and death combat." Peaceful coexistence fulfills the Communist objectives in this mortal combat by "insuring" that victory is accomplished with minimal losses.

Soviet Strategy

Many observers were skeptical of Soviet proclamations of peaceful co-existence. In 1961 the Foreign Policy Research Institute at the University of Pennsylvania prepared a report for the U.S. Senate analyzing Soviet foreign policy and concluding that the Soviet Union still posed a threat to the United States.

Over the course of the last four decades, the Soviet leadership has refined its techniques of rule and developed a flexible approach to international power politics, but it has not shown the slightest inclination to relax its pressure on the free world as the power of the Communist camp has grown. On the contrary, each improvement in the Soviet position has been the signal for increased pressure on the non-Communist world in one form or another. . . .

Seen in this light, peaceful coexistence is the key to a strategy intended to remove the remaining—and still formidable—obstacles to Communist victory and security.

It follows from this statement that the Communists are prepared to accept some losses in propelling the revolution forward, but nowhere is it made clear just what these losses could entail. Despite the possibility of such setbacks, however, Khrushchev emphasizes the certainty of triumph.

The specific function of peaceful coexistence is not, as we have found, the establishment of a mere period of relative calm on a worldwide scale. Rather, it is to provide conditions favorable for waging a many-pronged offensive at and within the non-Communist world. Above all, it creates a degree of flexibility hitherto unknown to the Communist movement, inasmuch as it allows for harnessing and utilizing the most disparate forces to the revolutionary cause. . . .

The Challenge to the West

Faced with such a real and formidable opponent, the West must clarify and reaffirm the goals which it has so long sought to achieve. And if a just and lasting peace is foremost among those goals, then it will have to keep sight of that goal while steeling itself to meet even greater threats than those experienced in the past.

There can be little doubt about the goals which the Communists have set for themselves; they have been forthrightly stated on these pages by the Communists themselves, and were summarized by Khrushchev:

> Capitalism . . . wants to bury the Socialist system and we want—not only want but have dug—quite a deep hole, and shall exert efforts to dig this hole deeper and bury the capitalist system forever.

Whether there will continue to be room on the earth for the opposing systems of capitalism and Communism is a question which history alone will answer. For our part, we are willing to examine serious proposals for peace at any time; but "peace" on the basis of the Communist doctrine of "peaceful coexistence" is clearly an impossibility.

There is, however, a very real danger to the free world should it fail to judge accurately the intentions of the Communists. After some eight years of peaceful coexistence as the principal strategic line of the international Communist movement, we have no evidence that it seeks genuine peace with the rest of the world. Above all, it is clear that the Communists have not given up their long-range goal of world domination, and in the final analysis we must judge their motivations according to that goal. An intervening period of "peace" and relaxation, regardless of how inviting it may seem, must not be allowed to lower the guard of the free world.

End of the Cold War?

It is clear that when Communists employ the language of "peace," they do so to mask their true strategic purpose: the isolation, encirclement, weakening, and final destruction of the free world and its way of life. The cold war has not concluded, but has entered a new and still more complex phase in which the spectrum of psychological, political, economic, and class warfare will be radically expanded. Such classic techniques as subversion, espionage, propaganda, sabotage, terrorism, deceit, and incited disorder will remain and be refined; but the new techniques of nuclear blackmail are also to be employed whenever feasible. It would be totally unrealistic to hold, as some do, that nuclear weapons have only a military purpose. Long ago the Soviet Union appreciated fully the political purposes of these enormously destructive modern weapons, and their early decisions to invest huge sums of money and manpower into their development indicates their willingness to attain real supremacy over the West.

During the period of peaceful coexistence, the Communists also hope to reap the benefits of a worldwide "détente," i.e., a relaxation of tensions. Under such conditions they would hope not only to gain through an American and Western slowdown in armaments, but also to subvert and paralyze hostile governments in the hope that at the critical moment such governments will capitulate or will be incapable of offering effective resistance.

The great paradox of our time may well turn out to be our inability to recognize that the cold war has in reality become more intense despite the increasing appearances of peace. It need not be emphasized that the overwhelming sentiment of the free world is to live in peace. But to mistake the illusion of peace for genuine peace would be a profoundly dangerous, perhaps fatal mistake.

Our purpose in this great struggle imposed upon us by the Communist world is, as our Presidents and statesmen have repeatedly stressed, the victory of our way of life. If the clash between the two systems is, as the Communists never tire of stating, irreconcilable, then our victory will not be achieved until freedom and justice prevail everywhere in the world.

VIEWPOINT 3

"I believe the first step is for the President of the United States to declare officially that it is our purpose to win the cold war, not merely wage it in the hope of attaining a standoff."

The U.S. Should Aim for Total Victory in the Cold War

Barry Goldwater (1909-)

Barry Goldwater served for many years as Republican senator from Arizona and was the Republican nominee for president in 1964. He was well-known for his strongly conservative views, and his books *The Conscience of a Conservative* and *Why Not Victory* sold millions of copies.

In the following viewpoint, taken from remarks Goldwater made in Congress on July 14, 1961, a few months after John F. Kennedy was inaugurated as president of the United States, Goldwater offers a conservative critique of U.S. policy toward the Soviet Union. He argues that the U.S. policy has been marked by vacillation, and that America should aim for nothing less than total victory in the Cold War.

Goldwater's views as expressed here helped him to win the 1964 Republican presidential nomination. During the general election campaign, however, his opponent, Lyndon B. Johnson, sought to portray Goldwater as an extremist who would lead the

United States into a nuclear war. Johnson won a decisive victory. Goldwater returned to the Senate in 1968 and remained there until his retirement in 1986.

Mr. President, I should like to see us get on the right track, once and for all, in our approach to foreign policy matters. And I believe the first step is for the President of the United States to declare officially that it is our purpose to win the cold war, not merely wage it in the hope of attaining a standoff. Further, I would like to see the chairman of the Senate Foreign Relations Committee [J. William Fulbright] urge this action on the President, and back him to the hilt if he agrees.

Mr. President, it is really astounding that our Government has never stated its purpose to be that of complete victory over the tyrannical forces of international communism. I am sure that the American people cannot understand why we spend billions upon billions of dollars to engage in a struggle of world-wide proportions unless we have a clearly defined purpose to achieve victory. Anything less than victory, over the long run, can only be defeat, degradation, and slavery. Are not these stakes high enough for us? Is not this reason enough for us to fight to win?

Official Timidity

I suggest that our failure to declare total victory as our fundamental purpose is a measure of an official timidity that refuses to recognize the all-embracing determination of communism to capture the world and destroy the United States. This timidity has sold us short, time and time again. It denied us victory in the Korean war, when victory was there for the taking. It refused General [Douglas] MacArthur the right to prosecute a war for the purpose of winning, and caused him to utter these prophetic words:

> The best that might be said for the policy-makers responsible for these monumental blunders is that they did not comprehend the truism, as old as history itself, that a great nation which voluntarily enters upon war and does not fight it through to victory must ultimately accept all of the consequences of defeat—that in war, there is no substitute for victory.

Mr. President, we would do well to heed those words of General MacArthur, and apply them to the present—apply them to our position in this cold war, for if we engage in this cold war, and do not fight it through to victory, we must be prepared to ac-

151

cept the consequences of defeat. And, the consequences of such a defeat, I can assure you, Mr. President, will be slavery for all the peoples of the world.

In addition to an over-all objective of victory, we need a careful appraisal of what such an effort will cost, and a priority list of essentials to measure against the willy-nilly demands for spending on all sectors. This is a clarification which the American people are demanding. In this respect, I refer to the findings of Mr. Samuel Lubell, a public opinion expert who recently took samplings in 19 States. He reached these conclusions:

> If President Kennedy is to gain public support for a more intensive cold war effort, two basic reforms seem needed:
> 1. Existing programs must yield better results.
> 2. All of the Government spending effort, domestic and foreign, must be unified into a thought-through, first-things-first system of priorities.

Mr. President, I am not one who ordinarily takes the findings of public-opinion pollsters as the last word in popular sentiment; but I must say that the findings of Mr. Lubell are in keeping with everything which my office mail, as well as conversations I have had with people across the face of this country, have been telling me. There is a great restiveness among our people, because they have the feeling that the administration's programs have been thrown together without sufficient regard for an overall objective or for final costs. They are disturbed at reports that the State Department is toying with a so-called two-China policy; at indications that we may negotiate with Khrushchev on Berlin instead of standing firm; at the possibility that a flimsy, "phony" pretext will be found for diplomatic recognition of Communist Outer Mongolia.

Stand Up to Communism

To date, Mr. President, the American people have nothing to which they can point as a positive indication that the New Frontier means to stand up to the forces of international communism, after the fashion of a great world power. They have waited patiently—and in vain—for this Government to resume nuclear testing, against growing evidence that the Soviet Union is already secretly engaged in this vital activity. Let me say that I believe right here is where the New Frontier could act to show us that it does not intend to be hoodwinked forever by Soviet negotiators. I do not think there is any longer a reason for even fixing a deadline for the resumption of these tests. I believe the United States should just pull its representatives back from the test meetings, and begin work—work that has been delayed too long in the face of new and greater Communist threats around the world.

These are things, I believe, that our Nation needs right now, instead of more excuses for inaction and more justifications for an expanding foreign-aid program, which needs drastic alterations before it can yield results. We need a declaration that our intention is victory. We need a careful cost-accounting of what will be required to meet this objective within the framework of our economic ability. And we need an official act, such as the resumption of nuclear testing, to show our own people and the other freedom-loving peoples of the world that we mean business.

These are minimum requirements, Mr. President, in the nature of first steps. But they are essential if we are to chart a positive course aimed at total victory in a struggle for the future of freedom.

VIEWPOINT 4

"There are limitations to foreign policy. We are neither omniscient nor omnipotent, and we cannot aspire to make the world over in our image."

The U.S. Should Not Aim for Total Victory in the Cold War

J. William Fulbright (1905-)

J. William Fulbright was U.S. senator from Arkansas from 1944 to 1974, and was named chairman of the Senate's Committee on Foreign Relations in 1959. He gained a reputation as an independent and intelligent analyst of U.S. foreign policy, and in the latter stages of his career became well-known as an outspoken critic of the Vietnam War.

The following viewpoint is taken from a speech Fulbright gave in Congress on July 24, 1961. It is in part a response to a speech by Barry Goldwater which had called for the United States to make total Cold War victory an official U.S. objective. Fulbright argues that Goldwater and others calling for total victory have not spelled out any concrete means for achieving it, and that even if a total victory over the Soviet Union and China were possible, it might create more problems than it would solve. Fulbright states the United States should not consider itself an omnipotent country that can dictate world affairs, and that it should avoid military intervention in other countries.

Mr. President, I should like to comment briefly today on certain themes contained in the remarks concerning our foreign policy made by the junior Senator from Arizona [Mr. GOLDWATER] on July 14. The Senator's views are, as usual, forthright and provocative. They are of special significance, in that the Senator is an acknowledged spokesman and leader of opinion in his party. The Senator says that our fundamental objective must be "total victory" over international communism. I must confess to some difficulty in understanding precisely what "total victory" means in this age of ideological conflict and nuclear weapons. Certainly the term is a stirring one. It has a romantic ring. It quickens the blood like a clarion call to arms, and stimulates the imagination with a vision of brave and gallant deeds.

Unanswered Questions

It would be beneficial and instructive, I think, if those who call for total victory would spell out for us precisely how it might be achieved and, more important, what we would do with a total victory once we had won it. Is it to be won by nuclear war—a war which at the very least would cost the lives of tens of millions of people on both sides, devastate most or all of our great cities, and mutilate or utterly destroy a civilization which has been built over thousands of years?

Or can total victory be won without war—by some brilliant stroke of diplomacy or by arguments of such compelling logic that the Communists will acknowledge the error of their ways and abandon their grand imperialistic design? Perhaps the advocates of total victory believe that we can achieve it by abandoning our efforts toward disarmament and engaging in an unrestricted nuclear arms race, even though such a policy would provoke similar measures by the Communist powers.

The Senator from Arizona suggests that the periphery of freedom "is growing steadily smaller in direct ratio to our failure to act from strength." What would a policy of strength involve? Does it mean a military invasion of Cuba which would destroy the Castro dictatorship, but which would also alienate the rest of Latin America and necessitate the stationing of Marines in Cuba to protect an American-imposed regime against Fedelista rebels and guerillas? Does it mean the commitment of American forces to interminable guerilla warfare in the jungles of Laos, a war in which all the advantages of geography would be on the side of the Communists?

Even more perplexing than the question of how to win a total victory is the problem of what we would do with it once it was

155

won. Would we undertake a military occupation of Russia and China and launch a massive program to reeducate 200 million Russians and 600 million Chinese in the ways of Western democracy?

Advice for the President

In January 1961, the Atlantic *magazine published an open letter to newly elected president John F. Kennedy. The author of the letter was William R. Mathews, editor of the* Arizona Daily Star. *Mathews called on Kennedy to seek compromise with the Soviet Union and to educate the American public about the dangers of seeking total victory in the Cold War—nuclear destruction.*

Your big job is to prepare the American people to make peace. They are prepared morally and militarily to make war, but they are poorly prepared to make peace. They have been taught to expect a rigid perfection in the conduct of our foreign policy. They need to be told that perfection is not only impossible but dangerous. Although they accept compromises constantly in their everyday domestic lives, they reject them as "appeasement" in our foreign policy. . . .

A widespread belief prevails that unless we defeat Communism, Communism will take over the whole world, and that if we defeat Communism, our troubles will be over. Therefore, so the reasoning goes, there can be no compromises. The Communist must give in; we must never give in. The resulting deadlock, coupled with the intensified armament race, creates an increasing danger of hydronuclear war. . . .

The big issue before these two giant political powers is whether it might not be best for the leaders of each to try to get along with the other rather than to try to destroy each other. It is better for us to get along just halfway than to expect perfection from each other. That means compromise. That there must be concessions by both sides is scarcely understood. If the American people could see that it is to their own self-interest to make concessions in return for concessions by the Soviets, as a means of avoiding hydronuclear war, a more peaceful climate might result.

Political objectives must be framed in terms of time and circumstance. In the Middle Ages, when military combat took the form of jousts between chivalrous knights, total victory was perhaps a reasonable objective. One combatant bested the other with his sword or lance or mace, and that was the end of it. In our own time the chivalrous encounter has been relegated to the football field or the boxing arena, and it is a dangerous illusion to confuse the rules of a college football game with those that apply to the arena of world politics.

We have had total victories in the past, and their examples offer little encouragement. We fought the First World War to make the world safe for democracy, and prosecuted the Second World War to achieve the unconditional surrender of our enemies. Both World Wars ended in total victory, but the world is far less safe for democracy today than it was in 1914, when the current era of upheavals began. One of the principal lessons of two World Wars is that wars, and total victories, generate more problems than they solve. Apparently we have not yet fully accepted the fact that there are no absolute solutions, that we can hope to do little more than mitigate our problems as best we can and learn to live with them.

A Double Standard

As I said in my remarks of June 29, there is a double standard in the struggle between communism and the free nations. While Communist tactics include terror, subversion, and military aggression, the world demands a higher order of conduct from the United States. Our policies must be consistent with our objectives, which are those of constructive social purpose and world peace under world law. Were we to adopt the same mischievous tactics as those employed by the Communists, the principal target of these tactics would be our own principles and our own national style.

The Senator says that world opinion "is an area of official concern which has no reason for existing," that world opinion actually countenances international communism. The Senator does an injustice to the hopes and aspirations of peoples throughout the world and he credits communism with a far greater appeal than it actually has. It is not communism which appeals to the hearts and minds of the emergent peoples of Asia, Africa, and Latin America. These people hope for peace, for a decent material life, and for national self-determination. Only insofar as communism succeeds in identifying itself with these aspirations does it win prestige, allegiance, and respect.

World opinion is eminently worth courting—because the hopes of millions of people for world order and for economic and social reform are our hopes as well. Where world opinion seems to us to be feeble or ill-informed, our proper task is to seek to develop and inform it, not to dismiss it as unworthy of our concern.

We have much to learn, as well as to teach, from the opinions of peoples throughout the world. Our own judgments are not infallible, and there is much to be gained by a decent respect for the opinions of mankind.

World opinion is a civilizing force in the world, helping to restrain the great powers from the worst possible consequences of their mutual hostility. To disavow and override the opinions of other peoples because they do not always agree with our own is to destroy a potentially powerful force for peace and to return to the laws of the jungle.

The Senator says that I favor a policy of "nonintervention." I am indeed opposed to policies that would overextend the United States, especially when such policies find little or no support elsewhere in the non-Communist world. By refusing to permit our national strength to be sapped by peripheral struggles, we maximize our power to honor our obligations and commitments all over the world. We are committed to military and political alliances with many nations and we are committed to assist many more nations toward the fulfillment of their legitimate political, economic, and social aspirations. Such policies are the diametric opposite of any doctrine of nonintervention. Their basic concept is one of intervention—but not indiscriminate military intervention in response to every provocation and every disorder, regardless of its character and cause. The latter approach is one of rigid and negative reaction, one which would leave every initiative to our adversaries. The program which I support is one of long-range intervention in depth, one which employs all of the instrumentalities of foreign policy, the political and economic as well as the military. Its object is the realization of our national interests and not merely the piecemeal frustration of Communist ambitions.

Limits to U.S. Power

There are limitations to foreign policy. We are neither omniscient nor omnipotent, and we cannot aspire to make the world over in our image.

Our proper objective is a continuing effort to limit the world struggle for power and to bring it under civilized rules. Such a program lacks the drama and romance of a global crusade. Its virtue is that it represents a realistic accommodation between our highest purposes and the limitations of human capacity. Its ultimate objective is indeed total victory, not alone for our arms in a nuclear war or for the goal of a world forcibly recast in our image, but rather for a process—a process of civilizing international relations and of bringing them gradually under a world-wide regime of law and order and peaceful procedures for the redress of legitimate grievances.

VIEWPOINT 5

"The United States has a role to play . . . in learning to deter guerrilla warfare, if possible, and to deal with it, if necessary."

The U.S. Should Counter Communist Revolutions in the Third World

Walt W. Rostow (1916-)

The years of the Cold War coincided with massive changes on the world scene as the former colonial empires of Great Britain, France, and other European powers broke up. Between 1945 and 1960 more than forty new nations with a population of over a billion achieved independence. This development helped turn the Cold War between the Soviet Union and the United States into a worldwide competition for power and influence. Historian John Spanier writes:

> The cold war had started in Europe after World War II; the fall of nationalist China and the Korean War had extended it to Asia after later 1949. But the birth of so many new states, as Western colonialism collapsed after 1945, underline the importance of this new Third World. The international system was no longer divided into the First World, or Western world of industrial states, and the Second World, led by the Soviet Union. . . . In a bipolar world, the "in-between" Third World was not a center of power but an attraction for the two superpowers. The United States and the Soviet Union extended the cold war in their rivalry for the support, if not the allegiance, of the former colonial states. . . . Moscow perceived the anticolonial revolt against

the West as proof that the international capitalist order was disintegrating. The Soviet Union saw an opportunity for taking the new states into a partnership to build a Soviet-led Communist international order. . . .

The developing countries' choice of which path to follow was seen as critical to American security. . . . The United States thought it vital to help the new countries develop, and it was a matter of basic self-interest rather than humanitarian concern for the poor.

U.S. presidents had differing policies toward the Third World. Truman in his 1949 inaugural address called for economic and technical assistance to developing nations in what became known as the Point Four program, which, due partially to domestic opposition, had limited success. Eisenhower and his secretary of state John Foster Dulles vigorously opposed neutralism in the Third World and sought to create a system of alliances similar to NATO in Europe; among the treaty organizations made were CENTO in the Middle East and SEATO in southeast Asia. The Eisenhower administration also used the Central Intelligence Agency for covert operations designed to counter governments or revolutionary movements seen as too sympathetic to communism. Among the countries affected by U.S. covert operations were Guatemala, Iran, and the Philippines.

President John F. Kennedy, through programs such as the Peace Corps and the Alliance for Progress, sought to reemphasize economic assistance to encourage developing countries, while at the same time using military counterinsurgency strategies to counter communist guerrilla armies in places like Vietnam. The following June 28, 1961, speech by Kennedy adviser Walt W. Rostow provides a good overview of U.S. policies and views at the beginning of the 1960s. In the speech, given at graduation ceremonies at the United States Army Special Warfare School at Fort Bragg, North Carolina, and taken from the August 7, 1961 issue of the *Department of State Bulletin*. Rostow emphasizes the importance of preventing communist revolutions in the Third World. Rostow held several government and adviser posts in the Kennedy and Johnson administrations, including chairman of the Policy Planning Council at the Department of State. He later was a professor of economic history at the University of Texas at Austin.

It does not require much imagination to understand why President Kennedy has taken the problem of guerrilla warfare seriously. When this administration came to responsibility it faced four major crises: Cuba, the Congo, Laos, and Viet-Nam. Each represented a successful Communist breaching—over the previous 2 years—of the cold-war truce lines which had emerged from the Second World War and its aftermath. In different ways each had arisen from the efforts of the international Communist movement to exploit the inherent instabilities of the underdeveloped areas of the non-Communist world, and each had a guerrilla-warfare component.

Cuba, of course, differed from the other cases. The Cuban revolution against Batista was a broad-based national insurrection. But that revolution was tragically captured from within by the Communist apparatus; and now Latin America faces the danger of Cuba's being used as the base for training, supply, and direction of guerrilla warfare in the hemisphere.

More than that, Mr. Khrushchev, in his report to the Moscow conference of Communist parties (published January 6, 1961), had explained at great length that the Communists fully support what he called wars of national liberation and would march in the front rank with the peoples waging such struggles. The military arm of Mr. Khrushchev's January 1961 doctrine is, clearly, guerrilla warfare.

Faced with these four crises, pressing in on the President from day to day, and faced with the candidly stated position of Mr. Khrushchev, we have, indeed, begun to take the problem of guerrilla warfare seriously.

Revolutionary Process in Southern Hemisphere

To understand this problem, however, one must begin with the great revolutionary process that is going forward in the southern half of the world; for the guerrilla warfare problem in these regions is a product of that revolutionary process and the Communist effort and intent to exploit it.

What is happening throughout Latin America, Africa, the Middle East, and Asia is this: Old societies are changing their ways in order to create and maintain a national personality on the world scene and to bring to their peoples the benefits modern technology can offer. This process is truly revolutionary. It touches every aspect of the traditional life—economic, social, and political. The introduction of modern technology brings about not merely new methods of production but a new style of family life, new links between the villages and the cities, the beginnings of national politics, and a new relationship to the world outside.

Like all revolutions, the revolution of modernization is disturbing. Individual men are torn between the commitment to the old familiar way of life and the attractions of a modern way of life.

The power of old social groups—notably the landlord, who usually dominates the traditional society—is reduced. Power moves toward those who can command the tools of modern technology, including modern weapons. Men and women in the villages and the cities, feeling that the old ways of life are shaken and that new possibilities are open to them, express old resentments and new hopes.

Communist Exploitation

This is the grand arena of revolutionary change which the Communists are exploiting with great energy. They believe that their techniques of organization—based on small disciplined cadres of conspirators—are ideally suited to grasp and to hold power in these turbulent settings. They believe that the weak transitional governments that one is likely to find during this modernization process are highly vulnerable to subversion and to guerrilla warfare. And whatever Communist doctrines of historical inevitability may be, Communists know that their time to seize power in the underdeveloped areas is limited. They know that, as momentum takes hold in an underdeveloped area—and the fundamental social problems inherited from the traditional society are solved—their chances to seize power decline.

It is on the weakest nations, facing their most difficult transitional moments, that the Communists concentrate their attention. They are the scavengers of the modernization process. They believe that the techniques of political centralization under dictatorial control—and the projected image of Soviet and Chinese Communist economic progress—will persuade hesitant men, faced by great transitional problems, that the Communist model should be adopted for modernization, even at the cost of surrendering human liberty. They believe that they can exploit effectively the resentments built up in many of these areas against colonial rule and that they can associate themselves effectively with the desire of the emerging nations for independence, for status on the world scene, and for material progress.

This is a formidable program; for the history of this century teaches us that communism is not the longrun wave of the future toward which societies are naturally drawn. On the contrary. But it is one particular form of modern society to which a nation may fall prey during the transitional process. Communism is best understood as a disease of the transition to modernization.

What is our reply to this historical conception and strategy? What is the American purpose and the American strategy? We, too, recognize that a revolutionary process is under way. We are dedicated to the proposition that this revolutionary process of modernization shall be permitted to go forward in independence, with increasing degrees of human freedom. We seek two results: first, that truly independent nations shall emerge on the world scene; and, second, that each nation will be permitted to fashion, out of its own culture and its own ambitions, the kind of modern society it wants. The same religious and philosophical beliefs which decree that we respect the uniqueness of each individual make it natural that we respect the uniqueness of each national society. Moreover, we Americans are confident that, if the independence of this process can be maintained over the coming years and decades, these societies will choose their own version of what we would recognize as a democratic, open society.

Unconventional Warfare

Franklin A. Lindsay was a foreign policy analyst and vice president of ITEK Corporation. In this 1962 article in Foreign Affairs *he argued that the United States needed to develop new methods to deal with communist revolutions in the Third World.*

The West needs to acquire the ability to conduct unconventional warfare successfully, and it must do so quickly. The Communists have evolved a highly effective strategy combining grass-roots political organization and guerrilla warfare which they are employing against the non-Communist world. They have devised a totalitarian political structure that is highly resistant to counter-attack. The creation by the West of an adequate defensive and offensive capability for political and guerrilla warfare will require time and effort. It must be pursued vigorously and without further delay.

These are our commitments of policy and of faith. The United States has no interest in political satellites. Where we have military pacts we have them because governments feel directly endangered by outside military action and we are prepared to help protect their independence against such military action. But, to use Mao Tse-tung's famous phrase, we do not seek nations which "lean to one side." We seek nations which shall stand up straight. And we do so for a reason: because we are deeply confident that nations which stand up straight will protect their independence and move in their own ways and in their own time toward human freedom and political democracy.

Protecting Revolutionary Process

Thus our central task in the underdeveloped areas, as we see it, is to protect the independence of the revolutionary process now going forward. This is our mission, and it is our ultimate strength. For this is not—and cannot be—the mission of communism. And in time, through the fog of propaganda and the honest confusions of men caught up in the business of making new nations, this fundamental difference will become increasingly clear in the southern half of the world. The American interest will be served if our children live in an environment of strong, assertive, independent nations, capable, because they are strong, of assuming collective responsibility for the peace.

The diffusion of power is the basis for freedom within our own society, and we have no reason to fear it on the world scene. But this outcome would be a defeat for communism—not for Russia as a national state, but for communism. Despite all the Communist talk of aiding movements of national independence, they are driven in the end, by the nature of their system, to violate the independence of nations. Despite all the Communist talk of American imperialism, we are committed, by the nature of our system, to support the cause of national independence. And the truth will out.

The victory we seek will see no ticker tape parades down Broadway, no climactic battles, nor great American celebrations of victory. It is a victory which will take many years and decades of hard work and dedication—by many peoples—to bring about. This will not be a victory of the United States over the Soviet Union. It will not be a victory of capitalism over socialism. It will be a victory of men and nations which aim to stand up straight, over the forces which wish to entrap and to exploit their revolutionary aspirations of modernization. What this victory involves, in the end, is the assertion by nations of their right to independence and by men and women of their right to freedom as they understand it. And we deeply believe this victory will come—on both sides of the Iron Curtain.

If Americans do not seek victory in the usual sense, what do we seek? What is the national interest of the United States? Why do we Americans expend our treasure and assume the risks of modern war in this global struggle? For Americans the reward of victory will be, simply, this: It will permit American society to continue to develop along the old humane lines which go back to our birth as a nation—and which reach deeper into history than that—back to the Mediterranean roots of Western life. We are struggling to maintain an environment on the world scene which will permit our open society to survive and to flourish.

U.S. Responsibilities

To make this vision come true places a great burden on the United States at this phase of history. The preservation of independence has many dimensions.

The United States has the primary responsibility for deterring the use of nuclear weapons in the pursuit of Communist ambitions. The United States has a major responsiblity to deter the kind of overt aggression with conventional forces which was launched in June 1950 in Korea.

We Shall Bear Any Burden

John F. Kennedy's inaugural address in 1961 featured stirring promises that America would resist communism and promote freedom worldwide, including in the developing nations in Africa, Asia, and Latin America.

Let every nation know, whether it wishes us well or ill, that we shall pay any price, bear any burden, meet any hardship, support any friend, oppose any foe to assure the survival and the success of liberty.

This much we pledge—and more. . . .

To those new states whom we welcome to the ranks of the free, we pledge our word that one form of colonial control shall not have passed away merely to be replaced by a far more iron tyranny. We shall not always expect to find them supporting our view. But we shall always hope to find them strongly supporting their own freedom—and to remember that, in the past, those who foolishly sought power by riding the back of the tiger ended up inside. . . .

To our sister republics south of our border, we offer a special pledge—to convert our good words into good deeds—in a new alliance for progress—to assist free men and free governments in casting off the chains of poverty. But this peaceful revolution of hope cannot become the prey of hostile powers. Let all our neighbors know that we shall join with them to oppose aggression or subversion anywhere in the Americas. And let every other power know that this hemisphere intends to remain the master of its own house.

The United States has the primary responsibility for assisting the economies of those hard-pressed states on the periphery of the Communist bloc, which are under acute military or quasi-military pressure which they cannot bear from their own resources; for example, south Korea, Viet-Nam, Taiwan, Pakistan, Iran. The United States has a special responsibility of leadership in bringing not merely its own resources but the resources of all the free world to bear in aiding the longrun development of those nations which are serious about modernizing their economy and their social life. And, as President Kennedy has made clear, he regards no program of his administration as more important than his program for long-term economic development, dramatized, for example, by the Alliance for Progress in Latin America. Independence cannot be maintained by military measures alone. Modern societies must be built, and we are prepared to help build them.

Finally, the United States has a role to play—symbolized by

your presence here and by mine—in learning to deter guerrilla warfare, if possible, and to deal with it, if necessary.

I do not need to tell you that the primary responsibility for dealing with guerrilla warfare in the underdeveloped areas cannot be American. There are many ways in which we can help—and we are searching our minds and our imaginations to learn better how to help; but a guerrilla war must be fought primarily by those on the spot. This is so for a quite particular reason. A guerrilla war is an intimate affair, fought not merely with weapons but fought in the minds of the men who live in the villages and in the hills, fought by the spirit and policy of those who run the local government. An outsider cannot, by himself, win a guerrilla war. He can help create conditions in which it can be won, and he can directly assist those prepared to fight for their independence. We are determined to help destroy this international disease; that is, guerrilla war designed, initiated, supplied, and led from outside an independent nation.

Leader of the Free World

Although as leader of the free world the United States has special responsibilities which it accepts in this common venture of deterrence, it is important that the whole international community begin to accept its responsibility for dealing with this form of aggression. It is important that the world become clear in mind, for example, that the operation run from Hanoi against Viet-Nam is as clear a form of aggression as the violation of the 38th parallel by the north Korean armies in June 1950. . . .

The sending of men and arms across international boundaries and the direction of guerrilla war from outside a sovereign nation is aggression; and this is a fact which the whole international community must confront and whose consequent responsibilities it must accept. Without such international action those against whom aggression is mounted will be driven inevitably to seek out and engage the ultimate source of the aggression they confront.

In facing the problem of guerrilla war, I have one observation to make as a historian. It is now fashionable—and I daresay for you it was compulsory—to read the learned works of Mao Tse-tung and Che Guevara on guerrilla warfare. This is, indeed, proper. One should read with care and without passion into the minds of one's enemies. But it is historically inaccurate and psychologically dangerous to think that these men created the strategy and tactics of guerrilla war to which we are now responding. Guerrilla warfare is not a form of military and psychological magic created by the Communists. There is no rule or parable in the Communist texts which was not known at an earlier time in his-

166

tory. The operation of Marion's men in relation to the Battle of Cowpens in the American Revolution was, for example, governed by rules which Mao merely echoes. Che Guevara knows nothing of this business that T.E. Lawrence did not know or was not practiced, for example, in the Peninsular Campaign during the Napoleonic wars, a century earlier. The orchestration of professional troops, militia, and guerrilla fighters is an old game whose rules can be studied and learned.

My point is that we are up against a form of warfare which is powerful and effective only when we do not put our minds clearly to work on how to deal with it. I, for one, believe that with purposeful efforts most nations which might now be susceptible to guerrilla warfare could handle their border areas in ways which would make them very unattractive to the initiation of this ugly game. We can learn to prevent the emergence of the famous sea in which Mao Tse-tung taught his men to swim. This requires, of course, not merely a proper military program of deterrence but programs of village development, communications, and indoctrination. The best way to fight a guerrilla war is to prevent it from happening. And this can be done.

Similarly, I am confident that we can deal with the kind of operation now under way in Viet-Nam. It is an extremely dangerous operation, and it could overwhelm Viet-Nam if the Vietnamese— aided by the free world—do not deal with it. But it is an unsubtle operation, by the book, based more on murder than on political or psychological appeal.

When Communists speak of wars of national liberation and of their support for "progressive forces," I think of the systematic program of assassination now going forward in which the principal victims are the health, agriculture, and education officers in the Viet-Nam villages. The Viet Cong are not trying to persuade the peasants of Viet-Nam that communism is good; they are trying to persuade them that their lives are insecure unless they cooperate with them. With resolution and confidence on all sides and with the assumption of international responsiblity for the frontier problem, I believe we are going to bring this threat to the independence of Viet-Nam under control.

My view is, then, that we confront in guerrilla warfare in the underdeveloped areas a systematic attempt by the Communists to impose a serious disease on those societies attempting the transition to modernization. This attempt is a present danger in southeast Asia. It could quickly become a major danger in Africa and Latin America. I salute in particular those among you whose duty it is—along with others—to prevent that disease, if possible, and to eliminate it where it is imposed.

VIEWPOINT 6

*"[O]ur Cold War with Communism. . . . [has]
created an American machine for suppressing revolt
wherever it may occur in the so-called 'free world.' "*

The U.S. Should Not Counter Communist Revolutions in the Third World

D.F. Fleming (1893-1980)

D.F. Fleming was a professor of international relations at Vanderbilt University in Nashville, Tennessee, from 1928 to 1961. He also served as an adviser to the State Department on atomic energy matters and wrote several books on U.S. foreign policy, including *The Cold War and Its Origins*.

In the following viewpoint, an article first published in 1965, he takes a sharply critical view of American involvement in the Third World. He states that it is the United States rather than the Soviet Union that is seeking to impose its own order on the rest of the world. A need to project U.S. power and protect corporate profits, Fleming states, is pitting the United States against nationalist forces in the Third World that are seeking economic justice. He cites Vietnam, where the United States was becoming increasingly involved in a protracted and divisive war, as a prime example of U.S. imperialism.

In the [past] twenty years the already vast power of our corporate enterprise has increased tremendously. Powered by enormous orders for defense and space exploration purposes, the end products of which are mostly sterile economically, and stimulated by Keynesian policies applied by the government, they have expanded into all the non-Communist world.

Today the economy of Canada has been substantially taken over, many Latin American states are largely our economic fiefs, Europe is organizing against our business take-overs and we fight long and exhausting wars in Asia in no small part to keep areas of investment open to our corporate enterprises.

This is a matter of deep concern, since our corporations earn huge profits each year which must be invested somewhere, and the greatest returns can often be found abroad. Then they must be reinvested and the new profits must find employment indefinitely into the future. The dynamism of our war-directed economy is so great that it needs the whole world as its province, certainly the non-Communist part of it. The same dynamism moves also, or tries to move, against any additional country, no matter how small, going Communist.

From this standpoint a Communist Cuba or Vietnam means two calamitous things: (1) it confiscates American corporate properties and (2) it closes the door to any future American economic expansion. A new and mutually beneficial trade could grow up, but there could be no new private investment for private profits. This is the mortal sin which Communism commits and there is no forgiving it.

A Huge Counterinsurgency Apparatus

It is universally known that our Cold War with Communism generated the mightiest arms race of all time with the Soviet Union, in all the big weapons that had ever been invented or that are even theoretically possible. But it is not so well known that it also created an American machine for suppressing revolt wherever it may occur in the so-called "free world." In it other freedoms may be permitted so long as they do not interfere with freedom of investment, but they do not include the basic irreplaceable right to change any hated system of social oppression by force. Having forbidden this, we most naturally went on to build a great counterinsurgency apparatus to go out into the world and stamp out guerrilla rebels. It centers on the Army's Special Forces which [Roger Hagan writes] is "primarily a teaching corps of about 6,000 men."

In his unforgettable report in *Viet-Report*, Roger Hagan explains that this corps not only teaches our own troops all the techniques of killing social dissenters abroad but teaches these tactics to other armies on the spot, as in Bolivia and Thailand, and to foreigners in army schools both here and abroad. Our own schools are normally training about 24,000 foreign military men, about a tenth of them exclusively in counterinsurgency, while others are trained in three army schools abroad: a jungle warfare school in Panama, a counterinsurgency school in Okinawa, and one in Germany to train both Americans and Europeans to suppress revolt in Africa.

No Military Threat

Robert Heilbroner was for many years professor of economics at the New School for Social Research in New York City. His many books include The Future as History *and* Behind the Veil of Economics. *In April 1967 he wrote an article in* Commentary *magazine questioning U.S. policy of aiding anticommunist governments.*

Suppose that most of Southeast Asia and much of Latin America were to go Communist, or to become controlled by revolutionary governments that espoused collectivist ideologies and vented extreme anti-American sentiments. Would this constitute a mortal threat to the United States?

I think it fair to claim that the purely *military* danger posed by such an eventuality would be slight. Given the present and prospective capabilities of the backward world, the addition of hundreds of millions of citizens to the potential armies of Communism would mean nothing when there was no way of deploying them against us. The prospect of an invasion by Communist hordes—the specter that frightened Europe after World War II with some (although retrospectively, not too much) realism—would be no more than a phantasm when applied to Asia or South America or Africa.

Thus we train forces around the world to put down men who might have Communist ideas about property or, more likely, nationalists who want social reform of various kinds. In addition, other lesser programs deal with counterinsurgency. [According to Hagan,] "One, called Public Safety, trains police forces in a couple of dozen countries. There are two Inter-American Police Academies, in Panama and Washington, as well as much exporting of specialists to train on locale." All this is buttressed by special training programs for counterinsurgency in our Army, Navy, Air Force and Marine Corps, each of which has a research program in the CI field, as does the Defense Department separately.

Abroad "there is the vast and least visible effort of the CIA, which conducts what is called 'black' psychological warfare, infiltrating insurgent groups which might threaten established governments and feeding in false information." Since the Bay of Pigs fiasco the actual handling of subversive *operations* appears to have been transferred to the Defense Department, which may, for example, develop "guerrilla forces within a Communist state." Even the State Department runs a course for generals and ambassadors at the Foreign Service Institute. State prefers to call its CI activities "Overseas Internal Defense," a concealing newspeak title.

This entire program of counterinsurgency activity throughout the world is directed by a general staff of civilians called the Special Group, which meets every Thursday in Washington to coordinate the various CI activities. It is chaired by an Under Secretary of State and includes half a dozen of the highest officials in Washington, or their representatives, whom Hagan names. It surveys the world and assigns CI work to military or civilian agencies, since one side of the global campaign is concerned with civic action—every kind of activity designed to separate insurgent leaders from their followers or potential followers, and to forestall insurgency.

Reformist Governments Overthrown

It is well known that this global activity, largely clandestine, has already upset leftist nationalist governments in Iran, Guatemala and the Congo—all of which threatened foreign investments—to name only some of its main successes. To these one should now add Santo Domingo, where in May, 1965, a revolt to restore a democratically elected government was crushed by a swift American occupation, in painful violation of the most explicit provisions of the OAS [Organization of American States] and UN charters and other treaties. To exclude the bare possibility that weak Communist leadership might seize control of a powerful army movement, some 30,000 United States sea and land forces were quickly dispatched to the island to take control, as President Johnson declared on May 3, 1965: "We don't intend to sit here in our rocking chair with our hands folded and let the Communists set up any government in the Western Hemisphere."

The affirmation of our right to defeat any revolution that may break out in the "free world" is therefore complete, since at least a few Communists will infallibly be involved in, or join, any revolution (or we will say there are). The Truman and Johnson Doctrines are welded together, for all the world to see, as the guiding light and purpose of our national life. Our long-term purpose for living is summed up in the great negation: *There shall be no more revolutions, less they turn Red.*

Less than a month earlier, on April 7, Johnson had declared his immutable will to prevail in Vietnam, saying: "We will not be defeated. We will not grow tired. We will not withdraw, either openly or under the cloak of a meaningless agreement."

He insisted that "Armed hostility is futile. Our resources are equal to any challenge. . . . Our patience and determination are unending. . . . We will use our power with restraint and with all the wisdom we can command. *But we will use it.*" (Italics added.)

Losing Our Place in the Sun

Noted economist and author Robert Heilbroner wrote in the April 1967 issue of Commentary *magazine that the United States might have to accept the fact that communism could be the wave of the future in Third World nations.*

It is, I think, the fear of losing our place in the sun, of finding ourselves at bay, that motivates a great deal of the anti-Communism on which so much of American foreign policy seems to be founded. In this regard I note that the nations of Europe, most of them profoundly more conservative than America in their social and economic dispositions, have made their peace with Communism far more intelligently and easily than we, and I conclude that this is in no small part due to their admission that they are no longer the leaders of the world.

The great question in our own nation is whether we can accept a similar scaling-down of our position in history. This would entail many profound changes in outlook and policy. It would mean the recognition that Communism, which may indeed represent a retrogressive movement in the West, where it should continue to be resisted with full energies, may nonetheless represent a progressive movement in the backward areas, where its advent may be the only chance these areas have of escaping misery. Collaterally, it means the recognition that "our side" has neither the political will, nor the ideological wish, nor the stomach for directing those changes that the backward world must make if it is ever to cease being backward. It would undoubtedly entail a more isolationist policy for the United States vis-à-vis the developing continents, and a greater willingness to permit revolutions there to work their way without our interference. It would mean in our daily political life the admission that the ideological battle of capitalism and Communism had passed its point of usefulness or relevance, and that religious diatribe must give way to the pragmatic dialogue of the age of science and technology.

There was not the faintest suggestion of conceding any right of self-determination by revolution in Vietnam; or any right to conduct a war of independence against Western, white control; or any right of one-half of Vietnam to be involved in the affairs of the other half. Indeed, these issues were begged in the sweeping affirmation: "we will always oppose the effort of one *nation* to conquer another" (italics added), implying that South Vietnam was already one nation and North Vietnam another, in the plainest violation of the Geneva Conference of 1954 which temporarily divided Vietnam only for the purpose of ending the French war of reconquest. . . .

In South Vietnam every kind of terrible firepower has been used on our real opponents, the peasants—bombs of every size, including great quantities of the big ones from B52s; napalm by the shipload, that maims for life if it does not kill, melting the flesh on people's faces, causing it to run down on their bodies where it sits and grows again; phosphorus that keeps on burning until it eats to the bone, chemicals that kill foliage and crops and also old and young people; artillery fire of all types; naval gunfire reaching many miles inland; villages shot up at night with machine guns that pour out 18,000 rounds a minute, a one-second burst laying down "enough lead to cover a football field"; everything except atomic bombs—all propelled by the mightiest engines of war, the most efficient means of communication and the most scientific means of detection, even at night. Yet much of this incessant destruction is blind, killing far more civilians than peasant fighters. More than a million people have been driven out of their homes as pitiable refugees, some think 3,000,000.

What Our Conquest Means

All the while the vast weight of our troops on the people, especially the women and children, and of avalanches of goods and money dumped on a primitive economy, is disintegrating the whole fabric of Vietnamese society, which has had its own internal health, beauty and viability for many centuries. French officials who know Vietnam think that we will so destroy it that in the end there will be only ruins and refugees, and that the Americans will never be able to revive or run a Vietnamese state.

The Nazis called the Slavs of Europe *Untermenschen*, subhuman, and tried to exterminate them to make way for blond German humans. We have degraded our alleged enemies in Vietnam to the status of vermin, killing them both blindly and personally, and celebrating an alleged body count each day and week. We assume that the patriots fighting for their lives and homes are only Communists, or at least led by Communists. Doesn't that justify all? And in some vague way are we not containing China by killing Vietnamese?

Standing on this queasy terrain we must press on to conquer South Vietnam, inch by inch. "The war cannot be won," wrote R. W. Apple, Jr. to *The New York Times* on December 12, 1966, "until the Vietcong guerrillas are rooted out of the 11,000 rural hamlets of South Vietnam." We propose to train the South Vietnamese army to do this while we hold the ring, but since they have little stomach for the effort it will be up to us to go out into the jungles and rice paddies and execute the main thrust.

What it will mean was explained by our Ambassador [Henry Cabot] Lodge in Saigon, on December 4, 1966. Pacification, he said, will involve elaborate peace precautions, a thorough census, identity cards and systematic curfews. In other words, we must establish the sternest and most elaborate police state over the whole of South Vietnam—in the name of freedom, liberty and anti-Communism.

Then we shall proceed to construct a new society in our own image. We have poured riches into the hands of a small new class in Saigon, perhaps gaining their loyalty. By inundating the few cities with goods we have also produced a huge black market, based on thefts of at least 20 percent of all arriving materials, and we have corrupted Vietnamese society in every way, up to the very top. However, after pacification we will continue to pour capital into Vietnam until an economic "takeoff" has been achieved. Until this point democracy is impossible; then it will take care of itself—so the story goes.

This is the theory of Walt W. Rostow, "one of the initial architects of the paramilitary program" for Vietnam, who elaborated the capitalism first and democracy last program in his book *The Stages of Economic Growth* (Cambridge University Press, 1960). Fittingly enough, Rostow is now Chairman of the Policy Planning Council in the State Department, since his marriage of "military style" and capitalist theory "has had as great an impact as any other single intellectual endeavor we might think of in shaping the direction of United States policy in the sixties.". . .

It has been argued cogently that, in spite of its stark brutality, our imperialism is different from the traditional, exploitative kind; it is welfare imperialism, which seeks to impose Americanism, economic and otherwise, on underdeveloped peoples, ignoring the peasant majorities and supporting the social classes and values that we approve. In this drive John McDermott sees United States economic interests growing "daily more intertwined with government policy and more committed to its objectives." But he expects "to see the bureaucratic power of the United States government more and more opposed by armed resistance as native peoples seek to control their own future." And as they see our "overwhelming influence and resources" compromise their independence we must expect to find ourselves creating Vietnams everywhere.

If, too, the pulverization of Vietnam, and the giant bases we have built in Vietnam and Thailand, do not lead on into a war with China, our leaders will have, after the "war" is over, a great supply of troops trained to suppress rebellion. The *New Republic* noted with well-justified foreboding on September 10, 1966, that "The Pentagon has got so guerrilla-conscious that the world's

174

mightiest military structure spends most of its time brooding on insurgency and counterinsurgency. What will this country do with the enormous numbers of men who are being trained in guerrilla warfare tactics?"...

We may well continue along the same road of arousing increasing antagonism among the lesser peoples, since the effect of our capitalist embrace is to *decapitalize* the underdeveloped countries. Our great corporations act as huge suction pumps, drawing out great quantities of raw materials at low prices and selling back processed goods at their own prices. The result is, in the words of *The New York Times* editorial on January 18, 1966, that "The developing countries are burdened with huge debts and soaring interest rate payments," to which there is added the withdrawal of the dividends of our business. Indeed our investors take out each year twice as much profits as we grant in "loans," all of which ["loans"] are in the form of credits which must be spent in the United States. Even the operation of our foreign aid in Latin America is strongly imperialistic.

The traditional, agrarian and underdeveloped societies accordingly remain poor while we grow steadily richer, and they are thus driven to some kind of revolt both to protect their independence and to stave off the inroads of hunger by pushing their own development.

Our response is that if they are to develop, it must be by our method and under our control which means, essentially, they will not develop. This is why, in Barrington Moore's memorable words, the American government is "quite literally trying to burn these revolutionary movements off the face of the earth." As exploding populations compel the peoples to rise against parasitic, political landlordism, the United States has emerged as "the military bastion of counterrevolution, willing and able to rain fire on those made impatient by hunger." In the process we are destroying Western democracy's clearest claim upon humanity's allegiance, "that it was no terrorist society." Rejecting the myth that we are fighting in Vietnam (and now in Thailand) to counter a Chinese outthrust, he observes tellingly that "the United States is desperately trying to *establish* vital interests close to China rather than to defend interests it already has."(Italics added.)

The Military's Need for War

This is the military-industrial complex which President Eisenhower in his farewell address feared would take us over, operating full blast with the throttle wide open. The military need wars to keep their dominance over the national budget; the corporations must have foreign expansion indefinitely to employ swollen profits....

It was illusory to think after 1945 that we could deny Russia the political and military security in Eastern Europe which she had so tragically won, or that we could contain her influence in the world with vast rings of pacts and fortresses. The example of her internal success was bound to leap over all barriers that we could construct. It is a great illusion to think that we can do the same thing all over again to China. If she continues to build a society which distributes the necessities of life fairly and without corruption, all the world will know about it, especially if we support corrupt regimes, as in Saigon and elsewhere, interminably. Above all, it is a delusion to think that we can move into the shoes of all the defunct empires, from the Congo to Southeast Asia, restore the *Pax Britannica* and repress the social upheavals through which many of the world's peoples are fated to pass. In the words of Arnold Toynbee, the leading historian of the rise and fall of empires, it is futile for the United States to challenge "a force stronger than either Communism or capitalism. She is challenging the Asian, African, and Latin American determination—the majority of mankind's determination—to recover equality with the Western minority.". . .

Pax Americana was foreordained to fail, after nationalism had become universal and colonialism almost swept from the earth. Fortress America would be an intolerable, suffocating end to the American dream. Only a world united to deal with its common problems can offer us a role of leadership that its peoples will accept and honor.

VIEWPOINT 7

"Over this war—and all Asia—is another reality: the deepening shadow of Communist China. . . . The contest in Viet-Nam is part of a wider pattern of aggressive purposes."

U.S. Actions in Vietnam Are Necessary to Fight Communist Aggression

Lyndon B. Johnson (1908-1973)

Lyndon B. Johnson was president of the United States from 1963 to 1969, having previously been vice president under John F. Kennedy. The conflict in Vietnam was a dominant issue throughout his administration.

Vietnam had formerly been under French colonial rule, but in 1954 Ho Chi Minh defeated the French and established a communist government in what became North Vietnam. Determined not to let all of Vietnam become communist, the United States under President Dwight Eisenhower supported a noncommunist regime in what became South Vietnam. Eisenhower pledged to support and defend South Vietnam and sent several hundred military advisers and millions of dollars in economic aid to that country. John F. Kennedy increased the number of U.S. troops in Vietnam to sixteen thousand during his brief presidency.

Under Johnson, U.S. involvement in Vietnam greatly increased. The Tonkin Gulf Resolution, passed by Congress in August 1964 after two naval incidents between the United States and North Vietnam, served as the main legal basis for U.S. escalation. Johnson began extensive bombing campaigns against North Vietnam in early 1965 and increased the number of U.S. troops deployed there to 267,000 by 1966, and eventually to a peak of 543,000 in 1969.

As U.S. involvement escalated, the war became an increasingly divisive topic within the United States A growing number of people questioned the necessity of United States involvement in Vietnam and the U.S.' continued efforts to fight communism worldwide. The following viewpoint is taken from an April 7, 1965, speech by Johnson delivered at the Johns Hopkins University, and later reprinted in *Public Papers of the Presidents: Lyndon B. Johnson, 1965* (Washington, DC: Government Printing Office, 1966). Johnson defends his actions, arguing that communists in Vietnam are being supported by communist China, and that American involvement is necessary to fight communism in that area of the world. He argues that American actions are meant to preserve peace and to improve the lives of those in South Vietnam.

Tonight Americans and Asians are dying for a world where each people may choose its own path to change.

This is the principle for which our ancestors fought in the valleys of Pennsylvania. It is the principle for which our sons fight tonight in the jungles of Viet-Nam.

Viet-Nam is far away from this quiet campus. We have no territory there, nor do we seek any. The war is dirty and brutal and difficult. And some 400 young men, born into an America that is bursting with opportunity and promise, have ended their lives on Viet-Nam's steaming soil.

Why must we take this painful road?

Why must this Nation hazard its ease, and its interest, and its power for the sake of a people so far away?

We fight because we must fight if we are to live in a world where every country can shape its own destiny. And only in such a world will our own freedom be finally secure.

This kind of world will never be built by bombs or bullets. Yet the infirmities of man are such that force must often precede reason, and the waste of war, the works of peace.

We wish that this were not so. But we must deal with the world as it is, if it is ever to be as we wish.

The world as it is in Asia is not a serene or peaceful place.

The first reality is that North Viet-Nam has attacked the independent nation of South Viet-Nam. Its object is total conquest.

Of course, some of the people of South Viet-Nam are participating in attack on their own government. But trained men and supplies, orders and arms, flow in a constant stream from north to south. This support is the heartbeat of the war.

Responding to North Vietnamese Aggression

In February 1965 the U.S. State Department published a "White Paper" on Vietnam, arguing that South Vietnam was a victim of aggression analogous to the invasion of South Korea in 1950.

The record is conclusive. It establishes beyond question that North Vietnam is carrying out a carefully conceived plan of aggression against the South. It shows that North Vietnam has intensified its efforts in the years since it was condemned by the International Control Commission. It proves that Hanoi continues to press its systematic program of armed aggression into South Vietnam. This aggression violates the United Nations Charter. It is directly contrary to the Geneva Accords of 1954 and of 1962 to which North Vietnam is a party. It shatters the peace of Southeast Asia. It is a fundamental threat to the freedom and security of South Vietnam.

The people of South Vietnam have chosen to resist this threat. At their request, the United States has taken its place beside them in their defensive struggle.

And it is a war of unparalleled brutality. Simple farmers are the targets of assassination and kidnapping. Women and children are strangled in the night because their men are loyal to their government. And helpless villages are ravaged by sneak attacks. Large-scale raids are conducted on towns, and terror strikes in the heart of cities.

The confused nature of this conflict cannot mask the fact that it is the new face of an old enemy.

The Threat of China

Over this war—and all Asia—is another reality: the deepening shadow of Communist China. The rulers in Hanoi are urged on by Peking. This is a regime which has destroyed freedom in Tibet, which has attacked India, and has been condemned by the United Nations for aggression in Korea. It is a nation which is helping the forces of violence in almost every continent. The contest in Viet-Nam is part of a wider pattern of aggressive purposes.

Why are these realities our concern? Why are we in South Viet-Nam?

We are there because we have a promise to keep. Since 1954 every American President has offered support to the people of South Viet-Nam. We have helped to build, and we have helped to defend. Thus, over many years, we have made a national pledge to help South Viet-Nam defend its independence.

And I intend to keep that promise.

To dishonor that pledge, to abandon this small and brave nation to its enemies, and to the terror that must follow, would be an unforgivable wrong.

We're also there to strengthen world order. Around the globe, from Berlin to Thailand, are people whose well-being rests, in part, on the belief that they can count on us if they are attacked. To leave Viet-Nam to its fate would shake the confidence of all these people in the value of an American commitment and in the value of America's word. The result would be increased unrest and instability, and even wider war.

We are also there because there are great stakes in the balance. Let no one think for a moment that retreat from Viet-Nam would bring an end to conflict. The battle would be renewed in one country and then another. The central lesson of our time is that the appetite of aggression is never satisfied. To withdraw from one battlefield means only to prepare for the next. We must say in southeast Asia—as we did in Europe—in the words of the Bible: "Hitherto shalt thou come, but no further."

There are those who say that all our effort there will be futile— that China's power is such that it is bound to dominate all southeast Asia. But there is no end to that argument until all of the nations of Asia are swallowed up.

There are those who wonder why we have a responsibility there. Well, we have it there for the same reason that we have a responsibility for the defense of Europe. World War II was fought in both Europe and Asia, and when it ended we found ourselves with continued responsibility for the defense of freedom.

Our objective is the independence of South Viet-Nam, and its freedom from attack. We want nothing for ourselves—only that the people of South Viet-Nam be allowed to guide their own country in their own way.

We will do everything necessary to reach that objective. And we will do only what is absolutely necessary.

New Attacks

In recent months attacks on South Viet-Nam were stepped up. Thus, it became necessary for us to increase our response and to make attacks by air. This is not a change of purpose. It is a change in what we believe that purpose requires.

We do this in order to slow down an aggression.

President Lyndon Johnson, shown here greeting American troops in 1966, esca-lated U.S. military involvement in Vietnam.

We do this to increase the confidence of the brave people of South Viet-Nam who have bravely borne this brutal battle for so many years with so many casualties.

And we do this to convince the leaders of North Viet-Nam—and all who seek to share their conquest—of a very simple fact:

We will not be defeated.

We will not grow tired.

We will not withdraw, either openly or under the cloak of a meaningless agreement.

We know that air attacks alone will not accomplish all of these purposes. But it is our best and prayerful judgment that they are a necessary part of the surest road to peace. . . .

Because we fight for values and we fight for principles, rather than territory or colonies, our patience and our determination are unending.

Once this is clear, then it should also be clear that the only path for reasonable men is the path of peaceful settlement.

Such peace demands an independent South Viet-Nam—securely guaranteed and able to shape its own relationships to all others—free from outside interference—tied to no alliance—a military base for no other country.

These are the essentials of any final settlement.

We will never be second in the search for such a peaceful settle-ment in Viet-Nam.

There may be many ways to this kind of peace: in discussion or negotiation with the governments concerned; in large groups or in small ones; in the reaffirmation of old agreements or the strengthening with new ones.

We have stated this position over and over again, fifty times and more, to friend and foe alike. And we remain ready, with this purpose, for unconditional discussions. . . .

These countries of southeast Asia are homes for millions of impoverished people. Each day these people rise at dawn and struggle through until the night to wrestle existence from the soil. They are often wracked by disease, plagued by hunger, and death comes at the early age of 40.

Stability and peace do not come easily in such a land. Neither independence nor human dignity will ever be won, though, by arms alone. It also requires the work of peace. The American people have helped generously in times past in these works. Now there must be a much more massive effort to improve the life of man in that conflict-torn corner of our world.

Economic Development

The first step is for the countries of southeast Asia to associate themselves in a greatly expanded cooperative effort for development. We would hope that North Viet-Nam would take its place in the common effort just as soon as peaceful cooperation is possible.

The United Nations is already actively engaged in development in this area. As far back as 1961 I conferred with our authorities in Viet-Nam in connection with their work there. And I would hope tonight that the Secretary General of the United Nations could use the prestige of his great office, and his deep knowledge of Asia, to initiate, as soon as possible, with the countries of that area, a plan for cooperation in increased development.

For our part I will ask the Congress to join in a billion dollar American investment in this effort as soon as it is underway.

And I would hope that all other industrialized countries, including the Soviet Union, will join in this effort to replace despair with hope, and terror with progress. . . .

I also intend to expand and speed up a program to make available our farm surpluses to assist in feeding and clothing the needy in Asia. We should not allow people to go hungry and wear rags while our own warehouses overflow with an abundance of wheat and corn, rice and cotton.

So I will very shortly name a special team of outstanding, patriotic, distinguished Americans to inaugurate our participation in these programs. This team will be headed by Mr. Eugene Black, the very able former President of the World Bank.

In areas that are still ripped by conflict, of course, development will not be easy. Peace will be necessary for final success. But we cannot and must not wait for peace to begin this job. . . .

We often say how impressive power is. But I do not find it impressive at all. The guns and the bombs, the rockets and the warships, are all symbols of human failure. They are necessary symbols. They protect what we cherish. But they are witness to human folly.

A dam built across a great river is impressive.

In the countryside where I was born, and where I live, I have seen the night illuminated, and the kitchens warmed, and the homes heated, where once the cheerless night and the ceaseless cold held sway. And all this happened because electricity came to our area along the humming wires of the REA Electrification of the countryside—yes, that, too, is impressive. . . .

Every night before I turn out the lights to sleep I ask myself this question: Have I done everything that I can do to unite this country? Have I done everything I can to help unite the world, to try to bring peace and hope to all the peoples of the world? Have I done enough?

Ask yourselves that question in your homes—and in this hall tonight. Have we, each of us, all done all we could? Have we done enough?

We Must Choose

We may well be living in the time foretold many years ago when it was said: "I call heaven and earth to record this day against you, that I have set before you life and death, blessing and cursing: therefore choose life, that both thou and thy seed may live."

This generation of the world must choose: destroy or build, kill or aid, hate or understand.

We can do all these things on a scale never dreamed of before.

Well, we will choose life. In so doing we will prevail over the enemies within man, and over the natural enemies of all mankind.

VIEWPOINT 8

"The United States. . . . should realize that the independence and security of a nation do not always require Washington's protection or intervention."

U.S. Actions in Vietnam Are Not Justified

Young Hum Kim (1920-)

The Vietnam War was the United States' most extensive military involvement in its fight against communism. Between 1950 and 1975 the United States lost over fifty-eight thousand lives and spent more than $150 billion in a futile attempt to prevent the Asian country from becoming communist. As military intervention sharply escalated in the 1960s, peace demonstrations and debates swept the United States. Many opponents of the Vietnam conflict began to question basic assumptions about the Cold War.

The following analysis by Young Hum Kim argues that the reasoning behind U.S. involvement in Vietnam is seriously flawed. Kim states that communism is not a monolithic force that threatens to occupy all of Asia. He further asserts that the Vietnamese are motivated not so much by communism as by nationalistic desires to drive foreigners from their land. Kim advocates that the United States withdraw from Vietnam and open up diplomatic channels with China. Four years after this article was written, in 1972, President Richard Nixon did establish relations with China.

Young Hum Kim is a professor of history and international relations at United States International University in San Diego (formerly California Western University) and the author of several books including *Twenty Years of Crises: The Cold War Era* and *The War of No Return.*

In recent decades the American image of China has changed to one of a monstrous society of human insects, destined to take over the world under the banner of Communism. The American obsessive and groundless fear that the Chinese will devastate the earth with their nuclear bombs and that the surviving Chinese will emerge from atomic ashes like the phoenix to inherit this troubled world is driving the United States to the brink of war with the Chinese through escalation of the war in Vietnam. . . .

Is the United States really on a collision course with the People's Republic of China? If so, how can the United States avoid it? What course of action or policy should the United States take or formulate to rectify the present unhealthy state of affairs?

Finding Answers in History

Some of the guidelines, if not answers, to these crucial questions may be found in the pages of history. A realistic and sober reexamination and reevaluation of some of the fundamental issues and attitudes in United States-Chinese relations in the past two decades may provide helpful clues and insights into the immediate problems confronting the two countries. In formulating a foreign policy, a nation should look back upon the road it has trodden in order to chart a new route for the future.

The end of World War II left the United States in a position to assume unilaterally a stance of "free world leadership." In Europe, Britain, France and Italy were exhausted. Russia was no longer in that "free world." And Germany, having been put through the wringer of "unconditional surrender," was again supposed not to "come back" within the predictable future. And however that might turn out, Germany was partly under the "joint occupation" of non-"free world" Russia.

So, Washington underwrote the economic and political recovery of Western Europe through the Marshall Plan. Designed to be a military bulwark to contain an imaginary threat of Soviet expansion, the formation of the North Atlantic Treaty Organization followed the Marshall Plan. The extension of power and influence of the United States in Europe was only blocked by the power of the USSR at the direct line of contact.

In the Near East, effectuation of the Truman Doctrine is said to have thwarted Communist subversion and infiltration. In the Middle East, Soviet occupation of part of Iran was abandoned through a combination of factors.

In the Far East, the United States did not encounter much difficulty in filling the military power vacuum left by the fall of the Japanese Empire. The only major obstacle lay in China—a huge

185

land mass of Asia larger in area than the United States with a population of over 600 million, more than three times that of the United States.

No Honorable Intentions

Martin Luther King Jr. won the Nobel Peace prize for his civil rights leadership advocating nonviolence. On April 4, 1967, he preached a controversial sermon directly attacking U.S. involvement in Vietnam.

If we continue, there will be no doubt in my mind and in the mind of the world that we have no honorable intentions in Vietnam. It will become clear that our minimal expectation is to occupy it as an American colony, and men will not refrain from thinking that our maximum hope is to goad China into a war so that we may bomb her nuclear installations.

The world now demands a maturity of America that we may not be able to achieve. It demands that we admit that we have been wrong from the beginning of our adventure in Vietnam, that we have been detrimental to the life of her people.

In order to atone for our sins and errors in Vietnam, we should take the initiative in bringing the war to a halt.

Unfortunately, China was torn by a titanic civil war between the Nationalists and the Communists, a situation which presented the United States with four possible alternatives: (1) complete withdrawal from China; (2) military intervention on a major scale to aid the Nationalists to destroy the Communists; (3) efforts to avoid a civil war by working for a compromise between the two sides; and (4) wholehearted acceptance of the new Communist China.

In its adoption of the third alternative policy, the United States government was influenced by certain obvious realities: (1) the Nationalists had been unable either to destroy or to win over the Communists during the ten years preceding the war; (2) after the war the Nationalists were weak, demoralized, and corrupt, lacking popular support and prestige; (3) the Communists, in contrast, had strengthened their power, militarily and politically, and were in control of most of the rural areas; (4) because of the ineffectiveness of the Nationalist forces, the Communists probably could have been dislodged only by United States armed forces; (5) the American people might not have endorsed such a colossal commitment of their armies in China; and finally, (6) official and intellectual leadership in the States had launched an all-out cold war against Communism, as incarnate evil.

At first the United States understandably attempted to influence the course of events in favor of the Nationalists. Later, as the fortunes of war were turning in the Communists' favor, Washington endeavored to establish a Nationalist-Communist coalition government. Failing in this, the United States' dream of a friendly and unified capitalistic China as the basis for Far Eastern stability —and a place for profitable private corporate operations—was shattered.

By the summer of 1949, the Chinese Communists had swept the country and achieved victory. Americans were astounded; it was a frustrating reality for them to admit defeat. Critics called the United States' China policy "a tragic failure" and a "crime.". . .

Vietnam

In Vietnam the United States again faced the problem of making a fateful choice from available alternatives. The domestic situation in South Vietnam in the 1960s was somewhat comparable to that of China in the years immediately following World War II. The Diem regime, like Chiang Kai-shek's, was autocratic, undemocratic, and oppressive. It did not have a foundation of popular support and had been unable to destroy or check the rising influence and prestige of the Vietcong.

After the fall of the Diem government, the successive military coups further destroyed all vestiges of political stability in South Vietnam. On the other hand, like the Chinese Communists, the Vietcong steadily increased their power and ultimately controlled two-thirds of the area. They were inspired to the point of fanaticism by the revolutionary zeal of national independence and of liberation from colonial rule. To them, the presence of foreign troops, friendly or otherwise, on their soil symbolized the return of imperialism in the form of "neo colonialism." Against this background the United States determined to pursue the second alternative course—*military intervention on a major scale to assist the Saigon government and to destroy the Vietcong and their supporters.*

The United States' choice of this alternative seems to have been based upon five possible fallacies which should be carefully scrutinized.

The first was the misapplication of the containment policy to Southeast Asia. The United States had made the halting of Communist expansion, regardless of time, place, character, methods, and tactics, the supreme goal of its foreign policy. In the words of Secretary of State Dean Rusk:

> What we are seeking to achieve in South Vietnam is part of a process that has continued for a long time—a process of preventing the expansion and extension of Communist domination by the use of force against the weaker nations on the perimeter of Communist power.

With sweeping generalizations the United States extended the policy of so-called containment, erroneously considered successful in Europe, to Southeast Asia where Communist influence has direct appeal in these underdeveloped societies. To be sure, with the inauguration of the Southeast Asia Treaty Organization in 1954 as a military countermeasure to balance political settlements at Geneva, and the formation of the Baghdad Pact (which later became the Central Treaty Organization), the United States had created a superficial wall of containment of Communism, stretching from the Atlantic to the Pacific through Western Europe and the Middle East. But, it was destined to be ineffective.

The second fallacy was the underestimation of Vietcong and North Vietnamese strength, on several accounts: namely, their military capability to carry on the protracted war, their sense of dedication to what they believe to be a sacred cause, the potent force of their nationalism, their pride and stamina, and the cohesive strength of national unity. Believing that its industrial, technological, and military power was insurmountable, the United States naively expected the Communists to fall to their knees as soon as its power was introduced in the struggle. . . .

The third oversight was the failure to recognize the changing character of Communism. As the cold war crystallized in the wake of World War II, both the United States and the Soviet Union abandoned the spirit of cooperation and mutual understanding and sought to promote their respective interests, while assuming that a gain by one was ipso facto a loss to the other.

With the outbreak of the Korean War and through the subsequent years, United States leadership hardened in its conviction that Communism, as a monolithic and invincible force spearheaded in Asia by Communist China, was bent on a conquest of the entire world. A number of Americans failed to exercise reason and came to look upon any settlement, compromise, or ordinary diplomatic dealings with Communist nations as "evil" and "immoral."

A Divided Communist World

The United States poured money, manpower, and military hardware into the poor and unstable countries of the world so long as they professed to be anti-Communist. It justified alignment with any dictatorial, totalitarian, antidemocratic—even corrupt—regime of dubious color so long as it was not Red. Taking the attitude that "if you are not with us, you are against us," the United States neither tolerated neutralism nor recognized nationalistic anticolonialism, thus alienating many Jeffersonian nationalists in Asia and Africa. It talked so much of great crusades against Communism that it mesmerized itself into recklessly undertaking what were considered to be "messianic missions."

The United States should recognize that Communism comes in many shades and colors. There is no monolithic Communist world any more than there is a unified "free world." Yugoslavia, Albania, and Rumania are definitely defiant of the Soviet Union; North Korea has taken a neutral stance; Poland, Hungary, and Czechoslovakia have gained greater freedom of action than most Central American republics. The Sino-Soviet rift is so obvious and well known that it requires no elaboration. . . .

The fourth error was the attempt to bridge what may be called the "reliability gap." One of the principal arguments of the United States in justifying its presence in Vietnam is the contention that if Washington fails to honor its commitments, most Asian allies will lose confidence in the United States and will give second thoughts to their alignment with it. The truth is that, throughout the cold war period, the United States has created an immense "reliability gap" in its relations with those nations which have been placed under its protective assistance treaties. In the course of remaking these nations in its own image, and with anxiety and impatience, the United States has unilaterally assumed a leadership which was paternalistic and meddlesome as well as indifferent to the initiative of indigenous leaders and to the needs of the people. The United States has demanded their absolute loyalty and mistaken their self-assertion for anti-American posture. It fostered a sense of doubt and suspicion instead of one of trust and confidence in the minds of the leaders. To them, the American attitude has been frequently arrogant and domineering, but they dare not express their feelings overtly lest they incur American displeasure and anger.

When the Korean War broke out, the United States took up arms to repel the alleged aggressors. This action was based on the assumption that if the open aggression was unchecked and if South Korea's pleas for help went unanswered, the United States would demonstrate to the world that it was indeed a "paper tiger" unconcerned with the safety of its allies. Thus the United States returned to rescue the country which it had recently left unprotected. The pattern of United States diplomacy in its worst aspect may therefore be categorized as follows: (1) empty promises and slogans; (2) indecision and vacillation; and (3) impulsive reaction to the positive action taken by its adversaries.

The "reliability gap" was further widened after America's alliance partners witnessed the performance, or sometimes the nonperformance, of the United States with respect to such crucial issues as the East European uprisings in 1953, the Geneva Accords of 1954, the Anglo-French-Israeli invasion of Egypt, the Hungarian Revolution of 1956, the Laotian conflict of 1960, the Congo crisis, the handling of the U-2 incident, the Bay of Pigs, and the Dominican intervention, to name a few. From the standpoint of many Afro-Asian peoples, the "reliability gap" is so great that a single stroke of military operation in Vietnam will not be able to bridge it. On the contrary, it may have an adverse effect because they believe that rather than righting the wrongs committed in the 1950s, the American military campaign in Vietnam serves only to double the wrong. The United States must not entertain the illusion that military power is a panacea for all the political, social, and economic ills of a nation. Power demonstrated without humility is arrogance; power used without prudence is affront; and power mobilized without discretion is aggression. . . .

The United States Should Leave

John Kerry fought in Vietnam and later became the voice of Vietnam Veterans Against the War. In April 1971 Kerry testified before Congress on Vietnam. In 1984 he returned to Washington as a Democratic senator from Massachusetts.

In our opinion, and from our experience, there is nothing in South Vietnam, nothing which could happen that realistically threatens the United States of America. And to attempt to justify the loss of one American life in Vietnam, Cambodia, or Laos by linking such loss to the preservation of freedom, which those misfits supposedly abuse, is to us the height of criminal hypocrisy, and it is that kind of hypocrisy which we feel has torn this country apart. . . .

We found most people didn't even know the difference between communism and democracy. They only wanted to work in rice paddies without helicopters strafing them and bombs with napalm burning their villages and tearing their country apart. They wanted everything to do with the war, particularly with this foreign presence of the United States of America, to leave them alone in peace, and they practiced the art of survival by siding with whichever military force was present at a particular time, be it Vietcong, North Vietnamese, or American.

Fifth, and finally, the concept of Communist China as the ultimate enemy has certain pitfalls. In clarifying the purpose of America's involvement in Vietnam, Secretary of Defense Robert McNamara stated: "The choice is not simply whether to continue our efforts to keep South Vietnam free and independent, but rather, whether to continue our struggle to halt Communist expansion in Asia." He did not say that we *will* have a war with Communist China, but the implication is clear that the United States is determined to carry on the struggle, so long as Communism exists in Asia. . . .

No sane leader would contemplate sending millions of American troops to fight on the mainland of China. President Eisenhower expressed his conviction that there could be "no greater tragedy than for the United States to become involved in an all-out war in Indochina," let alone in China. General MacArthur advised President Kennedy not to send American soldiers to the Asian mainland to combat the Chinese. China has proved to be Asia's "quicksand" for foreign invaders, for no nation or people has ever really conquered China. . . .

Should the United States get itself entangled in hostilities with China, which is no longer a "paper tiger," but a "baby dragon with thermonuclear teeth," the tragic consequences are too horrendous to contemplate.

In view of these analyses, the United States' China policy should be reformulated on the basis of certain immediate essentials, including (1) de-escalation of the war in Vietnam, (2) and a normalization of Sino-American relations.

The first recommendation to be considered is de-escalation. As pointed out, since one of the most important features of escalation in the Vietnam war has been the process of eliminating the proxies, the first step toward de-escalation lies in reversing that process. Through a positive and imaginative diplomacy, means can be found to disengage the United States and North Vietnam forces from combat. A cessation of United States bombing of North Vietnam may be a beginning toward that goal, followed by gradual reduction or withdrawal of both forces from South Vietnam. The parties involved must come to believe that what they have failed to achieve on the battlefield can be achieved at the conference table. . . .

The United States should cast off the old habits of thought and rhetoric, and should introduce the virtues of flexibility and sophistication into the conduct of its foreign policy, especially with respect to the Communist world. It should realize that the independence and security of a nation do not always require Washington's protection or intervention. . . .

The United States must come to the realization that competitive coexistence with China is no more difficult than with the Soviet Union. Recognizing China's great power status, the United States should allow China to participate in major international parleys, and at the opportune moment, extend to it de jure recognition, admit its representatives to United Nations organs and processes, lift its embargo, and institute an exchange of personnel.

In conclusion, in this age of multirevolutions, the United States—"a nation conceived in liberty and dedicated to the proposition that all men are created equal"—should preach *and practice* the blessings of that liberty at home and abroad, and should respect and honor the principle of "sovereign equality," that all nations are equal.

CHAPTER 4

From Détente to the End of the Cold War

Chapter Preface

U.S. Cold War policy underwent major shifts and turnarounds during the 1970s and 1980s. Much of the debate over U.S. foreign policy at this time was over the status of the Cold War. Many analysts argued that the world was becoming a more complex place and that U.S. foreign policy should move beyond its emphasis on containing the Soviet Union. Others maintained that the Soviet Union remained the number one threat to U.S. national security and that containing the Soviet Union should remain the highest priority.

The 1970s started with a major turnabout in U.S.-China relations when U.S. president Richard Nixon visited China in February 1972. Since China's 1949 communist revolution the United States had refused to recognize the communist government of China and had broken off all travel and economic ties between the two nations. This policy of isolating the world's most populous nation was based on the belief that China had allied itself with the Soviet Union to spread communism worldwide and that any ties to or recognition of China would lend assistance to the communist goal. The nonrecognition policy persisted even after the Sino-Soviet alliance was broken in 1960. Nixon's visit, which was the culmination of months of secret meetings between the two governments, resulted in a joint agreement to work toward peace in Asia and to establish closer economic and diplomatic ties.

Nixon followed up his historic visit to China by becoming the first U.S. president to visit the Soviet Union. The May 1972 summit meeting with Soviet leader Leonid Brezhnev and subsequent meetings in 1972 and 1973 resulted in arms control treaties, cooperative research, and expanded trade. Soviet cooperation helped in the negotiation of a cease-fire in Vietnam in 1973 and a U.S. withdrawal from that region after years of fighting. *Détente*, a French word meaning "release from tension," became the term used to describe the new relationship between the Cold War adversaries. Some argued that the new cooperation indicated that the Cold War was over.

Détente was short-lived, however. Critics of détente in Congress and elsewhere argued that the Soviet Union was taking advantage of arms control talks to move ahead in the nuclear arms race. Others criticized what they viewed as U.S. tacit acceptance of Soviet human rights abuses. Soviet and American interests also clashed in such places as Angola and the Middle East, where the two superpowers competed for influence. Nixon himself was forced to resign in 1974 because of the Watergate affair, a series of domestic scandals involving political espionage by Nixon's election officials, illegal wiretapping of civilians, and other illegal actions. Nixon's successors, presidents Gerald Ford and Jimmy Carter, attempted to continue progress in trade and arms control talks. However, the Soviet invasion of Afghanistan in December 1979 resulted in U.S. economic sanctions and a halt in efforts to ratify arms control treaties. It also put an end to détente as Nixon had envisioned it.

The 1980 election to the American presidency of Ronald Reagan, a longtime critic of détente and advocate of tough measures toward the Soviet Union, signaled a new phase of the Cold War. In one famous speech, he referred to the Soviet Union as an "evil empire," and he called for renewed efforts to counter Soviet expansionism. Reagan presided over massive increases in defense spending to build up America's military strength. Under his eight-year administration America spent $2.2 trillion on its armed forces. Reagan imposed economic sanctions on the Soviet Union following its 1980 crackdown on Poland, and he provided aid for armed rebels against the government of Nicaragua, a small Central American nation that had undergone a communist revolution in 1979. Reagan's policies were opposed by many who said that his Cold War vision of a bipolar world divided between the United States and the Soviet Union was too simplistic for the complex realities facing the United States and that it perpetuated dangerous tensions between the two nuclear superpowers.

In 1985 the USSR gained a new leader, Mikhail Gorbachev, whose leadership marked dramatic improvements in Soviet-American relations. Gorbachev, realizing that the Soviet economy was collapsing and seeking improved economic relations with the United States and Western Europe, made major concessions in the areas of nuclear arms and human rights. Furthermore, Gorbachev's call for *glasnost* (openness) and *perestroika* (economic restructuring) blunted the ideological divide between the two superpowers. Reagan and Gorbachev met in four major summits, and in December 1988 they signed a major treaty banning a whole class of nuclear missiles in Europe. Debate within the United States focused on Gorbachev. Was he to be trusted when he spoke of a new era of peace between the superpowers, or was he to be feared as someone who merely wished to strengthen the Soviet Union's hand? The debate over Gorbachev was a new way of asking whether the Cold War was truly over.

VIEWPOINT 1

*"There can be no peaceful international order
without a constructive relationship between the
United States and the Soviet Union."*

Détente Is a Successful U.S. Policy Toward the Soviet Union

Henry A. Kissinger (1923-)

Henry A. Kissinger was a principal architect of U.S. foreign policy from 1969 to 1977 under presidents Richard Nixon and Gerald Ford. Kissinger entered public life at a time America was disillusioned with the Vietnam War and with global involvement in general. During his tenure relations between the United States and the Soviet Union were marked by *détente*, or relaxation of tensions. Kissinger was largely responsible for several U.S. initiatives to lesson Cold War tensions, including his and Nixon's visits to the People's Republic of China, negotiating a cease-fire with North Vietnam in 1973, and negotiating trade and nuclear arms agreements with the Soviet Union.

In the following viewpoint, taken from testimony before the Senate Foreign Relations Committee in September 1974, (*Department of State Bulletin*, October 14, 1974), Kissinger explains the purposes and accomplishments of détente. He states that the threat of nuclear weapons makes it imperative that the two superpowers work to reduce tensions between them, and that the policies of détente have successfully improved U.S.-Soviet relations without compromising U.S. national interests. He argues that the United States should replace Cold War concerns—containing and defeating the Soviet Union—with a realization that the two superpowers should learn to accept each other's existence and power and learn to live together without war.

Since the dawn of the nuclear age the world's fears of holocaust and its hopes for peace have turned on the relationship between the United States and the Soviet Union. . . .

The destructiveness of modern weapons defines the necessity of the task; deep differences in philosophy and interests between the United States and the Soviet Union point up its difficulty. These differences do not spring from misunderstanding or personalities or transitory factors:

• They are rooted in history and in the way the two countries have developed.

• They are nourished by conflicting values and opposing ideologies.

• They are expressed in diverging national interests that produce political and military competition.

• They are influenced by allies and friends whose association we value and whose interests we will not sacrifice.

Paradox confuses our perception of the problem of peaceful coexistence: if peace is pursued to the exclusion of any other goal, other values will be compromised and perhaps lost; but if unconstrained rivalry leads to nuclear conflict, these values, along with everything else, will be destroyed in the resulting holocaust. However competitive they may be at some levels of their relationship, both major nuclear powers must base their policies on the premise that neither can expect to impose its will on the other without running an intolerable risk. The challenge of our time is to reconcile the reality of competition with the imperative of coexistence.

There can be no peaceful international order without a constructive relationship between the United States and the Soviet Union. There will be no international stability unless both the Soviet Union and the United States conduct themselves with restraint and unless they use their enormous power for the benefit of mankind.

Principles of Détente

Thus we must be clear at the outset on what the term "détente" entails. It is the search for a more constructive relationship with the Soviet Union reflecting the realities I have outlined. It is a continuing process, not a final condition that has been or can be realized at any one specific point in time. And it has been pursued by successive American leaders, though the means have varied as have world conditions.

A New Era

Richard Nixon was president of the United States from 1969 to 1974. In May 1972, in an historic summit meeting, he met with Soviet leader Leonid Brezhnev. The meeting resulted in several historic treaties between the two nations, including the Strategic Arms Limitation Talks (SALT). On June 1 he gave a speech before Congress and the nation reporting the results of the summit and expressing his hopes for peace between the superpowers.

Recognizing the responsibility of the advanced industrial nations to set an example in combating mankind's common enemies, the United States and the Soviet Union have agreed to cooperate in efforts to reduce pollution and enhance environmental quality. We have agreed to work together in the field of medical science and public health, particularly in the conquest of cancer and heart disease.

Recognizing that the quest for useful knowledge transcends differences between ideologies and social systems, we have agreed to expand United States-Soviet cooperation in many areas of science and technology. . . .

Expanded United States-Soviet trade will also yield advantages to both of our nations. When the two largest economies in the world start trading with each other on a much larger scale, living standards in both nations will rise and the stake which both have in peace will increase. . . .

Most important, there is the treaty and the related executive agreement which will limit, for the first time, both offensive and defensive strategic nuclear weapons in the arsenals of the United States and the Soviet Union.

Some fundamental principles guide this policy:

• The United States cannot base its policy solely on Moscow's good intentions. But neither can we insist that all forward movement must await a convergence of American and Soviet purposes. We seek, regardless of Soviet intentions, to serve peace through a systematic resistance to pressure and conciliatory responses to moderate behavior.

• We must oppose aggressive actions and irresponsible behavior. But we must not seek confrontations lightly.

• We must maintain a strong national defense while recognizing that in the nuclear age the relationship between military strength and politically usable power is the most complex in all history.

197

• Where the age-old antagonism between freedom and tyranny is concerned, we are not neutral. But other imperatives impose limits on our ability to produce internal changes in foreign countries. Consciousness of our limits is recognition of the necessity of peace—not moral callousness. The preservation of human life and human society are moral values, too.

• We must be mature enough to recognize that to be stable a relationship must provide advantages to both sides and that the most constructive international relationships are those in which both parties perceive an element of gain. Moscow will benefit from certain measures, just as we will from others. The balance cannot be struck on each issue every day, but only over the whole range of relations and over a period of time. . . .

Changes in the International Environment

America's aspiration for the kind of political environment we now call détente is not new. . . .

In the postwar period, repeated efforts were made to improve our relationship with Moscow. The spirits of Geneva, Camp David, and Glassboro were evanescent moments in a quarter century otherwise marked by tensions and by sporadic confrontation. What is new in the current period of relaxation of tensions is its duration, the scope of the relationship which has evolved, and the continuity and intensity of consultation which it has produced.

A number of factors have produced this change in the international environment. By the end of the sixties and the beginning of the seventies the time was propitious—no matter what administration was in office in the United States—for a major attempt to improve U.S.-Soviet relations. Contradictory tendencies contested for preeminence in Soviet policy; events could have tipped the scales either toward increased aggressiveness or toward conciliation.

• The fragmentation in the Communist world in the 1960s challenged the leading position of the U.S.S.R. and its claim to be the arbiter of orthodoxy. The U.S.S.R. could have reacted by adopting a more aggressive attitude toward the capitalist world in order to assert its militant vigilance; instead, the changing situation and U.S. policy seem to have encouraged Soviet leaders to cooperate in at least a temporary lessening of tension with the West.

• The prospect of achieving a military position of near parity with the United States in strategic forces could have tempted Moscow to use its expanding military capability to strive more determinedly for expansion; in fact, it tempered the militancy of some of its actions and sought to stabilize at least some aspects of the military competition through negotiations.

UPI/Bettmann.

U.S. president Richard Nixon held summit meetings with Soviet leader Leonid Brezhnev in 1972, 1973, and 1974. During this time the two nations signed forty-one treaties on arms control, trade, and other areas.

• The very real economic problems of the U.S.S.R. and Eastern Europe could have reinforced autarkic policies and the tendency to create a closed system; in actuality, the Soviet Union and its allies have come closer to acknowledging the reality of an interdependent world economy.

• Finally, when faced with the hopes of its own people for greater well-being, the Soviet government could have continued to stimulate the suspicions of the cold war to further isolate Soviet society: in fact, it chose—however inadequately and slowly—to seek to calm its public opinion by joining in a relaxation of tensions.

Incentives for Peace

For the United States the choice was clear: To provide as many incentives as possible for those actions by the Soviet Union most conducive to peace and individual well-being and to overcome the swings between illusionary optimism and harsh antagonism that had characterized most of the postwar period. We could capitalize on the tentative beginnings made in the sixties by taking advantage of the compelling new conditions of the seventies. . . .

The course of détente has not been smooth or even. As late as

1969, Soviet-American relations were ambiguous and uncertain. To be sure, negotiations on Berlin and SALT [Strategic Arms Limitations Talks] had begun. But the tendency toward confrontation appeared dominant.

We were challenged by Soviet conduct in the Middle East ceasefire of August 1970, during the Syrian invasion of Jordan in September 1970, on the question of a possible Soviet submarine base in Cuba, in actions around Berlin, and during the Indo-Pakistani war. Soviet policy seemed directed toward fashioning a détente in bilateral relations with our Western European allies, while challenging the United States.

We demonstrated then, and stand ready to do so again, that America will not yield to pressure or the threat of force. We made clear then, as we do today, that détente cannot be pursued selectively in one area or toward one group of countries only. For us détente is indivisible.

Finally, a breakthrough was made in 1971 on several fronts—in the Berlin settlement, in the SALT talks, in other arms control negotiations—that generated the process of détente. It consists of these elements: An elaboration of principles; political discussions to solve outstanding issues and to reach cooperative agreements; economic relations; and arms control negotiations, particularly those concerning strategic arms. . . .

The Strategic Relationship

We cannot expect to relax international tensions or achieve a more stable international system should the two strongest nuclear powers conduct an unrestrained strategic arms race. Thus, perhaps the single most important component of our policy toward the Soviet Union is the effort to limit strategic weapons competition.

The competition in which we now find ourselves is historically unique:

• Each side has the capacity to destroy civilization as we know it.

• Failure to maintain equivalence could jeopardize not only our freedom but our very survival.

• The lead time for technological innovation is so long, yet the pace of change so relentless, that the arms race and strategic policy itself are in danger of being driven by technological necessity.

• When nuclear arsenals reach levels involving thousands of launchers and over 10,000 warheads, and when the characteristics of the weapons of the two sides are so incommensurable, it becomes difficult to determine what combination of numbers of strategic weapons and performance capabilities would give one side a militarily and politically useful superiority. At a minimum, clear changes in the strategic balance can be achieved only by efforts so enormous and by increments so large that the very attempt would be highly destabilizing.

• The prospect of a decisive military advantage, even if theoretically possible, is politically intolerable; neither side will passively permit a massive shift in the nuclear balance. Therefore the probable outcome of each succeeding round of competition is the restoration of a strategic equilibrium, but at increasingly higher levels of forces.

• The arms race is driven by political as well as military factors. While a decisive advantage is hard to calculate, the *appearance* of inferiority—whatever its actual significance—can have serious political consequences. With weapons that are unlikely to be used and for which there is no operational experience, the psychological impact can be crucial. Thus each side has a high incentive to achieve not only the reality but the appearance of equality. In a very real sense each side shapes the military establishment of the other.

If we are driven to it, the United States will sustain an arms race. Indeed, it is likely that the United States would emerge from such a competition with an edge over the Soviet Union in most significant categories of strategic arms. But the political or military benefit which would flow from such a situation would remain elusive. Indeed, after such an evolution it might well be that *both* sides would be worse off than before the race began. The enormous destructiveness of weapons and the uncertainties regarding their effects combine to make the massive use of such weapons increasingly incredible. . . .

The SALT Agreements

The SALT agreements already signed represent a major contribution to strategic stability and a significant first step toward a longer term and possibly broader agreement. . . .

The agreements signed in 1972 which limited antiballistic missile [ABM] defenses and froze the level of ballistic missile forces on both sides represented the essential first step toward a less volatile strategic environment.

• By limiting antiballistic missiles to very low levels of deployment, the United States and the Soviet Union removed a potential source of instability; for one side to build an extensive defense for its cities would inevitably be interpreted by the other as a step toward a first-strike capability. Before seeking a disarming capability, a potential aggressor would want to protect his population centers from incoming nuclear weapons.

• Some have alleged that the interim agreement, which expires in October 1977, penalizes the United States by permitting the Soviet Union to deploy more strategic missile launchers, both land based and sea based, than the United States. Such a view is misleading. When the agreement was signed in May 1972, the Soviet Union *already* possessed more land-based intercontinental ballistic missiles than the United States, and given the pace of its submarine construction program, over the next few years it could have built virtually twice as many nuclear ballistic missile submarines. . . .

The SALT I agreements were the first deliberate attempt by the nuclear superpowers to bring about strategic stability through negotiation. This very process is conducive to further restraint. For example, in the first round of SALT negotiations in 1970-72, both sides bitterly contested the number of ABM sites permitted by the agreement; two years later both sides gave up the right to build more than one site. In sum, we believed when we signed these agreements—and we believe now—that they had reduced the danger of nuclear war, that both sides had acquired some greater interest in restraint, and that the basis had been created for the present effort to reach a broader agreement. . . .

An Assessment of Détente

Détente is admittedly far from a modern equivalent to the kind of stable peace that characterized most of the nineteenth century. But it is a long step away from the bitter and aggressive spirit that has characterized so much of the postwar period. When linked to such broad and unprecedented projects as SALT, détente takes on added meaning and opens prospects of a more stable peace. SALT agreements should be seen as steps in a process leading to progressively greater stability. It is in that light that SALT and related projects will be judged by history.

Where has the process of détente taken us so far? What are the principles that must continue to guide our course?

Major progress has been made:

• Berlin's potential as Europe's perennial flashpoint has been substantially reduced through the quadripartite agreement of 1971. The United States considers strict adherence to the agreement a major test of détente.

• We and our allies are launched on negotiations with the Warsaw Pact and other countries in the conference on European security and cooperation, a conference designed to foster East-West dialogue and cooperation.

• At the same time, NATO and the Warsaw Pact are negotiating the reduction of their forces in Central Europe.

• The honorable termination of America's direct military involvement in Indochina and the substantial lowering of regional conflict were made possible by many factors. But this achievement would have been much more difficult, if not impossible, in an era of Soviet and Chinese hostility toward the United States.

• America's principal alliances have proved their durability in a new era. Many feared that détente would undermine them. Instead, détente has helped to place our alliance ties on a more enduring basis by removing the fear that friendship with the United States involved the risk of unnecessary confrontation with the U.S.S.R.

• Many incipient crises with the Soviet Union have been contained or settled without ever reaching the point of public disagreement. The world has been freer of East-West tensions and conflict than in the fifties and sixties.

• A series of bilateral cooperative agreements has turned the U.S.-Soviet relationship in a far more positive direction.

• We have achieved unprecedented agreements in arms limitation and measures to avoid accidental war.

• New possibilities for positive U.S.-Soviet cooperation have emerged on issues in which the globe is interdependent: science and technology, environment, energy.

These accomplishments do not guarantee peace. But they have served to lessen the rigidities of the past and offer hope for a better era. Despite fluctuations, a trend has been established; the character of international politics has been markedly changed.

It is too early to judge conclusively whether this change should be ascribed to tactical considerations. But in a sense, that is immaterial. For whether the change is temporary and tactical, or lasting and basic, our task is essentially the same: To transform that change into a permanent condition devoted to the purpose of a secure peace and mankind's aspiration for a better life. A tactical change sufficiently prolonged becomes a lasting transformation.

But the whole process can be jeopardized if it is taken for granted. As the cold war recedes in memory, détente can come to seem so natural that it appears safe to levy progressively greater demands on it. The temptation to combine détente with increasing pressure on the Soviet Union will grow. Such an attitude would be disastrous. We would not accept it from Moscow; Moscow will not accept it from us. We will finally wind up again with the cold war and fail to achieve either peace or any humane goal.

To be sure, the process of détente raises serious issues for many people. Let me deal with these in terms of the principles which underlie our policy.

First, if détente is to endure, both sides must benefit.

There is no question that the Soviet Union obtains benefits from détente. On what other grounds would the tough-minded members of the Politburo sustain it? But the essential point surely must be that détente serves American and world interests as well.

If these coincide with some Soviet interests, this will only strengthen the durability of the process. . . .

Second, building a new relationship with the Soviet Union does not entail any devaluation of traditional alliance relations.

The Odd Couple

Our approach to relations with the U.S.S.R. has always been, and will continue to be, rooted in the belief that the cohesion of our alliances, and particularly the Atlantic alliance, is a precondition to establishing a more constructive relationship with the U.S.S.R.

Crucial, indeed unique, as may be our concern with Soviet power, we do not delude ourselves that we should deal with it alone. When we speak of Europe and Japan as representing centers of power and influence, we describe not merely an observable fact but an indispensable element in the equilibrium needed to keep the world at peace. The cooperation and partnership between us transcend formal agreements; they reflect values and traditions not soon, if ever, to be shared with our adversaries. . . .

Third, the emergence of more normal relations with the Soviet Union must not undermine our resolve to maintain our national defense.

There is a tendency in democratic societies to relax as dangers seem to recede; there is an inclination to view the maintenance of strength as incompatible with relaxation of tensions rather than its precondition. But this is primarily a question of leadership. We shall attempt to be vigilant to the dangers facing America. This administration will not be misled—or mislead—on issues of national defense. At the same time, we do not accept the proposition that we need crises to sustain our defense. A society that needs artificial crises to do what is needed for survival will soon find itself in mortal danger.

Fourth, we must know what can and cannot be achieved in changing human conditions in the East.

The question of dealing with Communist governments has troubled the American people and the Congress since 1917. There has always been a fear that by working with a government whose internal policies differ so sharply with our own we are in some manner condoning these policies or encouraging their continuation. Some argue that until there is a genuine "liberalization"—or signs of serious progress in this direction—all elements of conciliation in Soviet policy must be regarded as temporary and tactical. In that view, demands for internal changes must be the precondition for the pursuit of a relaxation of tensions with the Soviet Union.

Our view is different. We shall insist on responsible international behavior by the Soviet Union and use it as the primary index of our relationship. Beyond this we will use our influence to the maximum to alleviate suffering and to respond to humane appeals. We know what we stand for, and we shall leave no doubt about it. . . .

We have accomplished much. But we cannot demand that the Soviet Union, in effect, suddenly reverse five decades of Soviet, and centuries of Russian, history. Such an attempt would be futile and at the same time hazard all that has already been achieved. Changes in Soviet society have already occurred, and more will come. But they are most likely to develop through an evolution that can best go forward in an environment of decreasing international tensions. A renewal of the cold war will hardly encourage the Soviet Union to change its emigration policies or adopt a more benevolent attitude toward dissent.

Détente is a process, not a permanent achievement. The agenda is full and continuing. Obviously the main concern must be to reduce the sources of potential conflict. This requires efforts in several interrelated areas:

• The military competition in all its aspects must be subject to increasingly firm restraints by both sides.

• Political competition, especially in moments of crisis, must be guided by the principles of restraint set forth in the documents described earlier. Crises there will be, but the United States and the Soviet Union have a special obligation deriving from the unimaginable military power that they wield and represent. Exploitation of crisis situations for unilateral gain is not acceptable.

• Restraint in crises must be augmented by cooperation in removing the causes of crises. There have been too many instances, notably in the Middle East, which demonstrate that policies of unilateral advantage sooner or later run out of control and lead to the brink of war, if not beyond.

• The process of negotiations and consultation must be continuous and intense. But no agreement between the nuclear superpowers can be durable if made over the heads of other nations which have a stake in the outcome. We should not seek to impose peace; we can, however, see that our own actions and conduct are conducive to peace. . . .

We have insisted toward the Soviet Union that we cannot have the atmosphere of détente without the substance. It is equally clear that the substance of détente will disappear in an atmosphere of hostility.

We have profound differences with the Soviet Union—in our values, our methods, our vision of the future. But it is these very differences which compel any responsible administration to make a major effort to create a more constructive relationship.

We face an opportunity that was not possible twenty-five years, or even a decade, ago. If that opportunity is lost, its moment will not quickly come again. Indeed, it may not come at all.

As President Kennedy pointed out: "For in the final analysis our most basic common link is that we all inhabit this small planet. We all breathe the same air. We all cherish our children's future. And we are all mortal."

VIEWPOINT 2

"Kissinger's détente amounts to giving . . . [U.S.] assets away without requiring any strategic benefits in return."

Détente Is a Flawed U.S. Policy Toward the Soviet Union

G. Warren Nutter (1923-1979)

Both the policy of détente and its most famous practitioner, Henry Kissinger, were controversial in the 1970s. Many conservative observers argued that the United States was being too cooperative with the Soviet Union, which they believed remained a dangerous Cold War adversary. Such a view is provided here by G. Warren Nutter, who was assistant secretary of defense for international security from 1969 to 1973. Both prior to and after that time he was a professor of economics at the University of Virginia at Charlottesville.

Nutter argues that the policies of détente as practiced by Richard Nixon and Henry Kissinger have compromised U.S. interests, and that the Soviet Union has taken advantage of détente to rebuild its military strength even as the United States has reduced its own defense spending. The nuclear arms balance between the two superpowers has tilted in favor of the Soviet Union, he writes, and he asserts that the diplomatic agreements between the two superpowers will have little substantive effect on ensuring peace. Nutter insists that in formulating U.S. policy toward the Soviet Union the United States must recognize Soviet power and the USSR's anti-U.S. goals. Nutter concludes that the Cold War between the United States and the Soviet Union has not been replaced or superseded by détente.

Secretary of State Henry A. Kissinger has implicitly renounced his earlier conviction that only the exercise of power can check Soviet strife with the Western world and that, unless Soviet weakness is exploited, détente will merely hasten Soviet hegemony by demoralizing the West. "Détente is an imperative," he now says. "In a world shadowed by the danger of nuclear holocaust, there is no rational alternative to the pursuit of relaxation of tensions." That is, avoidance of the *risk* of war must be the supreme and overriding goal of U.S. policy, almost regardless of cost in other respects.

This attitude stands in stark contrast to the sober warning on the opening page of Kissinger's first book:

> Those ages which in retrospect seem most peaceful were least in search of peace. Those whose quest for it seems unending appear least able to achieve tranquility. Wherever peace—conceived as the avoidance of war—has been the primary objective of a power or a group of powers, the international system has been at the mercy of the most ruthless member of the international community. Whenever the international order has acknowledged that certain principles could not be compromised even for the sake of peace, stability based on an equilibrium of forces was at least conceivable.

He made the same point in those early years when he noted that "the dilemma of the nuclear period can, therefore, be defined as follows: the enormity of modern weapons makes the thought of war repugnant, but the refusal to run any risks would amount to giving the Soviet rulers a blank check." . . .

The change in attitude between then and now may seem subtle, but it is fundamental. Kissinger's détente is conceived as a no-risk policy: it aims not merely at avoiding war or the risk of war, but at eliminating all risk of confrontation that could eventually generate a risk of war. Kissinger the public official could find no more severe a critic of his policy of détente than Kissinger the scholar, who would say that the search for a no-risk policy is self-defeating, that a so-called no-risk policy incurs the greatest risk of all. . . .

Secretary Kissinger hails agreements that Professor Kissinger would have strenuously opposed. Some are acclaimed as landmarks in détente: ratification of the status quo in Berlin, recognition of East Germany, and legitimization of the existing political order in Eastern Europe. SALT I is called an unqualified success in limiting nuclear arms even though it permits a sizable expansion of the Soviet arsenal and contains serious terminological loopholes, both the product of Soviet intransigence. The Soviet Union, once portrayed as a revolutionary power beyond reassurance and incapable of compromise, is now viewed as a conciliatory member of the family of nations practicing restraint in its economic, political, and military relations with others.

One can only speculate on what caused such a profound change in outlook. A case can be made that Kissinger simply saw no other way to turn as he watched the tide of history sweep away, one by one, the elements he had identified as essential for establishing an international order. . . .

There remains the question . . . of whether the substance of détente constitutes the best foreign policy for the United States. For brevity, we shall use "détente" to mean the already described configuration of policies and procedures specifically associated with Kissinger's stewardship of foreign affairs, not the relaxation of international tensions in the abstract. The issue is whether détente, so defined, is the best way to preserve the security of the West.

Détente involves a mixed strategy: interdependency is the carrot, deterrence the stick, and arms control the rein. Let us examine the relative importance of these elements, their mutual consistency, and the compatibility of this strategy with the attainment of peace and tranquillity.

Deterrence is obviously the key element, for without it security of the West would depend solely on Soviet goodwill and self-restraint, scarcely a strong reed to lean upon in the light of Soviet history and ideology. By definition, effective arms control would reduce the level of Western military strength required for deterrence, but the relation between deterrence and interdependency is far more complex. Greater gains from so-called interdependency might, by enhancing the Soviet stake in the existing international order, provide an incentive to the Soviet Union to restrain its expansionist instinct. But the unilateral concessions yielding those gains will cause us to appear all the more weak-willed in the eyes of Soviet leaders, while the gains themselves increase Soviet power commensurately. Soviet leaders will consequently be tempted to seek even greater gains through power politics and to treat the United States as a weakling deserving contempt. Meanwhile, the atmosphere of détente is certain, as we now witness, to sway Western psychology toward downgrading the Soviet threat, cutting defense budgets, and disrupting alliances, the effect being a further tipping of the power balance in the Soviet Union's favor. The dynamics of this process can, as Kissinger once constantly warned, lead to demoralization of the West and Soviet victory by default.

Kissinger's grand design rests on the thesis that the dominating effect of greater interdependency will be to restrain Soviet behavior, but he has little backing from history. Economic interdependence is scarcely new: on the eve of World War I, Norman Angell argued in *The Great Illusion* that the intricate network of world commerce had destroyed all possibility of gain from war. Yet the warring nations of Europe in the twentieth century, as in the nineteenth, normally were close trading partners. As Professor Gregory Grossman reminds us, "history provides little reassurance that trade ensures peace, and Russia's own history least of all. Germany was her largest trading partner just before each of the two World Wars, while China was her largest trading partner (and Russia China's) before the break between Moscow and Peking around 1960."

It is doubtful in any case that the interdependency seemingly envisaged by Kissinger can grow out of normal trading relations, since there is no reason to believe that the Soviet Union is about to abandon its traditional policy of autarky. Soviet planners are, however, eager for a generous infusion of Western technology if the price is right—which is to say, if available on cheap long-term credit or otherwise concessionary terms. The response called for is economic aid, which might seem to weld a stronger bond of dependency than a network of trade. But, historically, tribute has been no more successful than trade in preventing conquest or domination by a foreign power.

Perhaps the weakest link in Kissinger's argument is the insistence that any gains accruing to Soviet power from détente are irrelevant "because when both sides possess such enormous power, small additional increments cannot be translated into tangible advantage or even usable political strength." This does not make sense, as Professor Albert Wohlstetter succinctly demonstrates:

> The reasoning supporting this view of the present equilibrium proceeds from the notion that adding an increment of military power to the "overwhelming arsenals of the nuclear age" does not effectively change anything. But is it true that because both the Soviet Union and the United States have many thousands of nuclear warheads, it makes no difference at all if one of the superpowers adds to its arsenal wire-guided anti-tank weapons or surface-to-air missiles or laser-guided bombs or the like for use in limited contingencies? And, can neither gain some political end by transferring such weapons (or even some day a few nuclear weapons) to an ally? On the evidence of October 1973 the Soviet Union feels that one-sided gains are feasible. Statements about the sufficiency or stability of military balances cannot be derived from the mere size of the superpowers' nuclear stockpiles. "Power" is much more complex and varied than that. Neither military nor political nor economic power can be measured by one simple scalar number.

In other words, the power balance is still subject to infinite variation through "marginal adjustments."

Dividing the World

Attacks on Henry Kissinger's foreign policy came from liberal as well as conservative sources. Harvard University professor of government Stanley Hoffman, writing in 1979, argues that Kissinger's conception of the world caused him to view all global conflicts as aspects of Soviet-American rivalry, which Hoffman believes is a distortion of reality.

To Kissinger, the struggle between Moscow and Washington is not just global in scope, it absorbs, so to speak, every other conflict or issue. Peace, or containment, is therefore indivisible. Every crisis anywhere tests our ability to stand up to the Soviets. And the credibility of the US depends on our capacity to meet every test. Thus, in case after case, Kissinger's policy was to make the Soviets squarely responsible for what was happening, and to act in such a way that they would either put pressure on their clients to cease and desist, or dissociate themselves from their clients.

Is this the real world? Or does it not substitute for the real world an artificially simple and tidy one, in which friends and foes, radicals and moderates are neatly lined up, and in which nationalism—surely as important a force as communism—gets thoroughly discounted? If one sees the world as more complex and fluid than in Kissinger's scheme, if one realizes that most states are not simply the superpowers' proxies—India and Syria are described as waging "proxy wars" for the Soviets—but pursue their own interests, the notion of indivisible credibility and of a strategy geared exclusively to the Soviet Union becomes eminently questionable. A Soviet presence or privileged position is not necessarily permanent. We may have a good reason for being occasionally on the same side as the Soviets in order to prevent them from capturing a cause or movement. And we may have many incentives to deal with Soviet clients while they still are beholden to the Soviets, precisely because they may not want to mortgage their independence, or because their radicalism is rhetorical, or compatible with our concerns. Looking to Moscow for a key (as Kissinger did, in early 1969, when he wanted to send Cyrus Vance there with a peace plan for Vietnam) can be a mistake. On the other hand, as we discovered in Vietnam, some "proxies" are of such a hostile will of their own that neither Soviet pressure nor Soviet political disengagement helps us much.

Consider what has been happening to Soviet and American defense efforts in real terms. Ours has fallen by almost a sixth since 1964 while theirs (according to our official estimate) has risen by more than a third, coming to surpass ours by 1970. When the incremental cost of the Vietnam War is eliminated, our defense effort shows virtually a steady decline, year by year, since 1963. Theirs shows a steady rise. Are we to believe that this "marginal adjustment" has had no effect on the global power balance?

The most immediate impact has been on relative forces in being. In the strategic nuclear sphere, the Soviet Union has moved from a position of substantial inferiority to rough parity, a development that has made the balance of conventional forces, whose importance Kissinger has always stressed, all the more significant. The Soviet Union now has almost twice as many men under arms as we do; a decade ago it had only a sixth more than we did. Our surface combat fleet has shrunk in numbers to become smaller than the Soviet fleet; a decade ago it was a third larger. And so on and on. These divergent trends in military strength surely have implications for diplomacy as well as deterrence, as Kissinger, an avid practitioner of show of force, well knows. And, however unthinkable nuclear war has become, use of conventional force remains habitual: witness the instances of the last quarter century in Korea, Hungary, the Middle East, Africa, South Asia, Cuba, Southeast Asia, Czechoslovakia, and Cyprus.

Over the longer run, diverging defense efforts are likely to disturb the power balance more fundamentally, because the technology of weaponry, offensive and defensive, is in constant flux along with the military arts. There is no way to regulate this dynamic process through arms control without rigorous on-site inspection, and whichever power gains the upper hand in innovation achieves the potential for commanding the future heights of power. The nature of the military balance a decade hence is therefore being determined in the laboratories and on the proving grounds of today. Who knows what new miracles of horror science has in store for us? Perhaps they will metamorphose the balance of terror in the same way that nuclear explosives once did. Whether radical or not, change is certain in military art and science, and relative strength in research and development now is likely to be translated directly into future relative strength in being.

Alternatives to Détente

Much more could be said against détente, but it would repeat what can be found in a voluminous literature already in print. Enough has been said here to enable us to turn to the questions put by Secretary Kissinger to his critics:

> What is the alternative they propose? What precise policies do they want us to change? Are they prepared for a prolonged situation of dramatically increased international danger? Do they wish to return to the constant crises and high arms budgets of the cold war? Does détente encourage repression—or is it détente that has generated the ferment and the demands for openness that we are now witnessing? Can we ask our people to support confrontation unless they know that every reasonable alternative has been explored?

The questions are quite loaded, of course, because they imply that the critics must choose either white hat or black, either détente or cold war. If that is the only choice open, one wonders what has happened to the "new stable structure of peace" under construction these last six years. As Professor Wohlstetter points out, "what is odd about this metaphor is its desire to have it both ways. The Structure of Peace in the nuclear era is solid and unshakable. Yet we must tiptoe carefully to make sure that we do not bring the whole apparently ramshackle affair crashing down about our ears in the final apocalypse of shattered glass and toppling masonry."

The metaphor is wrong on both counts: the structure is in fact shaky, but there is no need to tiptoe around our relations with the Soviet Union. Not yet. An alternative stance is still achievable for American foreign policy that avoids the perils of Kissinger's détente at the one extreme and stark cold war at the other. It involves restoring Western confidence and resolve, reconstituting deterrence, basing negotiation firmly on the principles of reciprocal concession and unimpaired security, and bargaining accordingly.

As already stressed, Kissinger's diplomacy has created too much one-sided détente, an overrelaxation of tension in the United States and throughout the West. Tension is after all the natural defensive reaction to a perceived threat, and it alerts and stimulates the will to resist. Tension had become excessive in the West, Kissinger concluded, because the cold war associated with it contained a more perilous risk—nuclear annihilation—than the threat being resisted. Tension was relaxed by a diplomatic blitz that had the effect of accenting the nuclear risk while belittling the Soviet threat. The consequence has been a dangerous weakening of the will to resist, as a confused public tries to understand whether resistance is unnecessary or whether it is futile.

What needs to be done first is to restore a healthy state of alert based on appreciation of the external dangers threatening the Western way of life and a sense of confidence that they can be overcome. This can be done gradually by nudging diplomacy away from a quest for ways of getting the Soviet Union involved and toward the practice of quid-pro-quo bargaining. The differing nature of Eastern and Western problems provides a basis for reciprocal concessions benefitting both sides while improving Western security, or at least leaving it unimpaired.

The Soviet Union suffers chronically from a defective economy, which constantly thwarts the ambition of Soviet leaders to maximize power in the future as well as now. The economy simply cannot meet the heavy demands placed on it for both maintaining strength in being and providing growth, including a rising living standard. The problems stem from the inefficient organization and deficient incentives of a huge command economy hampered by, among other things, a policy of basic autarky. Hence the economy experiences periodic agricultural crises in the short run and inability to generate a broad front of technological innovation over the long run.

False Promises

Eugene V. Rostow served as under secretary of state for political affairs from 1966 to 1969 under Lyndon Johnson, and as director of the Arms Control and Disarmament Agency from 1981 to 1983 under Ronald Reagan. Writing in 1984 he argued that détente, rather than ushering in a new era of cooperation between the superpowers, resulted in Soviet gains and a worsening of the Cold War.

We have been negotiating and signing nuclear arms agreements with the Soviet Union for more than ten years while most of our politicians and experts assured us that such agreements would induce "restraint" in Soviet behavior, and help move world politics toward "detente" and even "peace." In 1972, when the SALT I agreements were signed, Nixon even proclaimed that "detente" had been achieved, and "cooperation" with the Soviet Union substituted for "confrontation." The history of the last decade makes those claims embarrassing. The Soviet Union treated its formal guarantee of the Indochinese peace agreement, dated March 2, 1973, as a scrap of paper. In the Middle East, Soviet behavior was equally a betrayal; in May 1972, the Soviet Union promised Nixon full support for cooperative efforts to achieve peace between Israel and its neighbors in accordance with Security Council Resolution 242. One month before, the Soviet Union had promised to help Egypt launch the aggression of October 1973—a promise it carried out faithfully. The record has been the same, with minor variations, in Africa, Afghanistan, and Kampuchea. Thus the 1970s and early 1980s turned out to be the worst period of the cold war, marked by Soviet and Soviet-sponsored aggression throughout the Third World on a larger and more serious scale than the probes and feints of the late '40s, and by the emergence of the Soviet attempt to separate the U.S. from Western Europe, Japan, and China through the achievement and acknowledgement of the Soviet nuclear hegemony.

One way out would be fundamental reform of the economic system, but the totalitarian rulers have carefully avoided such a venture for fear of undermining their monolithic power. Curing the patient might eliminate need for the doctor. And so they have turned predictably to the West for help.

Whatever economic help we give is bound to enhance Soviet power—to make it stronger than it otherwise would be. Gains to the West, if any, will be trivial economically and even more so strategically, because Western military and political strength is not constrained significantly by economic factors. Hence we should not help the Soviet Union economically and technologically unless we receive political concessions in return that leave our security at least unimpaired. In general we should insist on improvement of security since what the Soviet Union gains from economic aid and expanded trade strengthens the leadership internally as well as externally. It should be required to reduce the Soviet threat to the West in exchange for the gain in domestic power. It is on this basis that we should parley for Soviet movement on SALT, MBFR, arms control in the Middle East, neutralization of Southeast Asia, and so on.

We must not delude ourselves that our foreign policy has no effect on conditions inside the Soviet Union and Eastern Europe. On this score, Solzhenitsyn is right and Kissinger wrong. If Soviet rulers know the West will bail them out of every economic difficulty, they will be under no pressure to liberalize the regime. Similarly, the relaxing of external tension has always been accompanied in the East by a tightening internally. Kissinger asks whether détente encourages repression or ferment, and the answer is repression. Dissent reached its high mark in the Soviet Union before détente, and the movement has been virtually stamped out since. The various parts of Eastern Europe have experienced a like reactionary policy. Kissinger attacks a straw man when he stubbornly insists that Western foreign policy cannot transform the Soviet domestic structure, for no one seriously believes that outside pressure can cause democracy or anything like it to spring forth overnight in Soviet society. That is not the issue at all, but rather how best to endorse and strengthen the liberal cause in the East.

Businesslike bargaining based on the principle of unimpaired security is hardly confrontation or cold war. If Soviet leaders blindly reject opportunities to make arrangements yielding mutual gains but not undermining our strategic position, we have all the less reason to believe that they will behave responsibly merely to continue enjoying the goodies of involvement.

Raising Western Morale

A revitalized diplomacy will help raise Western morale and confidence and lay the way for repairing our crumbling ramparts and alliances. The downward trend of defense must be reversed or all else is in vain. NATO must be put back together again and its strategic dilemmas resolved. It is a sad fact that Western military strategy has lagged far behind technology, particularly in not appreciating the revolutionary significance of smart weapons, non-nuclear as well as nuclear. Selective strategic targeting, the product of intensive deliberation in the Pentagon in recent years, is an early sign of overdue revision of strategic doctrine.

The issue, then, is how to make best use of our assets in the continuing struggle to defend Western civilization against the threat from the East. Stripped of rhetoric, Kissinger's détente amounts to giving the assets away without requiring any strategic benefits in return, this being done on the premise that the Soviet rulers will so treasure what they are receiving that they will carefully avoid upsetting the strategic equilibrium. But, as we have argued, they will hardly need to do anything since the power balance will steadily move in their favor anyhow. The alternative proposed here would exchange our assets only for compensatory strategic benefits. Such a diplomacy of reciprocal concession holds far more promise for meaningful peace than the drift of détente.

VIEWPOINT 3

"Without bringing about an increasing measure of individual liberty in the Communist world . . . there can be no real movement toward a more peaceful world."

The U.S. Should Press the Soviet Union to Improve Human Rights

Henry M. Jackson (1912-1983)

A common criticism of détente during the Nixon/Ford/Kissinger era was that it deemphasized the importance of human rights within the Soviet Union in the name of superpower cooperation. As long as the Soviet Union repressed its own people, these people argued, any relationship of cooperation between the United States and the Soviet Union would lack a firm foundation. One of the most influential critics of détente on this and other grounds was Henry M. Jackson, senator from Washington from 1953 to his death in 1983 and an unsuccessful candidate for the Democratic presidential nomination in 1972 and 1976.

Jackson's views on human rights had a direct effect on U.S.-Soviet relations when Congress in 1972 passed the Jackson-Vanik amendment. The amendment restricted trade and economic concessions with the Soviet Union unless the USSR relaxed laws on emigration. The law was meant to force the Soviet Union to grant its citizens greater freedom to leave the country if they chose. Soviet leaders argued that the amendment was interference in their internal affairs and rejected the trade agreement it had previously negotiated with the United States. U.S. secretary of state Henry M. Kissinger criticized the amendment, arguing that it limited U.S. flexibility in its policy toward the Soviet Union and threatened to derail progress the United States had made in nuclear arms talks, economic cooperation, and other areas. In the following viewpoint taken from a speech he made on October 11, 1973, Jackson defends his amendment and the argument that an improvement in the Soviet Union's human rights record was essential for the United States to successfully pursue peaceful cooperation with it.

At no time since the end of world war II has the Western democratic world been more hopeful, or the struggling democrats in the East more apprehensive, at the prospects of the developing international détente. And nowhere should the fears and apprehensions of those whose love of freedom has survived behind the Iron Curtain find a more receptive and thoughtful consideration than at a gathering devoted to pacem in terris [peace on earth]. So my remarks this morning are devoted to the question of détente and human rights.

Trade and Human Rights

On Monday night the Secretary of State and the chairman of the Senate Foreign Relations Committee—who agree on little else—came before you to share their belief that it is wrong for the United States to condition trade concessions to the Soviet Union on adherence to the free emigration provision of the Universal Declaration of Human Rights.

Senator Fulbright, who is beguiled by the Soviets, and Dr. Kissinger, who believes that he is beguiling them, manage to find common ground in rejecting Dr. Andrei Sakharov's wise counsel against promoting a "détente" unaccompanied by increased openness and trust.

I believe in the Universal Declaration of Human Rights and I believe that now, twenty-five years after its adoption by the United Nations, it is not too late or too early to begin to implement it. And I am sustained in the belief that the best way to do this is through pressing my amendment to the trade bill by these brave words from the great Soviet physicist Andrei Sakharov:

The abandonment of a policy of principle would be a betrayal of the thousands of Jews and non-Jews who want to emigrate, of the hundreds in camps and mental hospitals, of the victims of the Berlin Wall.

Such a denial would lead to stronger repressions on ideological grounds. It would be tantamount to total capitulation of democratic principles in face of blackmail, deceit and violence. The consequences of such a capitulation for international confidence, détente and the entire future of mankind are difficult to predict.

I express the hope that the Congress of the United States, reflecting the will and the traditional love of freedom of the American people, will realize its historical responsibility before mankind and will find the strength to rise above temporary partisan considerations of commercialism and prestige.

I hope that the Congress will support the Jackson amendment.

In an age of nuclear weapons, Senator Fulbright suggests, the Soviet Union is "the one country whose cooperation is absolutely

The American Vision

Jimmy Carter, speaking in a television debate with President Gerald Ford during the 1976 presidential campaign, attacked the foreign policy of Ford and his secretary of state Henry M. Kissinger, and called for a renewed commitment to human rights.

We've lost in our foreign policy the character of the American people. We've ignored or excluded the American people and the Congress from participation in the shaping of our foreign policy. It's been one of secrecy and exclusion. In addition to that we've had a chance to become now—contrary to our longstanding beliefs and principles—the arms merchant of the whole world. We've tried to buy success from our enemies, and at the same time we've excluded from the process the normal friendship of our allies. . . .

I want to see our nation return to a posture and an image and a standard to make us proud once again. I remember the world of NATO and the world of Point Four and the world of the Marshall Plan and the world of the Peace Corps. Why can't we have that once again? We ought to be a beacon for nations who search for peace and who search for freedom, who search for individual liberty, who search for basic human rights. We haven't been lately. We can be once again.

We'll never have that world leadership until we are strong at home, and we can have that strength if we return to the basic principles.

It ought not to be a strength of bombast and threats. It ought to be a quiet strength based on the integrity of our people, the vision of the Constitution and in a strong will and purpose that God's given us in the greatest nation on earth—the United States.

essential." Dr. Kissinger, who recognizes that our traditional commitment to individual liberty poses moral dilemmas, implies that this commitment must be weighed against "the profound moral concern . . . of the attainment of peace." Senator Fulbright hints darkly that our very survival may depend on the pursuit of a détente without human rights.

A True Peace

But is the risk of nuclear war really going to increase if the Congress conditions most-favored-nation treatment to the Soviet Union on free emigration? Does Senator Fulbright believe that the Soviet Union will be any less cautious about the risks of a suicidal nuclear war if we choose not to subsidize their foreign borrowing? I concur in Dr. Sakharov's belief that "the danger of nuclear war continues to be the foremost concern for all of humanity," and with him I support "all measures to avert this danger including proposed measures of armament reduction." The process of reducing the risks of nuclear war can and will continue because it is in the mutual interest of both the United States and the Soviet Union to do so. But the development of more extensive mutual interest, of a closer and more cordial relationship between the two countries, must be based on something more solid and more enduring and more comprehensive than bargain-basement credits and one-sided commercial transactions.

A true peace, an enduring peace, can only be built on a moral consensus. What better place to begin building this consensus than on the principles embodied in the Universal Declaration of Human Rights, among which the right to choose the country one lives in—the right to emigrate freely—is perhaps the most basic.

We are asked to believe that the prospects for peace are enhanced by the flow of Pepsi-Cola to the Soviet Union and the flow of vodka to the United States. I say that we will move much further along the road to a stable peace when we see the free flow of people and ideas across the barriers that divide East from West—a flow unchecked by arbitrary and capricious power.

Now, at this time in history, we have been presented with an unparalleled opportunity. The growth of the Soviet economy— the means by which the Soviet Union has so long been hoping to "overtake and surpass" the United States—has begun to falter badly. The Soviet economy, despite enormous inefficiencies, had managed to sustain significant economic growth only by resort to a staggering rate of capital investments, twice that of the United States. In recent years, the productivity of that capital has declined drastically. The inflexible Soviet economy has found it increasingly difficult to assimilate modern technology. Even massive infusion of their own capital no longer promises to sustain economic growth.

If the Soviet Union were a minor country with no external ambitions, it might stagger along indefinitely with a no-growth or slow-growth economy. But she is not such a country—and therein lies our opportunity and our challenge. The task that the Soviet leaders wish to impose on their rigid economic system is nothing less than to make the Soviet Union the dominant world power—economically, militarily, and politically. They hope to achieve a high rate of economic growth and hold their economy up as a model for the less-developed world. They want to continue to divert a disproportionate share of their resources to military spending—more than twice the percentage of GNP as in our case—to sustain their buildup of strategic arms and conventional forces in Eastern Europe and on the Chinese border and to underwrite the military forces of their Arab allies. The Soviet Government needs desperately to improve the quality and quantity of goods available to the Soviet consumer, because it is only too aware of the political threat posed by the continued frustration of consumer demands. Yet the Soviet leaders are also afraid—or perhaps they do not know how—to relax their rigidly controlled economy, and so they have come to us for help. We would be ill-advised to treat this request as just another business proposition, or even as a routine request for foreign aid.

Reordering Soviet Priorities

In my judgment, the most abundant and positive source of much needed help for the Soviet economy should come, not from the United States, but through a reordering of Soviet priorities away from the military into the civilian sector. And in this connection, it is high time that we propose serious disarmament at the SALT negotiations—not the sort of fiddling at the margins that has characterized the approach to arms control thus far, but serious reductions of strategic weapons on both sides. I see no reason, for example, why we cannot, in concert with the Soviet Union, agree that 900 ICBMs and 35 nuclear submarines are adequate for both sides. Would this not be better than the present situation in which they have 1,600 ICBMs and are building toward 62 submarines and we have 1,000 ICBMs and 41 submarines?

The Soviets are seeking billions of dollars in U.S. Government subsidized credits—long-term loans at 6 percent interest. Neither Dr. Kissinger nor Senator Fulbright chose to dwell on this aspect of what the Secretary of State euphemistically termed "a carefully shaped, overall mosaic." What is involved here are credit transfers that will dwarf last year's grain deal—or, as I prefer to call it, the great grain robbery.

There are, in my judgment, countries and purposes more deserving of our assistance, whose needs are greater—in some cases dire—and whose use of our aid for humanitarian purposes is more readily assured. The drought-stricken nations of the African Sahel come immediately to mind.

Communism and Human Rights

James L. Payne, a professor of political science at Texas A&M University, wrote in the 1983 book Beyond Containment *that the United States should work to confront the human rights record not only of the Soviet Union but of other communist countries.*

The Communist challenge to freedom . . . is pervasive and predictable. Communist dictatorships are inspired and aided by the Soviet Union and its allies. Each one that comes into existence serves as both an example to be emulated and as a physical base for the implantation of more tyrannies of the same type. Furthermore, what non-Communist rulers and regimes may become is an open question. Some may allow considerable freedom; others may be more or less dictatorial. We cannot tell forehand. The outcome of a Communist takeover, on the other hand, is predictable. One of the few truly dependable generalizations in international affairs is that the level of brutality in a country goes up when Communists take over. Virtually every side-by-side and before-and-after comparison supports this point: South Korea and North Korea; Batista's Cuba and Castro's Cuba; South Vietnam (pre-1975) and North Vietnam; South Vietnam pre-1975 and South Vietnam post-1975; West Germany and East Germany; and so on.

Another deplorable but dependable generalization is that Communist tyrannies, once established, are particularly long-lived. Indeed, since Soviet troops prevent them from dying a natural death, we cannot even say for sure that they are not immortal.

For these reasons, a nation with humanitarian goals but limited resources should concentrate on anti-Communism: holding back the Soviets; holding back their allies; and keeping countries from falling under their sway. In the world today, anti-Communism is the number one human rights policy.

Let us not lose this opportunity to bargain hard for human rights. Let us not be misled by arguments that the time is not yet ripe or that we will be able to accomplish more later, after we have enmeshed the Soviets in some entangling web of investments and business deals. As Dr. Kissinger so eloquently stated here a few nights ago, opportunities once lost may never recur again. What are now clearly recognized by the Russians as concessions on our part will eventually be demanded as the normal way of doing things. Already we see Dr. Kissinger insisting that the discretion of the Congress to grant or deny or condition most-favored-nation status no longer exists because he has bargained it away, never minding that he had no authority to do so. Does anyone believe that American corporations will be more willing, when they have massive investments to protect, to insist on the rights of Soviet dissenters than they are now? At this moment we have an opportunity—which may not again be repeated—when the Soviet people are graced with men with the stature and prestige of Sakharov and Solzhenitsyn who have courageously spoken out on behalf of human rights. Their plea must not fall on deaf ears.

As Sakharov said in his open letter to the Congress:

> The Jackson amendment is made even more significant by the fact that the world is only just entering on a new course of détente and it is therefore essential that the proper direction be followed from the outset. This is a fundamental issue, extending far beyond the question of emigration.

I believe that we ought to press our traditional commitment to human rights in the emerging détente not only because this commitment is a most solemn pledge, not only because these values are right in themselves, but because it must be a purpose of the détente to bring the Soviet Union into the community of civilized nations, to hasten the end of what Sakharov has called "an intolerable isolation, bringing with it the ugliest consequences." The isolation of the Soviet Union, which, in Sakharov's words, "is highly perilous for all mankind, for international confidence and détente," is as dangerous as and comparable to the isolation of Germany in 1937. In that year the great German writer Thomas Mann wrote these words:

> Why isolation, world hostility, lawlessness, intellectual interdict, cultural darkness, and every other evil? Why not rather Germany's voluntary return to the European system, her reconciliation with Europe, with all the inward accompaniments of freedom, justice, well-being, and human decency, and a jubilant welcome from the rest of the world? Why not? Only because a regime which, in word and deed, denies the rights of man, which wants above all else to remain in power, would stultify itself and be abolished if, since it cannot make war, it actually made peace.

Too often, those who insist that the pace and development of détente should reflect progress in the area of human rights are accused of opposition to détente itself. Nothing could be further from the truth. The argument is not between the proponents and detractors of détente, but between those who wish a genuine era of international accommodation based on progress toward individual liberty and those who, in the final analysis, are indifferent to such progress.

We will have moved from the appearance to the reality of détente when East Europeans can freely visit the West, when Soviet students in significant numbers can come to American universities, and when American students in significant numbers can study in Russia. When reading the Western press and listening to Western broadcasts is no longer an act of treason, when families can be reunited across national borders, when emigration is free—then we shall have a genuine détente between peoples and not a formula between governments for capitulation on the issue of human rights.

Without bringing about an increasing measure of individual liberty in the Communist world there can be no genuine détente, there can be no real movement toward a more peaceful world. If we permit form to substitute for substance, if we are content with what in Washington is referred to as "atmospherics," we will not only fail to keep our own most solemn promises, we will, in the long run, fail to keep the peace.

VIEWPOINT 4

"It is because I see the nuclear question as always foremost that I cannot be sanguine about the human prospect in the long run, unless the human rights issue of the moment in this country is made less salient."

The U.S. Should Not Let Human Rights Issues Endanger Peace Between the Superpowers

David Riesman (1909-)

The issue of human rights in U.S.-Soviet relations continued in 1976 with the election of Jimmy Carter as president. Carter had criticized the policies of the previous administrations as being too insensitive to the issue of human rights. He pledged to make human rights a cornerstone of U.S. foreign policy and called for improved human rights in the Soviet Union.

In the following viewpoint, taken from a commencement address delivered in June 1977, David Riesman questions this renewed emphasis on human rights. He argues the primary goal of

U.S. policy toward the Soviet Union should be the prevention of nuclear war. Thus the United States should focus its efforts on reducing tensions between the two nations, not raising them on the basis of human rights or other issues. Riesman was a professor of sociology at Harvard University, and became noted for his use of social science techniques in analyzing U.S. foreign policy. His writings include the book *The Lonely Crowd.*

The concepts of human rights and human prospects suggest the possibility of conflicts among our ideals, that is, the possibility that the proclaimed goal of human rights may inadvertently risk the human prospects of survival itself. This is the risk of immediate destruction through what I have regarded, since Hiroshima, as the overarching danger to the species: the existence of nuclear weapons and the possibility to which these give rise of an escalating nuclear conflict among the superpowers. I supported the candidacy of President Carter on a number of grounds, chief among them the fact that he is the first president with a technical understanding of those weapons and with a serious and systematic interest in controlling and eventually banishing them—an effort that must begin between the Soviet Union and ourselves before we can hope to restrain proliferation among those other nations who now possess such weapons in actuality or potential.

At the same time, in lending his prestige and immense moral capital to the campaign for human rights vis-a-vis the Soviet Union, it is possible that President Carter has jeopardized his hopes on the all-important nuclear front, not only because prominent officialdom in the Soviet Union says so, but because of the long-run impact of the Carter campaign on *American* public opinion. Indeed, it is difficult to predict the possible impact of the human rights campaign, not so much on the vocal dissidents who have already suffered jeopardy, but on the generally silent but nonetheless in the long run influential public opinion of nonelites in the Soviet Union and its uneasy satellites.

The campaign for human rights vis-a-vis the Soviet Union of course did not begin with President Carter. In one sense it goes back to the very beginning of the Soviet regime, while long before that the insistence of many Americans on the proper moral conduct of other countries was a factor in launching us into both the Spanish-American War and the First World War. The contemporary campaign vis-a-vis the Soviet Union would seem to take its origin at the conclusion of the fighting in Vietnam, and, in some degree, to represent the unliquidated continuation of the American domestic conflict over that war by other means and with somewhat altered partisans.

A Quiet Diplomacy

Joseph S. Nye Jr. is a professor of government at Harvard University. In a 1984 article in Foreign Affairs *he wrote that rather than confronting the Soviet Union over human rights violations, the United States could best serve the cause of human rights by maintaining a cooperative relationship with the Soviet leadership.*

We need caution and realism in our expectations of bringing about social and political change in the Soviet Union. . . . [A] confrontation human rights policy is likely to be counterproductive in terms of the interests of Soviet citizens. Sometimes, however, minor improvements can be made through quiet diplomacy. In general, the fate of human rights in the Soviet Union is adversely affected by the worsening of the overall climate of U.S.-Soviet relations. Government actions that promote social contact and quiet diplomacy rather than public government efforts targeted at individuals or Soviet policies are more likely to serve both human rights and our long-term objective of enhancing the degree of transparency and communication in the relationship.

Liberal intellectuals, public officials, and interest groups ranging from influential American Zionists to longshoremen to the hard-liners who run the international division of the AFL-CIO have been in the forefront of the human rights issue, in some part as an attack on the efforts to achieve detente by former president Nixon and Henry Kissinger—an attack joined by the Republican Cold War Right, and the Democratic-liberal Left with its call for an open moral diplomacy, superior to realpolitik. The campaign appeals to our idealism: to our hope of living in a world without torture, without slavery, one where people are free to speak and to move about—although the current campaign against illegal immigrants and, indeed, against any further immigration at all fits in badly with a desire for greater freedom of movement across frontiers.

Competing Ideals

It is not sufficient argument against our human rights campaign that we ourselves often violate our own ideals in practice vis-a-vis immigration of other people. On another level we attempt to limit or keep out, through ever increasing efforts at protectionism, the importation of goods which others can make more efficiently than we. The purpose of an ideal is to express something not easily achieved. No American policy, foreign or domestic, is viable which rests on a definition of the national interest—a questionable concept—which fails to take account of our national idealism; the problem is to adjudicate among competing ideals.

The notion that ideals may not be compatible with each other is often difficult for Americans to accept; we are inclined to believe that all good things are compatible, that we can have *both* human survival and human rights without any risk to the former or compromise or delay with respect to the latter. Furthermore, the focus on human rights, though now voiced by a generally liberal Democratic administration, inevitably plays into the never wholly defeated Cold War mentality of ethnocentric and patrioteering Americans even while President Carter is seeking to open up our relations with Cuba and Panama, with Vietnam and even with North Korea.

The current generation of young people has not grown up with nightmares of the possibility of nuclear devastation. Vietnam was not seen as an issue of nuclear peril, as it was for me, but as a moral outrage and, for many, a personal threat and a personal moral dilemma.

My generation is the product of a different history. I did not share a number of attitudes that prevailed in this country during the Second World War. I never for a moment had any sympathy for Stalinism, and I regarded Soviet brutalities as quite as murderous as Hitler's. Yet, despite my fear lest Hitler emerge victorious, I believed at the time and still do that the British and American bombing of Dresden and Hamburg, as well as Tokyo and other large Japanese cities, transcended the limits which need to be placed on warfare and was not necessary for Allied survival....

Still, terrible as these mass bombings were, carried on with so-called conventional weapons, the use of nuclear bombs at Hiroshima and Nagasaki marked a perilous dividing line. In the decades since then I have fought those supposed realists like Edward Teller and many strategists who, pointing out that the largest conventional weapons were more deadly than the smallest nuclear ones, sought to erase the formal line between nuclear war and all other kinds of war. The idea, toyed with in Vietnam, that one could use tactical nuclear weapons, seemed a dangerous delusion; things generally go wrong with such calculations, and escalation to mutual annihilation could be the likely result.

A Feeling of Deja Vu

There have been many agonizing moments over the last thirty years in which hopes for rapprochement were shattered by internal politics of the Soviet Union or of the United States. Or just as a meeting was planned to discuss the end of nuclear testing, and the possibility of controlling nuclear weapons, something accidental prevented it—for example, the U-2 spy flight (which may not have been accidental, but undertaken by those prepared to risk and hence perhaps torpedo, the forthcoming summit meeting between Khrushchev and Eisenhower). In this context President Carter's raising of the human rights issue at the same time that he hoped to assure success of the SALT talks gives a feeling of *deja vu*.

Tribalism within nation-states and among nation-states remains the most powerful force at work in the world today, more powerful even than class conflicts although especially powerful when tribal and class divisions coincide. The recent American presidential election was fought along both lines of fission. When I became an early supporter of candidate Jimmy Carter, I found myself opposed by many on the grounds of both regional and religious tribalism—by people with no understanding of or sympathy with the complexities of southern theological traditions and suspicious of white southerners in general. Yet as C. Vann Woodward pointed out a number of years ago, white southerners are the only major American group to have suffered military defeat, and at least in some instances are therefore likely to have a sense of limits of tragedy. This has not been a general American characteristic, not even a southern one.

But President Carter is as American as he is southern. He has an all-American faith that problems are soluble and that they can be resolved not only within but among nations, especially when talked about candidly and openly. Candor can be both right conduct and successful strategy. Yet to believe that it will always work seems to me an often unconscious ethnocentric failure to appreciate that we cannot approach other countries in the same way that at times, in our cults of intimacy and of sharing, in our demolishing of the line between public and private, we approach each other both in adversary journalism and in many aspects of personal life.

The fact that the Soviet Union lacks adversary journalism (except in *Samizdat* or the privately circulated writings of dissidents) and is not an open society has been a stumbling block in the efforts to secure a test ban treaty which would cover underground testing, since our negotiators insisted at the time of negotiation of the 1963 partial test ban treaty that it would be impossible without such inspection to distinguish between an underground test and an earthquake. This was a mistaken and even tendentious judgment: the best seismic experts believe that a distinction is easily made between an underground test and an earthquake; moreover, our spy satellites and our intelligence can tell us what is going on in the Soviet Union, even though we do not always want to reveal how much we know because that will tip off the

Soviet Union as to how we know it. But above all, any analysis of this sort must distinguish between capabilities and intentions. Much of our thinking about the Soviet Union, like that of military men professionally, has been "worst case" thinking— a mode of thinking which can be self-confirming since it creates an alliance of the supposedly patriotic war party inside the United States with the patriotic war party within the Soviet Union, against the civilian population of both countries. . . .

A Perilous Campaign

The history of our relations with the Soviet Union over the control of nuclear weapons is a history of might-have-beens. When President Eisenhower, in what was for him an uncharacteristic act of boyish openness, accepted responsibility for the U-2 overflight, one possible moment of rapprochement was lost. Now Brezhnev may be forced out of office by his illness, giving still further power to other factions in the Soviet military-industrial complex, before a new SALT agreement has been reached.

It is in this situation that the launching of the human rights campaign against the Soviet Union seems so perilous. It was not begun by candidate or President Carter. It has been carried on by Senator Jackson and others in the Senate—and Senator Jackson is a man who, contrary to widespread cynicism, is not only the "Senator from Boeing Aircraft," but also a true believer in human rights, as are many other idealistic Americans. And just as Senator Jackson had been mistaken in insisting that the Soviet Union would on materialistic grounds accept our trade terms while accepting also our vocal criticism concerning the emigration of Jewish dissidents, so President Carter began his administration by insisting that the Soviet Union would come to terms on the SALT agreements because the USSR would so clearly gain by it (as we would also) while at the same time insisting on its accepting our standards of human rights as well.

Meantime, the Senate has already indicated where it stands by its vote of considerably less than two-thirds in favor of the confirmation of Paul Warnke as our disarmament negotiator. And the human rights issue itself vis-a-vis the Soviet Union can be taken up readily by the Congress to use against the President, who is himself now inclined to be more cautious on the issue—in other words, to use against a SALT agreement, as an all too easy argument to add to other arguments. In fact, the judgment of many experts is that we are more than amply protected by the mobile and dispersed weapons we already possess. By giving the movement for human rights full legitimacy at an earlier point, President Carter may have lost the ability to control and focus it.

But I now must enter an area where I can claim no expertise:

that of the internal politics of the Soviet Union—yet an area where I am guided by a certain skepticism bred by experience with American Sovietologists going back to the 1930s. I had the odd experience, during the height of the Cold War in the middle and late 1950s, of being told that I was "soft on communism" by people whom I had known when they were Communists, Trotskyites, Schachtmanites, and so on, and when I was, as I have remained, convinced of the brutality, corruption, and—in many areas—sheer incompetence of Soviet society. Some of these Russian experts were among the last to realize what Victor Zorza had long been pointing out: the likelihood of a Sino-Soviet split in what had been thought of as monolithic world communism. More important, the Soviet Union suffers even more from internal tribalism than we do, with many nationalities struggling to get out from under the control of the Great Russians, and in which the countries of the Eastern zone produce superior consumer goods and have a higher standard of living, despite having constantly to pay tribute to the Soviet Union, than do the citizens of the latter.

The Necessity for Restraint

I am not contending that Soviet citizens are ready to break out in open revolt, but rather that Soviet authorities see themselves as beleaguered by China, West Germany and the especially threatening dangers of French and Italian communism in Western Europe (threatening because they are not under Soviet hegemony), and then of course by the United States. The Soviet Union has never been able to achieve the kind of disciplined work force and the internalized as well as superficial obedience that the Chinese Communists appear to have been able to instill, drawing in part on long Confucian and other traditions. Hence, the fact that the Soviets have a long tradition of superiority in artillery, and that they can make and no doubt deliver huge bombs, is as much a sign of defensiveness as aggression—indeed, their foreign policy in recent years has brought a series of defeats—even though their defensiveness, in dialectic with ours, may, in the form of nuclear war, end their prospects and ours.

This outlook has meant (for me, at least) a necessary restraint in criticism of the Soviet Union, even while prior to today's era there remained in this country quite a few influential intellectuals and writers who, as currently in many European countries, blinded themselves to the cruelties of the regime because it called itself socialist and because of their awareness of the evils of their own nation-states. And today I am in a position of deep moral ambiguity because, on the one hand, I admire enormously the courage of the Soviet dissidents, whatever their personal ideologies, and share many of the values that inspire someone like the scientist [Andrei] Sakharov; but at the same time I have consistently refused to sign petitions or in any other way lend my name to the criticisms of the treatment of these dissidents. In a bipolar nuclear world we cannot afford to hold to a simple, straightforward, universalistic moral standard such as one might hope for in a world free of the threat of mass annihilation.

There are many students of the Soviet Union who would disagree with my analysis, who believe that the regime is fully effective, secure, and unthreatened, that its leaders only pretend to be stung by criticism—criticisms which are justified in any circumstances other than nuclear peril at the very moment when we are trying to reach across that chasm for some understanding. My position on human rights does not spring from cultural or moral relativism. While one must take account of local conditions, and of the perils and priorities of other peoples, that does not mean that one condones ancient Aztec human sacrifice or today's tribal murders in Bangladesh. To repeat: it is because I see the nuclear question as always foremost that I cannot be sanguine about the human prospect in the long run, unless the human rights issue of the moment in this country is made less salient.

VIEWPOINT 5

"During the past decade and a half, the Soviets have built up a massive arsenal of new strategic nuclear weapons—weapons that can strike directly at the United States."

The Soviet Union Is a Serious Threat to the U.S.

Ronald Reagan (1911-)

Ronald Reagan was president of the United States from 1981 to 1989. A former movie star and president of the Screen Actors' Guild, Reagan first gained national attention in politics as a supporter of 1964 Republican presidential candidate Barry Goldwater. Subsequently Reagan became governor of California and a leading figure of the right wing of the Republican party. His presidency encompassed several critical turning points in the Cold War.

Reagan, an ardent anticommunist since the 1950s, was critical of the détente policies of Republican presidents Nixon and Ford. In his 1980 presidential campaign against incumbent president Jimmy Carter, Reagan charged that the United States was failing to respond to the growing Soviet threat in nuclear arms capability and involvement in the Third World, especially Latin America. One of his first proposals as president was a five-year $1.7 trillion defense budget. While not all of Reagan's spending requests were passed by Congress, annual defense spending in the United States did rise from $135 billion in 1980 to $210 billion in 1983 and $234 billion in 1984, resulting in the largest military buildup in

American peacetime history. This buildup was partially responsible for massive increases in the U.S. budget deficits, which rose from $60 billion in 1980 to over $180 billion in 1984.

Reagan's military buildup and Soviet policies encountered sharp criticism. A growing political movement began calling for a nuclear freeze—a stop of U.S. development and deployment of nuclear weapons—and for a renewed emphasis on the nuclear arms talks with the Soviet Union that had stalled in the first years of Reagan's presidency. The following viewpoint is taken from an address to the nation televised on March 23, 1983. In it, Reagan repeats his reasons for a U.S. military buildup, emphasizing the Soviet threat to the United States.

I want to explain to you what this defense debate is all about, and why I am convinced that the budget now before the Congress is necessary, responsible and deserving of your support. And I want to offer hope for the future. . . .

Our Policy Is to Deter Aggression

The defense policy of the United States is based on a simple premise: The United States does not start fights. We will never be an aggressor. We maintain our strength in order to deter and defend against aggression—to preserve freedom and peace.

Since the dawn of the atomic age, we have sought to reduce the risk of war by maintaining a strong deterrent and by seeking genuine arms control. Deterrence means simply this: Making sure any adversary who thinks about attacking the United States or our allies or our vital interests concludes that the risks to him outweigh any potential gains. Once he understands that, he won't attack. We maintain the peace through our strength; weakness only invites aggression.

This strategy of deterrence has not changed. It still works. But what it takes to maintain deterrence has changed. It took one kind of military force to deter an attack when we had far more nuclear weapons than any other power; it takes another kind now that the Soviets, for example, have enough accurate and powerful nuclear weapons to destroy virtually all of our missiles on the ground. Now this is not to say the Soviet Union is planning to make war on us. Nor do I believe a war is inevitable—quite the contrary. But what must be recognized is that our security is based on being prepared to meet all threats.

There was a time when we depended on coastal forts and artillery batteries because, with the weaponry of that day, any attack would have had to come by sea. This is a different world and our defenses must be based on recognition and awareness of the weaponry possessed by other nations in the nuclear age.

We can't afford to believe we will never be threatened. There have been two world wars in my lifetime. We didn't start them and, indeed, did everything we could to avoid being drawn into them. But we were ill-prepared for both—had we been better prepared, peace might have been preserved.

The Soviet Buildup

For 20 years, the Soviet Union has been accumulating enormous military might. They didn't stop when their forces exceeded all requirements of a legitimate defensive capability. And they haven't stopped now.

During the past decade and a half, the Soviets have built up a massive arsenal of new strategic nuclear weapons—weapons that can strike directly at the United States.

As an example, the United States introduced its last new intercontinental ballistic missile, the Minuteman III, in 1969, and we are now dismantling our even older Titan missiles. But what has the Soviet Union done in these intervening years? Well, since 1969, the Soviet Union has built five new classes of ICBM's, and upgraded these eight times. As a result, their missiles are much more powerful and accurate than they were several years ago and they continue to develop more, while ours are increasingly obsolete.

The same thing has happened in other areas. Over the same period, the Soviet Union built four new classes of submarine-launched ballistic missiles and over 60 new missile submarines. We built two new types of submarine missiles and actually withdrew 10 submarines from strategic missions. The Soviet Union built over 200 new Backfire bombers, and their brand new Blackjack bomber is now under development. We haven't built a new long-range bomber since our B-52's were deployed about a quarter of a century ago, and we've already retired several hundred of those because of old age. Indeed, despite what many people think, our strategic forces only cost about 15 percent of the defense budget.

Another example of what's happened: In 1978, the Soviets had 600 intermediate-range nuclear missiles based on land and were beginning to add the SS-20—a new, highly accurate mobile missile, with three warheads. We had none. Since then the Soviets have strengthened their lead. By the end of 1979, when Soviet leader Brezhnev declared "a balance now exists," the Soviets had over 800 warheads. We still had none. A year ago this month, Mr. Brezhnev pledged a moratorium, or freeze, on SS-20 deployment. But by last August, their 800 warheads had become more than 1,200. We still had none. Some freeze. At this time Soviet Defense Minister Ustinov announced "approximate parity of forces continues to exist." But the Soviets are still adding an average of three new warheads a week, and now have 1,300. These warheads can reach their targets in a matter of a few minutes. We still have none. So far, it seems that the Soviet definition of parity is a box score of 1,300 to nothing, in their favor.

So, together with our NATO allies, we decided in 1979 to deploy new weapons, beginning this year, as a deterrent to their SS-20's and as an incentive to the Soviet Union to meet us in serious arms control negotiations. We will begin that deployment late this year. At the same time, however, we are willing to cancel our program if the Soviets will dismantle theirs. This is what we have called a zero-zero plan. The Soviets are now at the negotiating

The Surrender of America

Norman Podhoretz, editor of Commentary *magazine, was a member of the Committee on the Present Danger. Formed in 1976, the group of prominent conservative business executives, academics, and public officials believed United States military power was falling behind that of the Soviet Union. Many of the CPD's members obtained government positions in the Reagan administration. In the following excerpt from his 1980 book* The Present Danger, *Podhoretz speculates on what might happen should the Soviet Union attain direct or indirect control over Middle East oil supplies.*

What would the Finlandization of America look like?

In contrast to the traditional kind, this new species of surrender would not be accompanied by the arrival of Soviet troops or formalized in an unambiguous declaration. There would be no military occupation, and the closest thing to an announcement of surrender might be a speech by the President abrogating the Carter Doctrine in words similar to those already used in a letter published shortly after the invasion of Afghanistan in *The New York Times*: "Why . . . should we, at the risk of starting World War III, keep the Russians from displacing the present owners? They might be more efficient producers, and they might save us money by eliminating the corruption that is an element of the present price." Such words would be applauded by "responsible" people, and they would represent the beginning of a gradual but steady process of accommodation to Soviet wishes and demands.

For example, to forestall a cutoff of oil, we would immediately shelve any plans for deploying the new theater nuclear weapons in Western Europe. Then various SALT agreements, entirely skewed in the Soviet favor but universally described as "mutual" and "balanced," would be negotiated. Trade agreements involving the transfer of technology, grain, and anything else the Soviets might want or need would also be negotiated on terms amounting to the payment of tribute, and with an inexorably commensurate decline in the American standard of living. . . .

Politicians and pundits would appear to celebrate the happy arrival of a new era of "peace" and "friendship" and "cooperation" between the Soviet Union and the United States. Dissenters from this cheerful view would be castigated as warmongers and ways would be found to silence questions and criticisms, which could, after all, only result in making things worse for everyone. Only those politicians would run who could be depended upon to support the terms on which the threat of nuclear war had finally been banished from the earth. Of course, such politicians would work toward a sociopolitical system more in harmony with the Soviet model than the "unjust" and "reactionary" system we have today.

There is no need to go on filling in the details. A world in which the Soviet Union had the military power to seize control of the oil fields would be a world shaped by the will and tailored to the convenience of the Soviet Union.

table—and I think it's fair to say that without our planned deployments, they wouldn't be there.

Now let's consider conventional forces. Since 1974, the United States has produced 3,050 tactical combat aircraft. By contrast, the Soviet Union has produced twice as many. When we look at attack submarines, the Unites States has produced 27, while the Soviet Union has produced 61. For armored vehicles including tanks, we have produced 11,200. The Soviet Union has produced 54,000, a nearly 5-to-1 ratio in their favor. Finally, with artillery, we have produced 950 artillery and rocket launchers while the Soviets have produced more than 13,000, a staggering 14-to-1 ratio.

There was a time when we were able to offset superior Soviet numbers with higher quality. But today they are building weapons as sophisticated and modern as our own.

The Threat to Our Vital Interests

As the Soviets have increased their military power, they have been emboldened to extend that power. They are spreading their military influence in ways that can directly challenge our vital interests and those of our allies. The following aerial photographs, most of them secret until now, illustrate this point in a crucial area very close to home—Central America and the Caribbean Basin. They are not dramatic photographs but I think they help give you a better understanding of what I'm talking about.

This Soviet intelligence collection facility less than 100 miles from our coast is the largest of its kind in the world. The acres and acres of antenna fields and intelligence monitors are targeted on key U.S. military installations and sensitive activities. The installation, in Lourdes, Cuba, is manned by 1,500 Soviet technicians, and the satellite ground station allows instant communications with Moscow. This 28-square mile facility has grown by more than 60 percent in size and capability during the past decade.

In western Cuba, we see this military airfield and its complement of modern Soviet-built MIG-23 aircraft. The Soviet Union uses this Cuban airfield for its own long-range reconnaissance missions, and earlier this month two modern Soviet antisubmarine warfare aircraft began operating from it. During the past two years, the level of Soviet arms exports to Cuba can only be compared to the levels reached during the Cuban missile crisis 20 years ago.

This third photo, which is the only one in this series that has been previously made public, shows Soviet military hardware that has made its way to Central America. This airfield with its MI-8 helicopters, antiaircraft guns and protected fighter sites is one of a number of military facilities in Nicaragua which has received Soviet equipment funneled through Cuba and reflects the massive military build-up going on in that country.

On the small island of Grenada, at the southern end of the Caribbean chain, the Cubans, with Soviet financing and backing, are in the process of building an airfield with a 10,000-foot runway. Grenada doesn't even have an air force. Who is it intended for? The Caribbean is a very important passageway for our international commerce and military lines of communication. More than half of all American oil imports now pass through the Caribbean. The rapid build-up of Grenada's military potential is unrelated to any conceivable threat to this island country of under 110,000 people, and totally at odds with the pattern of other eastern Caribbean States, most of which are unarmed. The Soviet-Cuban militarization of Grenada, in short, can only be seen as power projection into the region, and it is in this important economic and strategic area that we are trying to help the governments of El Salvador, Costa Rica, Honduras and others in their struggles for democracy against guerrillas supported through Cuba and Nicaragua.

These pictures only tell a small part of the story. I wish I could show you more without compromising our most sensitive intelligence sources and methods. But the Soviet Union is also supporting Cuban military forces in Angola and Ethiopia. They have bases in Ethiopia and South Yemen near the Persian Gulf oilfields. They have taken over the port we built at Cam Ranh Bay in Vietnam, and now, for the first time in history, the Soviet Navy is a force to be reckoned with in the South Pacific.

The Question of Soviet Intentions

Some people may still ask: Would the Soviets ever use their formidable military power? Well, again, can we afford to believe they won't? There is Afghanistan, and in Poland, the Soviets denied the will of the people and, in so doing, demonstrated to the world how their military power could also be used to intimidate.

The final fact is that the Soviet Union is acquiring what can only be considered an offensive military force. They have continued to build far more intercontinental ballistic missiles than they could possibly need simply to deter an attack. Their conventional forces are trained and equipped not so much to defend against an attack as they are to permit sudden, surprise offensives of their own.

Our NATO allies have assumed a great defense burden, including the military draft in most countries. We are working with them and our other friends around the world to do more. Our defensive strategy means we need military forces that can move very quickly—forces that are trained and ready to respond to any emergency.

Every item in our defense program—our ships, our tanks, our

planes, our funds for training and spare parts—is intended for one all-important purpose—to keep the peace. Unfortunately, a decade of neglecting our military forces had called into question our ability to do that.

Military Weakness

When I took office in January 1981, I was appalled by what I found: American planes that could not fly and American ships that could not sail for lack of spare parts and trained personnel and insufficient fuel and ammunition for essential training. The inevitable result of all this was poor morale in our armed forces, difficulty in recruiting the brightest young Americans to wear the uniform and difficulty in convincing our most experienced military personnel to stay on.

There was a real question, then, about how well we could meet a crisis. And it was obvious that we had to begin a major modernization program to insure we could deter aggression and preserve the peace in the years ahead.

We had to move immediately to improve the basic readiness and staying power of our conventional forces, so they could meet—and therefore help deter—a crisis. We had to make up for lost years of investment by moving forward with a long-term plan to prepare our forces to counter the military capabilities our adversaries were developing for the future.

I know that all of you want peace and so do I. I know too that many of you seriously believe that a nuclear freeze would further the cause of peace. But a freeze now would make us less, not more, secure and would raise, not reduce, the risks of war. It would be largely unverifiable and would seriously undercut our negotiations on arms reduction. It would reward the Soviets for their massive military buildup while preventing us from modernizing our aging and increasingly vulnerable forces. With their present margin of superiority, why should they agree to arms reductions knowing that we were prohibited from catching up?

Believe me, it wasn't pleasant for someone who had come to Washington determined to reduce Government spending, but we had to move forward with the task of repairing our defenses or we would lose our ability to deter conflict now and in the future. We had to demonstrate to any adversary that aggression could not succeed and that the only real solution was substantial, equitable and effectively verifiable arms reduction—the kind we're working for right now in Geneva. . . .

We have not built a new long-range bomber for 21 years. Now we're building the B-1. We had not launched one new strategic submarine for 17 years. Now, we're building one Trident submarine a year. Our land-based missiles are increasingly threatened by the many huge, new Soviet ICBM's. We are determining how to solve that problem. At the same time, we are working in the START and I.N.F. negotiations, with the goal of achieving deep reductions in the strategic and intermediate nuclear arsenals of both sides.

We have also begun the long-needed modernization of our conventional forces. The Army is getting its first new tank in 20 years. The Air Force is modernizing. We are rebuilding our Navy, which shrank from about 1,000 in the late 1960's to 453 ships during the 1970's. Our nation needs a superior Navy to support our military forces and vital interests overseas. We are now on the road to achieving a 600-ship Navy and increasing the amphibious capabilities of our Marines, who are now serving the cause of peace in Lebanon. And we are building a real capability to assist our friends in the vitally important Indian Ocean and Persian Gulf region. . . .

Yes, we pay a great deal for the weapons and equipment we give our military forces. And, yes there has been some waste in the past. But we are now paying the delayed cost of our neglect in the 1970's. We would only be fooling ourselves, and endangering the future, if we let the bills pile up for the 1980's as well. Sooner or later these bills always come due, and the later they come due, the more they cost in treasure and in safety.

This is why I am speaking to you tonight—to urge you to tell your Senators and Congressmen that you know we must continue to restore our military strength.

If we stop midstream, we will not only jeopardize the progress we have made to date—we will mortgage our ability to deter war and achieve genuine arms reductions. And we will send a signal of decline, of lessened will, to friends and adversaries alike.

VIEWPOINT 6

"We already have enough strategic warheads to destroy all 218 Soviet cities with a population of 100,000 or more at least 40 times over."

The Soviet Threat Is Exaggerated

Sidney Lens (1912-1986)

The first years of Ronald Reagan's presidency were marked by a massive U.S. defense spending buildup and by increasing tensions between the United States and the Soviet Union. In his first press conference President Reagan said the Russians could not be trusted because "they reserve unto themselves the right to commit any crime, to lie, to cheat," in order to achieve world domination.

Many people were highly critical of Reagan's stance toward the Soviet Union. One example of such criticism came from Sidney Lens, who wrote the following article in response to Reagan's March 23, 1983, television address calling for higher defense spending.

Lens's views on the Cold War predated Reagan's presidency. A writer, union activist, and senior editor of the *Progressive* magazine, Lens had been an opponent of U.S. Cold War policies since the 1950s. He was a leading critic and organizer of resistance to the Vietnam War. In the following viewpoint he argues that Reagan and his advisers had exaggerated the Soviet threat to the American people. The Soviet Union, he asserts, is far more threatened by American policies and power than the United States is by the Soviet Union. The main danger facing the United States, according to Lens, is an uncontrolled nuclear arms race.

The substance of the president's claim was that the Russians are moving ahead of us. In the past decade and a half, he said, the Soviets "have built up a massive arsenal . . . that can strike directly at the United States." The fact is that in the past decade and a half, *both* powers have built up a massive arsenal. In 1968 the United States had 4,200 strategic nuclear warheads, the Soviets 1,100; today we have 9,300, they have 7,300—an increase of 5,100 for us and 6,200 for them.

What those figures prove is not that we need "more," but that we should have negotiated a freeze or a cutback in 1968, before our escalation sparked their escalation. Former Secretary of Defense Robert McNamara—by no means an apologist for the Kremlin—told the *Los Angeles Times* in 1982 that the Soviet buildup of the 1960s and 1970s was a "reaction to the earlier U.S. military buildup and to rumors that the U.S. was preparing to strike first at the Soviet Union. . . . If I had been the Soviet secretary of defense I would have been worried as hell at the imbalance of forces."

What President Reagan Didn't Say

As proof that the Russians are plunging ahead of us, Reagan produced a graph showing that the most recent new missile in our arsenal, the Minuteman III, was introduced in 1969, whereas the Soviets have developed and produced five new missiles since then. It sounded frightening, as though we had become militarily impotent.

But while it is true that we haven't built a new type of missile, we introduced the MIRV (multiple independently targetable reentry vehicle) in 1970, so that land-based missiles which once carried only a single warhead now carry three, and those on submarines, as many as 14. Of greater importance, our weapons now have guidance systems such as the MARV and the MARK 12-A, which make them at least twice as accurate as Soviet weapons. This development is of the utmost importance, for if the accuracy of a weapon is doubled, its "kill" capability increases by eight times.

The difficulty in making nuclear comparisons is that each side has different weapons for different strategies. Reagan made much ado about Soviet superiority in intermediate-range missiles. They had 600 before, he said; they have added hundreds of the new SS-20s—whereas the United States still has no such weapons at all in Europe, "none." "So far," he chided, "the Soviet definition of parity is a box score of 1,300 to nothing in their favor."

The president omitted a few pertinent facts, however. One is that the U.S. has a large number of F-111 airplanes in Britain capable of raining hundreds of nuclear bombs on the Soviet Union. Our allies, Britain and France, also have a few hundred warheads each (mostly on submarines), capable of hitting the Soviet Union. And although most of our 7,000 tactical nuclear warheads in Europe do not have the range to reach Soviet soil, we have a couple of dozen submarines in the Atlantic, Pacific, Mediterranean and Indian oceans which have at least 3,000 warheads targeted on the U.S.S.R. all the time—plus 2,000 more in home ports.

Government Lies

Tom Gervasi, journalist and director of the Center for Military Research and Analysis in New York, wrote The Myth of Soviet Military Supremacy *in 1986. The book castigated the Reagan administration and its views on Soviet military power.*

We have had a bomber gap and a missile gap and a military spending gap and a window of vulnerability—none of which ever existed. Yet we never learned that they didn't exist until after the political objectives they were designed to achieve had already been accomplished. After the missile gap helped elect President Kennedy, we learned there hadn't been one. After the military spending gap helped elect President Reagan, we learned there never was one. Time after time, Americans have had to accept each gap, each set of lies, and each cycle of military expansion. . . .

How has the Reagan administration persuaded America that the Soviets hold the lead in military power? Chiefly by saying that it does, and by systematically misrepresenting the balance of military power to reinforce its assertions. It simply selects whatever information best supports the conclusions it wishes the public to draw, and omits whatever information contradicts those conclusions. This means that a great deal of information must be omitted. Most of the information the administration presents is perfectly accurate; it is just incomplete. The result is a wholly different conclusion from the one that all of the facts would provide.

Our 41 nuclear submarines are invulnerable—which means that, unlike the situation with land-based missiles, no way has yet been found to track them down and destroy them. The Soviets also have nuclear submarines, of course, 61 of them, but almost all of their missiles carry single warheads; few are fully MIRVed. Thus the ratio in the United States' favor is nearly five to one—5,000 submarine-launched warheads for us, a thousand or 1,200 for them. Moreover, most Soviet ships of this class are in port; they have only 400 nuclear weapons at sea at any given time.

To emphasize how menacing the Soviet threat has become, Reagan showed classified pictures of a Soviet intelligence-gathering facility in Cuba, run, he said, by 1,500 Soviet technicians, and another in western Cuba for long-range Soviet reconnaissance. He also showed a 10,000-foot airstrip on the island of Grenada (population 110,000) being built by Cuba with Soviet help. These three facilities are supposed to represent a grave threat to American security.

A little reflection indicates how out of focus such claims are. The Russians may or may not have two bases and one airstrip near American soil. But the U.S. has had bases with nuclear weapons flush up against Soviet territory, in Turkey, for decades. Our troops and ships are ensconced in 400 major and 2,000 minor bases around the world, most of them part of a great circle around the Soviet Union. No nation in history has ever been encircled with more firepower than the Soviet Union is today—and we are tightening that circle constantly.

American Nuclear Threats

Reagan implied that our military machine is benevolent, for defensive purposes only; the Soviets' is malevolent, for offense. "Some people may still ask, 'Would the Soviets ever use their formidable military power?' Well, again, can we afford to believe they won't?" He pointed to Afghanistan and Poland, two instances in which the Soviets come off badly. But he omitted our own interventions in Lebanon, the Dominican Republic, Vietnam, our hundreds of covert CIA actions and—most grave—the 12 known occasions when the United States has considered or threatened limited or total nuclear war.

The first such instance, reported by Senator Henry Jackson more than 30 years after the event, occurred in 1946, when President Harry Truman gave Soviet Ambassador Andrei Gromyko a 48-hour ultimatum for the Russians to get out of two provinces in Iran, or have the Soviet Union itself atom-bombed. In October 1962 we again threatened nuclear war against the Soviet Union because it had placed missiles in Cuba. And in 1973 the superpowers almost came to a nuclear exchange when the Israelis were slow to observe a cease-fire in the Yom Kippur War.

Then there were nine occasions when limited nuclear war was planned or threatened: twice during the Korean War (once by Truman, once by Eisenhower); once in Vietnam, when we offered three nuclear bombs to France to use on China and the Viet Minh; a second time in Vietnam when our marines were surrounded at Khe Sanh; and yet a third time when Nixon sent secret messages through intermediaries that he would use nuclear weapons against North Vietnam unless the Vietnamese came to terms by November 1969. We weighed using the bomb to force the communists to join a tripartite government in Laos, to defend Quemoy and Matsu islands against China, during the Berlin blockade and during the 1957 "Lebanon crisis." Given this history, for Reagan to imply that only the Soviets contemplate using armed force and nuclear weapons—whereas we are quiescent—is more than a gross exaggeration.

The president failed to make a case for his requested $30 billion boost in the 1984 military budget, even from the point of view of a hawk. He didn't mention that we already have enough strategic warheads to destroy all 218 Soviet cities with a population of 100,000 or more at least 40 times over; and that the only purpose additional weapons might serve would be, in Winston Churchill's phrase, to "make the rubble bounce." . . .

Stop the Arms Race

Each side is furiously building its arsenal, and shouting that the other is untrustworthy. The U.S., for instance, is projecting 100 new B-1 bombers, 100 MX missiles, 15 Trident submarines, 464 ground-launched and 8,348 air- and sea-launched cruise missiles, 108 Pershing II missiles, 1,280 neutron bombs and two new aircraft-carrier battle groups—and the U.S.S.R. is no doubt matching us bomb for bomb. Also in the meantime, other nations are gaining the capability of making nuclear weapons—100 nations are expected to be members of the "nuclear club" by the year 2000—and the danger of a nuclear war beginning in a "small" conventional way—say, between Iran and Iraq—is growing apace. Germany and Japan can begin producing nuclear weapons within a couple of months after they make the decision to; if the present trade frictions intensify, the possibility that other great

246

powers will join the nuclear club mounts.

Against this background, Reagan's speech is seen not as a plea for strategic arms reduction but for making the U.S. so overpowering that Moscow would have no alternative but to cry uncle. That is the hope—though not the likelihood.

The arms race can be ended only by ending it. That means an immediate freeze without quibbling over the niceties of "verification." Better still is Jerome T. Wiesner's proposal for a "unilateral moratorium." Wiesner, a member of the National Security Council under Kennedy, suggests that we stop producing more nuclear weapons on our own, then invite the Russians to do the same. If they do, we would reduce our stockpiles by a certain percentage and again invite Moscow to match our effort, until there was complete disarmament.

Simultaneously we would have to disabuse ourselves of the ideological basis for the cold war—mainly, that "you can't trust the Russians." That thesis is irrelevant and obstructive. It is true that we cannot trust the Russian government, but then, we cannot trust *any* government, including our own. Nor should we. Whether we like the Soviet system or not, we and the Soviet people have a common destiny: finding a means of surviving together.

What America needs today is . . . a policy of abolition: we must abolish nuclear weapons. That would not mean scrapping those instruments of death tomorrow morning, but it would mean a *commitment* to do so, and taking certain unilateral initiatives (such as a freeze) while negotiating a quick timetable for abolition.

Reagan was right on one thing. The danger we face is monumental. The sickness is malignant.

247

VIEWPOINT 7

"The Soviet position has shifted more markedly than anyone expected. As a result we now have the opportunity to end this Cold War that has dominated our lives for almost half a century."

Gorbachev's Policies Signal the End of the Cold War

Robert Scheer (1936-)

Relations between the United States and the Soviet Union reached a low point in 1983. In March President Ronald Reagan called the Soviet Union "the focus of evil in the modern world." Later he proposed the funding of a Strategic Defense Initiative (SDI), a program to develop a defense against nuclear weapons. Many critics believed SDI threatened to increase the arms race and jeopardize arms control agreements between the superpowers. Superpower relations further deteriorated when on September 1, 1983, the Soviet Union shot down a Korean civilian jetliner killing all 269 passengers. Amidst the accusations and counteraccusations over the tragedy, Soviet leader Yuri Andropov declared that the United States was on "a militarist course that represents a serious threat to peace. . . . [I]f anyone had any illusions about the possibility of an evolution for the better in the policy of the present American administration," he said, "recent events have dispelled them once and for all."

Few predicted that by 1987 President Reagan would be hosting the Soviet leader in Washington and signing a treaty banning all intermediate-range nuclear missiles in Europe. Much of the change in U.S.-Soviet relations can be attributed to Mikhail Gorbachev, a little-known Soviet politician who took over leadership of the USSR in March 1985. Gorbachev sponsored internal reforms within Soviet society, dramatically recast Soviet positions on arms control, trade, and other issues, announced a moratorium on nuclear weapons testing, and proposed massive weapons cuts within the Soviet military.

Debates over the Cold War in the second half of the 1980s were largely focused on Gorbachev and his goals. His reforms and flexibility on such issues as arms control caused some Western observers to call for a relaxation of Cold War tensions between the United States and the Soviet Union, and some saw in Gorbachev's actions the beginning of the end of the Cold War. Other observers were more cautious, arguing that Gorbachev was simply using diplomatic skills as a tactic, and that fundamental antagonisms between the Cold War adversaries remained.

In the following viewpoint, written in 1988, Robert Scheer argues that the Soviet Union under Gorbachev was actively supporting the end of the Cold War and that it was the United States that was reluctant to make peace. Scheer argues that Soviet flexibility on nuclear arms control, its desire for economic reforms, and its willingness to allow greater political freedom all point to a new Soviet pragmatism that the United States should take advantage of. Scheer is the national correspondent for the *Los Angeles Times*. He composed this article shortly after a six-week trip to the Soviet Union in December 1987, during which he interviewed leaders of that country.

The argument between American doves and hawks is really very simple—either communism is complex, varied, divided and capable of change, or it isn't. The former view is obviously correct, as Deng Xiao Ping and Gorbachev have demonstrated. But American policy has most often been based on the simplistic "Marxist devil" theory, currently manifested in relations with Nicaragua.

It is important that we sort out our thinking in these areas because the Soviets are in possession of a secret weapon: they have let go of the rope in the tug of war, and we have been sent sprawling. Amazingly enough, it is they who have now embraced pragmatism, and we who adhere all too often to ideological rigidity.

For the Soviets there is an almost hypnotic appeal in the idea that they don't have to defend all of their previous positions all of the time. They have also learned they can get a great deal of power from letting go of the rope. Gorbachev, for example, is more popular in West Germany than Reagan. He is popular in Eastern Europe. He could probably even run for office in the United States and do as well as some of the Democratic candidates.

Challenging Basic Assumptions

The Soviets now in control have challenged the basic international power equation and recognize that influence and security are not directly tied to military might or the possession of satellite territories. They know it is much more of a check on US policy to have a popular Soviet leader than to have more troops or new weapons. They understand the initiatives of the US president and the ability of the US to respond to Soviet initiatives in an aggressive way are more limited by what our public thinks about the enemy—the nature of the beast—than by the weapons the Soviets possess.

The Cold War Is Outdated

George F. Kennan, the American diplomat whose 1947 "Mr X" article in many ways initiated the Cold War, states in a 1988 interview in New Perspectives Quarterly *that the United States should change its Cold War mentality.*

I feel very strongly that the extreme military anxieties and rivalries that have marked the high points of the Cold War have increasingly lost their rationale. Now, they are predominantly matters of the past. The Cold War is outdated.

Of far greater importance are areas which demand collaboration between the Soviet Union and the United States.

Of these, I would cite global environmental deterioration; the need to control the revolution in electronic communication; North-South economic relationships; and the situations in the Near and Middle East. Compared with the dangers these situations present, the perceptions of danger that inspired the Cold War pale into insignificance. . . .

What worries me more than whether Gorbachev has changed the Soviet Union for the better is the American media's persistent dramatization of Cold War myths and stereotypes. The Soviets dropped the Cold War mentality. Now, it's up to us to do the same thing.

Recently, I was present when a number of our top Kremlinologists were questioning Giorgi Arbatov, head of Moscow's US-Canada Institute. It was a very strange encounter because our experts were pounding away and Arbatov was obviously having a ball. All his life he had been required to defend difficult positions. Suddenly, he was able to say, "This was a mistake and that was a mistake and we have to change things. This is a good idea, that is not, and we have to rethink certain things."

Instead of being happy, the audience was miserable and angry. Finally a very famous Sovietologist stood up and said, with a real sense of personal betrayal, "How can you stand there and change your positions like that?" Arbatov just looked at him, savoring the moment, and then responded, "Well, maybe you people do need the Cold War more than we do."

Are we willing to call the Soviet's bluff? More often than not we hear moderate voices say, "No." They say, "Let's see the Russians cut conventional forces!" Then the Russians say, "Okay, let's cut conventional forces." Then the moderates respond, "Just wait a minute now. Let's see you cut chemicals." The Russians then say, "Let's cut chemicals." In fact, the Russians have agreed to everything we have ever asked for on a test ban treaty in terms of monitoring, verification, digging holes in the ground and putting in our equipment and *we* still have not accepted Gorbachev's offer of a comprehensive test ban.

Those who believe the Soviet Union has to be in tune with the world economy and that being in tune requires greater internal freedom—Anatoly Dobrynin, Aleksandr Yakovlev, Secretary Gorbachev—are pretty much in charge. And it will be very hard to put this genie of freedom back in the bottle because freedom is intoxicating.

When I make that point, Americans says, yes but could one do *that* in the Soviet Union. Low and behold, it turns out *that* can be done. Then I'm told the Soviets will never publish so-and-so. Then they publish so-and-so. I'm constantly being told the Soviets will never do certain things, and then they do them.

I was actually the first reviewer in the Soviet Union to review Gorbachev's book, *Perestroika.* I told a senior official they would never print the shot I took at Gorbachev for not mentioning the whole question of Soviet Jews wanting to leave. Well, my criticism was printed in *Moscow News*—a very clear statement criticizing the book for not dealing with the question of those Jews who want to go to Israel.

Discovering Freedom

What the Soviets have finally found after all these years of secretly believing otherwise is that their system is not a house of cards. They are finding that they can have a great deal more openness and freedom without the whole system crumbling. They have learned they can have Xerox machines and computers

Soviet Views Are Changing

Robert S. McNamara, U.S. secretary of defense from 1961 to 1968 and later president of the World Bank, wrote in his 1989 book Out of the Cold *that the Soviet Union wants the Cold War to end.*

The Soviets' view of the world and of the U.S.-Soviet competition is clearly changing. In their New Thinking they are now in the process of reevaluating a broad range of policies and potential costs, including reconsideration of the nature of security in the contemporary world; the U.S.-Soviet military competition; the dangers inherent in growing nuclear arsenals; the importance of cooperative solutions to regional and global problems; Soviet relations with Eastern Europe; Soviet activity in the Third World; human rights in the Soviet Union; market incentives in the Soviet economy; and the role of the Soviet economy in the international economic system of the twenty-first century. In every one of these areas, the Soviets are reaching conclusions that, if implemented, will have profound consequences for U.S.-Soviet relations.

It is important to understand that if the Soviets are pursuing cooperative and accommodative policies, they are doing so for Soviet interests. Soviet offers to reduce armaments and improve relations are not founded in altruism, but on the current Soviet calculation that a peaceful environment will offer better prospects for the Soviet reform program and other policies. But we should also recognize that the fact that such an environment is good for the Soviet Union does not automatically mean that it is bad for the United States.

Indeed, here is the very essence of the answer to the question "Can we end the Cold War?" The Soviets are stating, in effect, that they desire it, and that it is in the interests of both the Soviet Union and the United States. In the words of Richard H. Ullman, "Soviet objectives are real and concrete rather than ideological and transcendental." The missing factor is our response: the expression of an American desire to work toward reducing tension and increasing cooperation and a statement of an American vision of our nation's role in a world free of domination by the Cold War ideology.

without anarchy or the loss of their power base.

As a result, they have new priorities. A top Soviet general gave me an afternoon to talk, and I was driving him nuts with questions like, "Don't tell me you don't like being a general. What would you do if peace broke out? What about your military-industrial complex?" He pounded the table and said, "Look, our security depends on our people finding the same quantity and quality of goods in the store that your people find. It depends on that more than anything else. If we cannot meet the needs of our people, we cannot have their loyalty."

Where will this lead? I predict the Soviets will continue to let go of the rope. Politburo member Aleksandr Yakovlev told me they

U.S. president Ronald Reagan and Soviet leader Mikhail Gorbachev meet in Geneva, Switzerland. The November 1985 summit was the first of four major meetings over the next three years.

will call for deep cuts in conventional weapons. We will see proposals to go beyond deep cuts in strategic weapons. A top person in the Foreign Ministry outlined what he thought was a potential deal: The Soviets knew Reagan was committed to Star Wars and needed a face-saving formula, the formula would be no mention of Star Wars, 50% cuts and US agreement to continued strict interpretation of the ABM treaty.

I told the Soviet diplomat they would guarantee the election of a Republican president if they could actually push that deal through. And he said, "Yes, but why not? What have the Democrats ever been able to do for peace?"

At that point I realized the Soviets are really beginning to understand the American political process. Even they sense that irony of American history—that the Republicans are better at making arms deals than the Democrats. For that reason, the Soviets very much want Reagan's fingerprints on a treaty, even if it does not contain everything the Soviets desire.

It may well be the Republicans who will negotiate the end of the Cold War, in reality if not formally. And the Cold War is, in effect, over if the Soviets are not interested in expansionism.

The Soviets are very serious about this new thinking. If I were to use an American analogy, I would recall Nixon's speech in

1968 that defined the limits of American power—a policy known as the Nixon Doctrine. They are equally serious about defining the limits on their power because they recognize the Soviet Union cannot restructure its economy and develop arms agreements if it acts in the same ways it has in the past.

An Opportunity

So we are at a moment of truth. The Soviet position has shifted more markedly than anyone expected. As a result we now have the opportunity to end this Cold War that has dominated our lives for almost half a century.

It is also a moment when we should ask ourselves if we mean what President Eisenhower said when he warned that the military-industrial complex shouldn't run our foreign policy. Do we mean what Kennedy said when, after the Cuban missile crisis, he reminded us we have to learn to coexist in the world with the Soviets? Do we even mean what Richard Nixon said about *detente*? Are we really, as Ronald Reagan has said, committed to a nuclear free world? Are we really committed to a world with fewer armaments? If not, why not?

VIEWPOINT 8

"In the West we so discount Communist ideology that we fail to see the extent to which it continues to underpin Soviet actions."

Gorbachev's Policies Do Not Signal the End of the Cold War

Charles Krauthammer (1950-)

The closing years of the Cold War were marked by debates as to whether it safely could be declared finished, and specifically whether policies of Soviet leader Mikhail Gorbachev signaled an end to the long conflict. Gorbachev himself declared that the Cold War was over and that the Soviet Union had no hostile intentions toward the United States. In a 1986 speech he said, "We can never be secure while the U.S. feels insecure." He called for nuclear arms reductions and increased economic ties between the two countries. There was much debate within the United States as to whether the Soviet Union's policies under Mikhail Gorbachev were designed to end the Cold War or whether they were simply a Cold War tactic to keep the United States off guard.

The following viewpoint was written in late 1987 by Charles Krauthammer, an influential columnist for *Newsweek*, the *New Republic*, and other publications. Krauthammer argues that Gorbachev's reforms up to that time do not signal the end of the Cold War, and that the United States should be cautious in responding to Gorbachev's initiatives. Krauthammer lists several conditions necessary for the Cold War to end. They include significant improvements in the Soviet Union's human rights record, a cessation of Soviet support of regional conflicts in Afghanistan and elsewhere, and ideological change within the Soviet Union's government. Only when the Soviet Union clearly repudiates its hostile intentions toward the West, Krauthammer states, should the United States take steps to end the Cold War.

Mikhail Gorbachev's performance over the last two-and-a-half years has been remarkable: not just *glasnost* and *perestroika*, but INF [intermediate-range nuclear forces] concessions, Middle East peace feelers, pressure for reform in Soviet satellites, selective release of dissidents, and a whole new public face toward Europe and the United States. This performance has occasioned two reactions. On the one hand, it has been interpreted as the beginning of a fundamental turn in Soviet history and thus a fundamental change in East-West relations, which in turn warrants a fundamental change in American foreign policy. Hawks, on the other hand, tend to define *glasnost* more literally to mean publicity, public relations, an attempt at cosmetic change that will lure the West into a second period of détente, from which Gorbachev will extract Western credits and technology and a respite from the arms race.

Which is it? Despite the raging in the op-ed pages and in the foreign policy journals, no one knows. We don't know if Gorbachev is sincere. If he is, we don't know whether he will succeed in winning over his bureaucracy. If he does, we don't know if he will last. We have, after all, seen Khrushchev undertake domestic liberalization, while at the same time proclaiming the doctrine of national liberation, putting up the Berlin Wall, and sneaking SS-4s into Cuba.

Criteria to End the Cold War

Still, it is important for hawks to declare that they are open to evidence of change in the Soviet system and to specify what kind of evidence they would find convincing. Otherwise they are operating within a system as intellectually closed and impervious to refutation as the perverse ideology they so militantly oppose. There *are* criteria of Soviet behavior that warrant rethinking the U.S.-Soviet relationship, indeed, calling off the cold war. But they are not the two conditions—economic reform and arms control flexibility—most promiscuously cited by the cold-war-is-over school to prove that the Soviet Union has already reformed and

The Cold War Is Not Over

Former president Richard Nixon expressed his skepticism about the end of the Cold War in a Winter 1988/89 article in Foreign Affairs.

Those who parrot today a fashionable slogan—"the cold war is over"—trivialize the problems of Western security. Gorbachev's public relations experts have made many Western policymakers forget that a more benign Soviet image does not mean a more benign Soviet foreign policy. As a result, the race to Moscow is already on. Western leaders have jetted off to the Kremlin with planeloads of eager bankers and industrialists in tow, and Soviet leaders have gleefully lined up more than $10 billion in easy credit. Unless the West steps back and designs a coherent strategy, we will squander our leverage and lose the historic opportunity presented by events in the Soviet Union.

therefore that American foreign policy too needs overhauling.

Economic reform. There are two ways to go from economic reform to détente. One way is to argue that economic liberalization must inevitably lead to political liberalization. Allow people to make economic choices and they will hunger for political choices. Soon you have on your hands a revolution in human liberty. It is a nice theory. It is rarely correct. Most of the world's dictatorships, despite their fondness for socialist nomenclature, are capitalist to some degree or other. Economic liberty can engender an appetite for political liberty, but modern dictators have the necessary repressive apparatus to deal with appetites. Some degree of economic freedom can coexist with an extraordinary degree of political repression. Witness Fascist Italy. And it is not at all clear that the economic reforms contemplated by Gorbachev will permit any more individual economic liberty than existed under Mussolini. . . .

Arguing in the alternative, doves point to another road from economic reform to détente. This one does not pass through political liberalization, but makes the link directly: because the ruling party wants an economic restructuring, it is compelled to reorder its priorities. In order for Gorbachev to produce growth and renewal, he must turn inward, and is forced to seek a decrease in international tension, a halt in the arms race, a reduction in military expenditures, and general international calm. . . .

Peace for the Soviets is not a choice but a necessity.

A Faulty Analysis

There are several problems with this analysis. First, it has been heard before. One cannot remember a time when Soviet peace overtures did not come with the explanatory footnote that the Soviets could not sustain the strain of the arms race but needed peace to feed their people. All that time, however, as we later learned, they were doing little feeding and much building and survived quite nicely. The Western assumption that domestic appetites must be satisfied before a country can build militarily is not a fact of life. It is a fact of democratic life.

Second, the analysis is not necessarily true. The inefficiencies of the Soviet system are so grotesque that even a minimal restructuring will eliminate the grosser inefficiencies and generate enough surplus capital for reinvestment and more restructuring—and might even leave something for the military. Moreover, if the Soviets do need huge sums of capital for their economic restructuring, it does not necessarily have to come out of their military budget. It can just as easily come out of generous Western banks, now short of reliable foreign borrowers. . . . In the '70s the West fell over itself trying to infuse capital into the Soviet bloc. The banks are quite capable of doing that again, which would ensure that even an expensive economic restructuring in the Soviet Union does not exact too high a price from the military.

Third, assume that, Western credits or not, Gorbachev indeed finds that he must reduce military spending in order to rebuild his economy, and thus needs international calm, arms reductions, and peace. This still proves nothing about fundamental change in Soviet intentions and ambitions in the world and thus carries no fundamental implications for American foreign policy vis-à-vis the Soviets. It is quite conceivable that now, as in the past, the maneuver is tactical and temporary. Gorbachev may feel that his hugely overdeveloped military superstructure cannot forever be sustained on so thin an economic base and that military retrenchment is necessary now to right the balance—in order to sustain Soviet military might in the longer run. To rebuild his economy on a firmer foundation he may be quite prepared to subject himself to a temporary halt to the relentless Soviet attempts over the last 20 years to achieve conventional, strategic, and geopolitical advantage over the United States. We would still have no evidence that the ultimate goal of achieving such advantage has been given up. And without that, any American declaration of an end to the cold war would be unilateral and dangerous.

Giving Up Useless Weapons

Arms control. The other major encouragement to the end-of-the-cold-war school is Gorbachev's flexibility on arms control. He began with a unilateral test ban. He has made breakthroughs on verification, allowing more on-site inspection than the United States will now apparently accept. He has made concession after concession on medium-range missiles, until Reagan finally had to take yes for an answer. He has bent somewhat on his opposition to testing of strategic defenses. He has gotten so cocky that he is prepared to fly the odd delegation of Democratic doves to places like Krasnoyarsk to show that he is not afraid to expose even treaty violations to *glasnost*.

In the realm of arms control these are significant moves. But what do they tell us about overall Soviet foreign policy ambitions and intentions? Very little. For one thing, these moves are inherently ambiguous. On INF, for example, the Soviets have gotten a very good deal. It is true that they tried for a much better deal in the early '80s, namely, that they keep their SS-20s and the West deploy no American Euromissiles. But when it became clear to the Soviets that they were not going to get that, they settled for the next best outcome, the zero option, which suits their 40-year-old goal of decoupling NATO from the United States rather well. . . .

Foreign-Policy Sideshow

Weapons so unusable are difficult to turn into political counters. If there is a gross imbalance of forces, as there was during the Cuban missile crisis, nuclear force can intimidate (though the more relevant intimidating factor, even in that crisis, was overwhelming American conventional superiority in the Cuban theater). But today there is no such imbalance. An offer of quantitative arms control, even, for example, a 50 percent cut in strategic nuclear arms, changes nothing in the balance of power and tells us nothing about Soviet intentions. (Nor American intentions, for that matter: Ronald Reagan and Richard Perle can be for 50 percent strategic cuts without in any way having to modify their view of American foreign policy objectives.)

On the other hand, some qualitative arms control offers can signal a change in superpower strategy. On the American side, for example, abandonment of SDI [strategic defense initiative] would constitute a significant shift in American strategy and intentions. On the Soviet side, an offer to reduce their first-strike force to a level below which it is a potential instrument of blackmail would be a significant signal of reduced aggressive intent or at least reduced ambition. Tellingly, the Soviets continue to resist such a measure.

Anything short of such a true qualitative change in the array of nuclear forces reduces arms control to a foreign-policy sideshow: a way to save some money, make nuclear planning easier, and win the battle for public (Western) opinion on the peace issue. It tells us nothing about the future of the cold war.

What then can Gorbachev do to convince the West that the cold war is over, that the conflict between the United States and the

Soviet Union is no longer a struggle about values but about power? The question is crucial, because if all that is at stake on U.S.-Soviet relations is a traditional great power rivalry, then that would dictate a wholly new, deideologized American foreign policy. For the past 40 years Americans have correctly perceived the contest between the United States and the Soviet Union to be not merely a great power but an ideological struggle. This is what gives the cold war moral purpose and what makes it worth fighting. Take away that difference between the societies and the cold war loses its moral dimension.

Can that happen? The totalitarian idea, as conceived by Western intellectuals, is an impressive theoretical edifice. But it is not infallible. The ideological torpor and spiritual ossification of the Communist world were not anticipated by classical totalitarianism theory as articulated almost 40 years ago in the original writings of [Hannah] Arendt, [Zbigniew] Brzezinski, and [Carl] Friedrich. Classical theory was impressed by the self-replicating nature of the totalitarianism apparatus. Thus far the theory has been generally correct. But it must in principle be capable of contradiction by facts. When and if that happens, we should not then deny the facts for the theory.

Need Significant Change

What kind of facts? What has to happen, what criteria must Gorbachev meet, that would and should force a rethinking of U.S.-Soviet relations, for calling off the cold war?

No one expects democracy in the Soviet Union. The United States lives with all kinds of dictatorships around the world and does not see conflict with them as a moral imperative. If the Soviet Union were to make fundamental changes in its Leninist apparatus—democratic centralism at home, "anti-imperialism" abroad—that should start Americans, and American hawks in particular, rethinking the ideological nature of the East-West conflict. I am talking not about the chimera of economic reform or arms control, but about far more significant areas: human rights and "regional conflicts" or, put another way, the way the Soviets treat their own people and the way they treat vulnerable non-Soviet people around the world.

Human rights. The two most abhorrent features of the Soviet system from the Western point of view are the repression of dissent and the denial of the right of free movement. These are related and synergistic. What defines a prison, no matter how cushy the accommodations, is the fact that one may not leave. What turns ordinary oppression into imprisonment is an impossibility of escape. In a political system, a bar on emigration defines a state of radical unfreedom. The fact that Soviet-bloc citizens from Moscow to Havana may not escape their oppression makes for a singular form of tyranny. One of the reasons Americans have few moral qualms about warm relations with a severely repressive Communist Yugoslavia, for example, is that it allows emigration. Adoption of a similar policy in the Soviet system would have far-reaching implications.

An equally significant change would have to come in Soviet treatment of dissent. Full pluralism is not the point. What is important is dismantling the apparatus of the centralized police state: closing the psychiatric prisons, evacuating the Gulag [labor camp], reducing the power of the KGB [Soviet secret intelligence], and allowing non-Party voices to be heard in official media, meaning not just the internal self-criticism of corruption and inefficiency now permitted on the letters-to-the-editor page, but criticism from without. These changes, and not a two-candidate election for sewer commissioner of Vladivostok, are the signs of change in the Soviet political structure that would warrant a rethinking of the ideological underpinnings of the cold war.

Regional Conflicts

Regional conflicts. The issue is Soviet expansionism. The question is at what point are the Soviets prepared to be a status quo power. To the West, Gorbachev seems to be saying: now.

"[I]f the statements made by the general secretary were to come to reflect a committed, sustained policy," writes Christoph Bertram, "this would be the kind of attitude that the West has always sought: the Soviet Union as a responsible superpower, conscious of its obligations to international order and no longer prepared to define its security interests at the expense of others."

What kind of policy would one look for? For starters: relaxation of control over Eastern Europe and a willingness to return Afghanistan to its condition of non-Communist neutrality before Soviet intervention in the '70s. One cannot expect the Soviet Union, or any great power for that matter, to give up all efforts to expand its influence. But the way it expands its influence is important. There is a difference between Findlandizing buffer states, i. e., assuring non-hostile foreign policies while permitting freedom of social organization, and forcibly communizing them. If the Soviet Union merely allied itself with Ethiopia, the United States would have to deal with the geopolitical implications of Soviet access to Red Sea ports. But the transformation of Ethiopian society, under Soviet, East German, and Cuban tutelage, is attended with such barbarity and suffering that the American interest in Ethiopia ceases to be coldly realpolitikal. It becomes ideological: preventing yet another society from falling into the long, dark night of totalitarian rule. Were the Soviets content to seek traditional alliances and renounce their doctrine of national liberation and their efforts at imposing Communist social transformation on their "fraternal allies," the nature of the contest between the United States and the Soviet Union would be radically transformed.

Soviet Ideology

Finally, there is ideology. Listening to what the Soviets say may be more important than watching what they do. And what is important is not what Georgi Arbatov says on "Nightline" but what Gorbachev says to the Central Committee and what Party ideologues say in the pages of *Pravda*. In China, in an editorial on the 38th anniversary of the Communist Revolution, the *People's Daily* announced that "we cannot and will not undertake political campaigns of class struggle." For a Communist Party, giving up the notion of class struggle is far more important than allowing self-management in factories. The West is fixated on economic reforms. But the question is not whether Gorbachev is determined to put a VCR in every basket. The real question is what is he determined to have his schoolteachers put in the heads of their students and editorialists feed their readers. In the West we so discount Communist ideology that we fail to see the extent to which it continues to underpin Soviet actions. Nothing could be more important to the United States in thinking about the cold war than the state of Soviet ideology, which legitimizes the Party's rule and justifies both repression at home and expansion abroad. De-Stalinization is a reason to tone down the cold war. De-Leninization is a reason—the only reason—for abandoning it. This is not just a pipe dream. It is not an impossible condition that hawks can invoke for the purpose of justifying an indefinite prolongation of the cold war. The process may already be starting in China, where the Central Committee is considering removing the Party from day-to-day governance. Were that process to take hold in the Soviet Union, it would justify a revolution in American foreign-policy thinking. What kind of revolution? We might call it a paradigm shift. In characterizing the current Soviet-American conflict, hawks and doves invoke two diametrically opposed historical analogies. For hawks the relevant historical paradigm is Munich. For doves it is Sarajevo. For hawks, we are engaged in a struggle against an inimical and implacable ideological adversary (with the important difference that while the Soviets are as unappeasable as Hitler, they are not as reckless). For doves, we are engaged in the blind and pointless collision of rival national and imperial ambitions that will eventuate in unintended, senseless general destruction.

A de-Leninization of the Soviet system would totally deideologize the cold war. There would simply be no point in carrying it on. We would all have to agree that we are living at Sarajevo and the great task of both American and Soviet diplomacy is to manage jointly the inevitable rivalry of two great powers in such a way as to ensure peace. That is how détente was defined when it was declared, prematurely, a decade and a half ago.

When hawks insist that the only way to pursue a lasting peace between the Soviet Union and the United States is through improvements in human rights and a moderation of Soviet expansionism they are not being disingenuous. They are not imposing a false and opportunistic linkage. They are not avoiding the real issues of peace, such as, we are told, nuclear arms control. They are stating what is plain for all to see: the cold war may end simply because the West wearies of the twilight struggle, but it *should* end when there is no more reason to pursue it. And that will come only when the moral distance between East and West has narrowed, not before.

CHAPTER 5

The Cold War: Two Reflections

Chapter Preface

U.S. president Ronald Reagan was succeeded by his vice president, George Bush, in January 1989. At the time Bush took office, the Cold War was still a major element of the world scene in spite of increasing cooperation between the United States and the Soviet Union. Within the next three years, however, a rapid sequence of events in Europe and elsewhere drastically altered the picture. By November 1990 Bush could safely proclaim, "The Cold War is over."

The events leading up to this proclamation were largely unforeseen in their suddenness. Communism's eclipse began with the fall of European communism in 1989. In some countries, such as Hungary, reforms had gradually liberalized the country's economy and government over a period of years, culminating in the peaceful replacement of the communist leaders. In other countries, such as Czechoslovakia, massive protests resulted in the overthrow of the communist regime over a period of six weeks. People in Eastern Europe had attempted to democratize or resist communist rule before. This time, however, the Soviet Union, weakened by internal problems and determined to maintain good relations with the United States and Western Europe, did not intervene with tanks or demand a government crackdown as it had in Hungary in 1956, Czechoslovakia in 1968, and Poland in 1981. The Iron Curtain first named by Winston Churchill in 1946 was lifted.

In Germany, the Berlin Wall, symbol of East-West division for almost thirty years, was opened in November 1989 and eventually was torn down. In May 1990 the foreign ministers of the old World War II allies, the Soviet Union and the United States, got together with Great Britain, France, and East and West Germany to finally dispose of unfinished World War II business—Germany's reunification. The treaty uniting Germany was signed in October, taking effect in early 1991.

By the end of 1991 the Soviet Union was no more. Democratically elected governments in the component Soviet republics were increasingly asserting their independence from the central Soviet government. An abortive coup in August 1991 staged by Communist party officials attempted but failed to recentralize control in the Communist party. The republics of the Soviet Union separated into independent nations, of which the largest was Russia, under the leadership of Boris Yeltsin, a former communist who sought closer relations with Europe and the United States. Mikhail Gorbachev, the Soviet leader whose reforms had set much of the previous years' events in motion, resigned from power. In some respects the prophecies of George Kennan—Mr. X of 1947—had finally come to pass. The Soviet Union, prevented from expanding into Europe, had been destroyed by its internal weaknesses and contradictions.

Communist governments remained entrenched in a few countries, including China, North Korea, Vietnam, and Cuba. Yet this did not evoke in the United States the same fear it once did. China never regained the enemy status it had prior to President Nixon's 1972 visit. China's communist leadership placed its emphasis on market reforms and trade with the United States and other nations rather than on exporting communist revolutions (although its reforms did not extend to liberalizing its internal rule). Vietnam, North Korea, and Cuba, impoverished and isolated, were no longer seen as serious threats to the United States. Disputes and tensions between these nations and the United States remain, but no longer in the context of a worldwide crusade against communism by the United States.

Historians have had a relatively short period to examine the Cold War in its entirety. Many questions remain to be explored in light of the dramatic events at the close of the conflict. Could cooperation between the United States and the Soviet Union have been maintained after World War II, thus evading a Cold War? What caused the Cold War to spread from a Europe-centered dispute to a worldwide conflict? Could the Cold War have been ended sooner? Were the results of the Cold War worth the cost to the United States and its allies? The historian's task in answering these questions has just begun. The two viewpoints presented here provide a sampling of historical perspectives on the Cold War.

VIEWPOINT 1

"The idea of freedom proved more durable than the practice of authoritarianism, and as a consequence, the Cold War ended."

The Cold War Was a Triumph of Democracy over Communism

John Lewis Gaddis (1941-)

John Lewis Gaddis is Distinguished Professor of History and director of the Contemporary History Institute at Ohio University in Athens. His books include *Strategies of Containment* and *The United States and the End of the Cold War.*

In the following viewpoint, Gaddis examines the Cold War in retrospect, noting that it paradoxically was a period of relative peace compared to the conflicts that had preceded it. He disagrees with historians who have argued that the Cold War was simply a struggle between two great powers or an example of American militarism. The Cold War was an ideological confrontation between the democracy of the United States and the communism of the Soviet Union, Gaddis states, and it ended when the ideological underpinnings of the Soviet Union collapsed. Gaddis writes that President Harry S Truman's 1947 declaration that the conflict was between the forces of freedom and authoritarianism was, in retrospect, more accurate than some other historians have believed.

When the fictional dictator Big Brother proclaimed the propaganda slogan "War Is Peace" in George Orwell's novel *1984*, first published in 1948, he turned out to be a better prophet than anyone, including his creator, could ever have imagined. For we can now see that the Cold War, the most dangerous, bitter, and protracted rivalry between Great Powers in modern history, did in time become the most protracted period of freedom from Great Power war in modern history. Whether or not one approves of the *means* by which this happened, whether or not one even agrees on the *way* in which it happened, the simple fact is that the Cold War did evolve into a Long Peace. Whether the Long Peace can survive the end of the Cold War is, however, quite another matter.

The Cold War was many things to many people. It was a division of the world into two hostile camps. It was a polarization of Europe in general, and of Germany in particular, into antagonistic spheres of influence. It was an ideological contest, some said between capitalism and communism, others said between democracy and authoritarianism. It was a competition for the allegiance of, and for influence over, the so-called Third World. It was a game of wits played out by massive intelligence organizations behind the scenes. It was a struggle that took place within each of its major adversaries as supporters and opponents of confrontation confronted one another. It was a contest that shaped culture, the social and natural sciences, and the writing of history. It was an arms race that held out the possibility—because it generated the capability—of ending civilization altogether. And it was a rivalry that even extended, at one point, beyond the bounds of earth itself, as human beings for the first time left their planet, but for a set of reasons that are likely to seem as parochial to future generations as those that impelled Ferdinand and Isabella to finance Columbus when he first set out for the New World five hundred years ago.

A Turning Point

The new world of the post-Cold War era is likely to have few, if any, of these characteristics: that is an indication of how much things have already changed since the Cold War ended. We are at one of those rare points of "punctuation" in history at which old patterns of stability have broken up and new ones have not yet emerged to take their place. Historians will certainly regard the years 1989-1991 as a turning point comparable in importance to the years 1789-1794, or 1917-1918, or 1945-1947; precisely what has "turned," however, is much less certain. We know that a series of geopolitical earthquakes has taken place, but it is not yet clear how these upheavals have rearranged the landscape that lies before us. . . .

Not a Zero-Sum Game

Arthur Schlesinger Jr. is Schweitzer Professor in the Humanities at City University of New York and the author of numerous books and articles on history and diplomacy. He also served as an aide to President John F. Kennedy. In an article in the Spring 1992 issue of Diplomatic History, *he speculates that the Cold War might have ended sooner had Kennedy not been assassinated.*

For many years, Cold War theology decreed that a gain for one side was by definition a defeat for the other. This notion led logically not to an interest in negotiation but to a demand for capitulation. In retrospect the Cold War, humanity's most intimate brush with collective suicide, can only remind us of the ultimate interdependence of nations and of peoples.

After President Kennedy and Premier Khrushchev stared down the nuclear abyss together in October 1962, they came away determined to move as fast as they could toward détente. Had Kennedy lived, Khrushchev might have held on to power a little longer, and together they would have further subdued the excesses of the Cold War. They rejected the zero-sum approach and understood that intelligent negotiation brings mutual benefit. I am not an unlimited admirer of Ronald Reagan, but he deserves his share of credit for taking Mikhail Gorbachev seriously, abandoning the zero-sum fallacy he had embraced for so long, and moving the Cold War toward its end.

And why indeed has it ended? If the ideological confrontation gave the geopolitical rivalry its religious intensity, so the collapse of the ideological debate took any apocalyptic point out of the Cold War. The proponents of liberal society were proven right. After seventy years of trial, communism turned out—by the confession of its own leaders—to be an economic, political, and moral disaster. Democracy won the political argument between East and West. The market won the economic argument. Difficulties lie ahead, but the fundamental debate that created the Cold War is finished.

No one can foretell, with any assurance, whether that is going to happen. But now that we can at last view the Cold War from beginning to end, it ought to be possible to get a clearer sense than we have had of what that conflict was all about, and to use that knowledge as a basis for attempting to anticipate what is to follow it. Projecting patterns from the past is, to be sure, an imperfect way of seeing into the future. But barring prophecy—whether of divine, ideological, or astrological inspiration—it is the only such means we have: history has always been a less than perfect teacher. This essay deals, therefore, with patterns and probabilities. It makes no assumptions about "laws" of history or the alleged certainties that flow from them. It should, as a consequence, be read with all the caution the phrase *caveat emptor* has always implied. But one has to start somewhere.

When President Harry S. Truman told the Congress of the United States on 12 March 1947 that the world faced a struggle between two ways of life, one based on the will of the majority and the other based on the will of a minority forcibly imposed upon the majority, he had more than one purpose in mind. The immediate aim, of course, was to prod parsimonious legislators into approving economic and military assistance to Greece and Turkey, and a certain amount of rhetorical dramatization served that end. But President Truman also probably believed what he said, and most Americans and Europeans, at the time, probably agreed with him. Otherwise, the United States would hardly have been able to abandon its historic policy of peacetime isolationism and commit itself, not only to the Truman Doctrine, but to the much more ambitious Marshall Plan and eventually the North Atlantic Treaty Organization as well. Those plans worked, in turn, because most Europeans wanted them to. The danger at the time seemed to be real, and few people at the time had any difficulty in explaining what it was: freedom was under attack, and authoritarianism was threatening it.

In the years that followed, though, it became fashionable in academic circles to discount this argument. The Cold War, for many scholars, was not about ideology at all, but rather balances of power and spheres of influence; hence it differed little from other Great Power rivalries in modern and even ancient history. Others saw the Cold War as reflecting the demands of an unprecedentedly powerful American military-industrial complex that had set out to impose its hegemony over the rest of the earth. Students of Cold War origins never entirely neglected issues of ideology and principle, but few of them were prepared to say, as Truman had, that that conflict was *primarily* about the difference between freedom and its absence. Such a view seemed too naïve, too simplistic, and, above all, too self-righteous: politicians might say that kind of thing from public platforms, but professors in the classroom and in their scholarly monographs should not.

What the Cold War Was About

As a result, it was left to the people of Eastern Europe and now the Soviet Union itself—through their own spontaneous but collective actions over the past three years—to remind us of a fact that many of us had become too sophisticated to see, which is that the Cold War really was about the imposition of autocracy and the denial of freedom. That conflict came to an end only when it became clear that authoritarianism could no longer be imposed and freedom could no longer be denied. That fact ought to make us look more seriously at how ideology contributed to the coming of the Cold War in the first place.

Much of twentieth-century history has revolved around the testing of a single idea: that one could transform the conduct of politics, government, and even human behavior itself into a "science" which would allow not only predicting the future but even, within certain limits, determining it. This search for a "science" of politics grew out of the revolution that had long since occurred in physics and biology: if scientific laws worked so well in predicting motions of the planets, the argument ran, why should similar laws not govern history, economics, and politics? Karl Marx certainly had such an approach in mind in the 1840s when he worked out his theory of dialectical materialism, which explicitly linked political and social consciousness to irreversible processes of economic development; his collaborator Friedrich Engels insisted in 1880 that the progression from feudalism through capitalism to socialism and ultimately communism was as certain as was the Darwinian process of natural selection.

This movement to transform politics into a science began, it is important to emphasize, with the best of intentions: its goal was to improve the human condition by making human behavior rational, enlightened, and predictable. And it arose as a direct response to abuses, excesses, and inequities that had grown out of the concept of freedom itself, as manifested in the mid-nineteenth century *laissez-faire* capitalism Marx had so strongly condemned.

But the idea of a "science" of politics was flawed from the beginning for the simple reason that human beings do not behave like the objects science studies. People are not laboratory mice; it is impossible to isolate them from the environment that surrounds them. They make judgments, whether rational or irrational, about the probable consequences of their actions, and they can change these actions accordingly. They learn from experience: the inheritance of acquired characteristics may not work in biology, the historian E. H. Carr once pointed out, but it does in history. As a result, people rarely act with the predictability of molecules combining in test tubes, or ball bearings rolling down inclined planes, or even the "dependent variables" that figure so prominently in the writings—and, increasingly, the equations— of our contemporary social scientists.

It was precisely frustration with this irritating unpredictability of human beings that led Lenin at the beginning of this century to invert Marx and make the state the instrument that was supposed to secure human freedom, rather than the obstacle that stood in the way of it. But that same problem of human intractability in turn caused Stalin to invert Lenin and make the state, its survival, and its total control of all its surroundings an end in itself, with a consequent denial of freedom that was as absolute as any autocrat has ever managed to achieve. A movement that had set out in 1848 to free the workers of the world from their chains had wound up, by 1948 and through the logic of its "scientific" approach to politics, insisting that the condition of being in chains was one of perfect freedom.

Anyone contemplating the situation in Europe at the end of World War II would have had good reason, therefore, to regard the very nature of Stalin's regime as a threat, and to fear its possible expansion. That expansion had already taken place in Eastern Europe and the Balkans, not so much because of Stalinism's accomplishments in and of themselves, but rather because of the opportunity created for it by the foolish behavior of the Europeans in allowing another flight from freedom—fascism—to take root among them. In one of history's many paradoxes, a successful, necessary, and wholly legitimate war against fascism created conditions more favorable to the spread of communism than that ideology could ever have managed on its own.

A Real Danger

The dangers Truman warned against in 1947, hence, were real enough. There is such a thing as bending before what one mistakenly believes to be the "wave of the future": fascism had gained its foothold in Europe by just these means. Many Europeans saw communism as such a wave following Hitler's defeat, not because they approved of that ideology, and not because they really expected the Red Army to drive all the way to the English Channel and the Pyrenees; the problem rather was that Europe had fallen into a demoralization so deep and so pervasive that Communists might have found paths to power there by constitutional means, much as the Nazis had done in Germany in 1933. Had that happened there is little reason to believe that constitutional procedures would have survived, any more than they did under Hitler; certainly the experiences of Poland, Romania, Hungary, and, after February 1948, Czechoslovakia do not suggest otherwise. Stalin's system could have spread throughout Europe without Stalin having to lift a finger: that was the threat. The actions the United States took, through the Truman Doctrine, the Marshall Plan, and NATO, were seen at the time and I think will be seen by future historians as having restored self-confidence among the Europeans, as having preserved the idea of freedom in Europe by a narrow and precarious margin at a time when Europeans themselves, reeling from the effects of two world wars, had

Gorbachev and the Cold War

Raymond L. Garthoff is a senior fellow at the Brookings Institution. A retired diplomat, his books include Détente and Confrontation: American-Soviet Relations from Nixon to Reagan. *Writing in the Spring 1992 issue of* Diplomatic History, *he argues that Mikhail Gorbachev, leader of the Soviet Union from 1985 to 1991, deserves most of the credit for ending the Cold War.*

The West did not, as is widely believed, win the Cold War through geopolitical containment and military deterrence. Nor was the Cold War won by the Reagan military buildup and the Reagan Doctrine, as some have suggested. Instead, "victory" for the West came when a new generation of Soviet leaders realized how badly their system at home and their policies abroad had failed. What containment did was to successfully stalemate Moscow's attempts to advance Soviet hegemony. Over four decades it performed the historic function of holding Soviet power in check until the internal seeds of destruction within the Soviet Union and its empire could mature. At that point, however, it was Gorbachev who brought the Cold War to an end.

Despite the important differences among them, all Soviet leaders from Lenin until Gorbachev had shared a belief in an ineluctable conflict between socialism and capitalism. Although Gorbachev remained a Socialist, and in his own terms perhaps even a Marxist-Leninist, he renounced the idea of inevitable world conflict. His avowed acceptance of the interdependence of the world, of the priority of all-human values over class values, and of the indivisibility of common security marked a revolutionary ideological change. That change, which Gorbachev publicly declared as early as 1986 (though insufficiently noted), manifested itself in many ways over the next five years, in deeds as well as in words, including policies reflecting a drastically reduced Soviet perception of the Western threat and actions to reduce the Western perception of the Soviet threat....

In the final analysis, only a Soviet leader could have ended the Cold War, and Gorbachev set out deliberately to do so.

almost given up on it.

To be sure, some historians have claimed that Europe might have saved itself even if the Americans had done nothing. There is no way now to prove that they are wrong. But few Europeans saw things this way at the time, and that brings us to one of the most important distinctions that has to be made if we are to understand the origins, evolution, and subsequent end of the Cold War: it is that the expansion of American and Soviet influence into Europe—the processes that really began that conflict—did not take place in the same way and with the same results. The Soviet Union, acting from primarily defensive motives, imposed its sphere of influence directly on Eastern Europe and the Balkans, against the will of the people who lived there. The United States, also acting for defensive reasons, responded to invitations from desperate governments in Western Europe, the Mediterranean, and even the Middle East to create countervailing spheres of influence in those regions. Compared to the alternative, American hegemony—for there is no denying that such a thing did develop—definitely seemed the lesser of two evils.

This distinction between imposition and invitation—too easily lost sight of in too much of the writing that has been done about Cold War history—proved to be critical in determining not only the shape but also the ultimate outcome of the Cold War. The system the United States built in Western Europe quickly won legitimacy in the form of widespread popular support. The Warsaw Pact and the other instruments of Soviet control in Eastern Europe never did. This happened because Europeans at the time understood the difference between authoritarianism and its absence, just as more recent Europeans and now citizens of the former Soviet Union itself have come to understand it. Survivors of World War II had no more desire to embrace the Stalinist model of "scientific" politics than their children and grandchildren have had to remain under it. Moscow's authority in Eastern Europe turned out to be a hollow shell, kept in place only by the sheer weight of Soviet military power. Once it became apparent, in the late 1980s, that Mikhail Gorbachev's government was no longer willing (or able) to prop it up, the system Stalin had imposed upon half of Europe almost half a century earlier collapsed like a house of cards.

The way the Cold War ended, therefore, was directly related to the way in which it had begun. Perhaps Harry Truman had it right after all: the struggle really was, ultimately, about two ways of life, one that abandoned freedom in its effort to rationalize politics, and another that was content to leave politics as the irrational process that it normally is, thereby preserving freedom. The idea of freedom proved more durable than the practice of authoritarianism, and as a consequence, the Cold War ended.

The Nuclear Threat

The Cold War did, however, go on for an extraordinarily long period of time, during which the world confronted extraordinary perils. . . . How close we came to not surviving we will probably never know; but few people who lived through the Cold War took survival for granted during most of its history. The vision of a future filled with smoking, radiating ruins was hardly confined to writers of science fiction and makers of doomsday films; it was a constant presence in the consciousness of several generations after 1945, and the fact that that vision has now receded is of the utmost importance.

I do not mean to imply by this that the nuclear threat itself has gone away. With the proliferation of lethal technology to more and more nations possessing less and less wisdom, the probability that someone may actually use a nuclear weapon someday against someone else could well be increasing. But although horrible enough, such an event would be far from what most people feared during most of the Cold War, which was the prospect of thousands of Soviet and American nuclear warheads raining down upon the territories of the United States, the USSR, and much of the rest of the world. The use of one or two nuclear weapons, in the post-Cold War world, would not end the world as we have known it. During the Cold War, it might have.

Nuclear weapons have evolved from their initial status in our minds as the ultimate instrument of the Apocalypse to, first, a means of deterrence, and then a method of reassurance, and then an object for negotiation, and then an inconvenience to be circumvented, and finally an embarrassment of such magnitude that old Cold War antagonists now race to divest themselves of what they once raced each other so avidly to possess. From having worried about how nuclear weapons could destroy us we have progressed to worrying about how we can safely destroy them, and that is undeniably progress.

How, though, did this happen? How did we get from the world of Dr. Strangelove and "The Day After" to what would have seemed—not so long ago—an even more improbable world in which the leaders of former Soviet republics, including Russia itself, report dutifully to a peripatetic American Secretary of State on how they propose to spend funds allocated by the United States Congress for the purpose of dismantling and disposing of the once formidable Soviet nuclear arsenal?

Nuclear weapons have for so long been the subject of our nightmares—but sometimes also of our delusions of power—that it is difficult to answer this question dispassionately. We have tended to want to see these devices either as a Good Thing or a Bad Thing, and hence we have talked past one another most of the time. But the role of nuclear weapons in Cold War history was neither wholly good nor bad, which is to say, it was more interesting than either the supporters or the critics of these weapons have made it out to be.

Nuclear weapons were, of course, a very bad thing for the people of Hiroshima and Nagasaki; but those Americans and Japanese spared the necessity of additional killing as a result of their use might be pardoned for seeing some good in them. Nuclear weapons were a bad thing in that they greatly intensified the fears the principal Cold War adversaries had of one another, and that much of the rest of the world had of both of them. But they were a good thing in that they induced caution on the part of these two Great Powers, discouraging irresponsible behavior of the kind that almost all Great Powers in the past have sooner or later engaged in. Nuclear weapons were a bad thing in that they held the world hostage to what now seems the absurd concept of mutual assured destruction, but they were a good thing in that they probably perpetuated the reputations of the United States and the Soviet Union as superpowers, thereby allowing them to "manage" a world that might have been less predictable and more dangerous had Washington and Moscow not performed that function. Nuclear weapons were a bad thing in that they stretched out the length of the Cold War by making the costs of being a superpower bearable on both sides and for both alliances: if the contest had had to be conducted only with more expensive conventional forces, it might have ended long ago. But nuclear weapons were a good thing in that they allowed for the passage of time, and hence for the education of two competitors who eventually came to see that they did not have all that much to compete about in the first place.

It is important to remember, though, that the peaceful end to the Cold War we have just witnessed is not the *only* conceivable way the Cold War could have ended. In adding up that conflict's costs, we would do well to recognize that the time it took to conclude the struggle was not time entirely wasted. That time—and those costs—appear to us excessive in retrospect, but future historians may see those expenditures as long-term investments in ensuring that the Cold War ended peacefully. For what we wound up doing with nuclear weapons was buying time—the time necessary for the authoritarian approach to politics to defeat itself by nonmilitary means. And the passage of time, even if purchased at an exorbitant price, has at last begun to pay dividends.

One of those dividends is that, now that the Cold War has finally ended, we can see just how useless nuclear weapons really are for most purposes most of the time. President Bush, in his television address of 27 September 1991, wiped out more nuclear warheads in a single unilateral gesture than decades of negotiations over arms control have managed to remove, and President Gorbachev quickly offered to go even further. But these decisions do not necessarily mean that the weapons whose numbers both leaders have promised to reduce, and in some categories to eliminate altogether, never had any useful purpose. It could be that their purpose—ensuring a peaceful end to the Cold War—simply took a long time to achieve.

VIEWPOINT 2

"The United States has paid dearly for its Cold War victory."

The Cold War Exacted Great Costs from the U.S.

Richard J. Barnet (1929-)

Richard J. Barnet is a senior fellow and former co-director of the Institute for Policy Studies, a research and analysis institute known for its criticisms of U.S. Cold War policy. Barnet's books include *Global Reach* and *The Rockets' Red Glare*. In the following viewpoint, he reexamines two documents from the beginning of the Cold War featured in this book, George Kennan's "X" article, and Walter Lippmann's book *The Cold War*. He argues that Lippmann presented a realistic alternative to the forty-year Cold War and that he correctly predicted the enormous domestic costs the Cold War would have on the United States. Barnet concludes that the Cold War resulted in a hollow victory for the United States that left the nation economically and morally exhausted.

Such reputations as present-day pundits enjoy owe much to the fact that the newspaper columns they wrote forty-three days ago have already become recycled paper. Re-reading Walter Lippmann's columns on George Kennan's "X" article forty-three years after they were first published—in my case on the very day that the World War II conquerors relinquished their powers over Germany—is an unsettling experience. What are we to make of these twelve columns that Lippmann published a few months later as *The Cold War*? The clarity, the intellectual power, and the breadth of the analysis cannot fail to impress the reader, whatever one thinks of Lippmann's argument. As the United States stands on the threshold of another series of fateful choices, the contemporary relevance of the Lippmann-Kennan debate is striking.

Striking Questions

The Cold War lays out a surprisingly coherent view of politics and diplomacy. It is a traditionalist, realist argument for a path not taken. Embedded in these columns and in Kennan's "Sources of Soviet Conduct" are many of the concerns that are likely to engage future historians of the Cold War. What was the Cold War? Was it inevitable? Could it have ended sooner? Is it reasonable to think that it could have ended differently under happier circumstances? (It is easy to imagine it ending under far worse.) What were the costs? Were any of them avoidable?

It is most unlikely that these questions will ever be put to rest. Probably the best we can hope for from historians are intimations of truth, not answers. Why, then, are the questions even interesting? Just as Lippmann and Kennan viewed the conflict with the Soviet Union and its Communist ideology through the prism of the struggle against Hitler and fascism, so today political analysts and politicians view the emerging order of the 1990s through the prism of the Cold War. The understanding of what that struggle was about, what was gained and what was lost, will have a profound influence on the paths to national security that will be taken in the months ahead.

Both Kennan and Lippmann cast themselves in the twin roles of prognosticator and counsellor. As prognosticator about the trajectory of the Soviet Union, Kennan has the better of the argument. Lippmann takes aim at Kennan's prediction that "Soviet power... bears within itself the seeds of its own decay, and that the sprouting of these seeds is well advanced." All of this seemed to fly in the face of Stalin's vaunted monolithic power, his huge standing armies, and the fanatical devotion demonstrated by the Russian masses to the Great Genius, impassive in his marshal's uniform atop Lenin's mausoleum. According to Lippmann, Kennan's prescription of "containment" ended up in political aeschotology— the faith that when the Kremlin is forced to "face frustration indefinitely" the result will be "either the breakup or the gradual mellowing of the Soviet power." Kennan suggests, however, that it would take ten or fifteen years for Stalin's empire to mellow, not forty-three.

Lippmann ridicules Kennan's optimism since the policy prescriptions he wishes to discredit depend on it. According to the columnist, Kennan's position of "holding the line and hoping for the best" is utterly dependent on "an extra strong dose of wishful thinking about the United States." By his own admission Kennan's policies would take many years to work, and the notorious impatience of the American people—a favorite Lippmann theme—would render the strategy unworkable. But in fact, the United States maintained the "containment" policy for forty-three years. The Soviet Union not only mellowed but no longer exists.

Spin Doctors

But how much did U.S. Cold War policy have to do with what has happened to the Soviet Union? The spin doctors are already at work on the history books. Ronald Reagan's defenders argue that the willingness of the United States to challenge the Soviet Union to a technological arms race and a spending race strained the Communist system to the breaking point. The president's insistence on spending almost $2 trillion over five years, on confronting the Soviet leadership with Hollywood fantasies of miracle weapons, and on mounting an ideological offensive against communism and all forms of statism caused Mikhail Gorbachev to throw in the towel. The eight-year Cold War II that began even before the Afghanistan invasion was more than the Soviet system could take. In short, the Cold War ended in a military victory for the United States, a historic triumph because for all the threats and feints, a shooting war between the United States and the Soviet Union was avoided.

This judgment appears to contradict most of the evidence. The arms race actually increased both the risk and the perception of risk of a war between the superpowers. It did not deter a Soviet intention to challenge the United States to a test of arms because, as virtually all U.S. intelligence estimates concluded in the years 1945-1950, the Soviet Union had neither the intention nor the capability of resorting to war. The U.S. nuclear monopoly neither contained Soviet expansion outside of Europe—that is, the acquisition of clients, spies, and propaganda assets—nor prevented Stalin from consolidating his hold over Eastern Europe. From the first the United States took the lead in the arms race. The Soviets struggled to keep up and thereby created the only military threat to the United States taken seriously by U.S. planners—the threat that Stalin's successors would acquire enough intercontinental planes and missiles to deter the United States from the vigorous pursuit of containment in the political arena. The extreme case, as

NSC-68 put it, contemplated the possibilily that the Kremlin might in some future "year of maximum danger" achieve the capability of launching a surprise attack. Should that happen, given the fundamentally evil nature of the system, the Soviets would resort to nuclear blackmail or "pre-emptive" war. These ideas kept the nuclear arms race going, raised the risk of war by miscalculation, and contributed to the proliferation of nuclear and nonnuclear military technology throughout the world.

The Cold War ended because internal failures and disappointments forced fundamental changes in the Soviet system. The Communist party lost legitimacy because it felt compelled to confirm the realities of Stalinist terror, to admit the widespread corruption of its leadership, and to come to terms with the fact that the system was working badly. The disastrous war in Afghanistan and the dawning realization that the Soviet Union would never develop a strong economic base as an autarchic command economy and could never compete in the global economy as a nation of regimented, unmotivated, or terrorized workers pushed Gorbachev down the road to *perestroika* and *glasnost*.

Kennan's Predictions

The disintegration of the Soviet system came about exactly in the way that Kennan had predicted. The system contained the seeds of its own destruction. The expensive pursuit of military equivalence no doubt accelerated the process, and for this the United States can take some dubious credit for hooking the Soviets into a spending race that was more precipitously disastrous for the Soviet system than for American society and its economic base. But the Cold War also helped to strengthen the hard-line leadership. Indeed, some reformist historians in the former Soviet Union believe that an earlier readiness of the United States to negotiate with Stalin's successors, or even with Stalin, over the fate of Europe would have caused the winds of change to blow earlier, harder, and faster, and that some Soviet leader might well have taken the risks of *perestroika* in the 1950s or the 1960s. Who knows? But as Kennan noted, the myth of capitalist encirclement was an important Stalinist weapon of social control. Beginning in the late 1940s, the extravagant rhetoric of officials, generals, and politicians in the United States about the inevitability of war with the Soviet Union—and the need to get it over with before the year of maximum danger arrived—served to confirm Stalinist paranoia and to reinforce the climate of fear on which the dictator built his regime. The hostility of the West also served to explain to two Soviet generations why the workers' government could not deliver on its promises to the workers.

But George Kennan neither predicted nor advocated a military

Cold War Concealed Domestic Problems

The Cold War concealed fundamental domestic problems of U.S. society which are only now beginning to emerge, write historians Gar Alperovitz and Kai Bird in the Spring 1992 issue of Diplomatic History. *Alperovitz and Bird are both with the Institute for Policy Studies in Washington, D.C.*

[T]he shift in the nuclear threat and the reduced likelihood of large limited wars may mean that the Cold War will no longer dominate domestic political discourse in the United States. If this is the case—if the Cold War no longer overhangs the American economy and American politics—fundamental issues that have been obscured for more than four decades are likely to resurface. From the 1940s onward, the Cold War played an important role in at least three fundamental areas: It provided the rationale for major, economy-simulating arms spending, thereby concealing deeper problems in the economic system; it repeatedly occupied center stage in America's media-dominated politics, thereby preempting other important domestic political debates; and it distorted our understanding of the real choices available to developing Third World countries. If the Cold War fades, the shroud of misconceptions, political hysteria, and war fears that has prevented serious discussion of these critical issues is likely to be slowly lifted.

victory, not even one that rested on a spending race and the demonstration of superior technological prowess. He has spent the second half of his life explaining away his "X" article, apologizing for its excessively militaristic ring and lamenting the uses to which it was put. Yet, it was Kennan's eloquent distillations of his complex, contradictory thought (backed by a reputation for expertise on the Soviet Union that few could match)—in such phrases as the "adroit and vigilant application of counter-force," or "the Russians look forward to a duel of infinite duration," or the emphasis on the Soviets' "neurotic view of world affairs," or the "instinctive Russian sense of insecurity"—that took official Washington by storm in early 1946. The picture that emerged from Kennan's analysis was of an ambitious power in the grip of an irrational ideology and impervious to conventional diplomacy. His "Long Telegram" was leaked to *Time* a year before the "X" article appeared, and his message was amplified and distorted as a brief for policies that he never supported, and indeed would at a much later stage publicly oppose. . . .

The Case for Negotiation

Lippmann is unwilling to assume that the "neurotic world view" and the totalitarian organization of Stalinist society meant that the Soviet Union was so inexorably committed to an expansionist course as to be beyond the influence of adroit diplomacy. Given the obvious Soviet weakness that Kennan identified, why was it so clearly impossible for the most powerful nation on earth to press the heirs of the Russian empire to accept a settlement?

> I am contending that the American diplomatic effort should be concentrated on the problem created by the armistice—which is on how the continent of Europe can be evacuated by the three non-European armies which are now inside Europe. This is the problem which will have to be solved if the independence of the European nations is to be restored. Without that there is no possibility of a tolerable peace. But if these armies withdraw, there will be a very different balance of power in the world than there is today, and one which cannot easily be upset. For the nations of Europe, separately and in groups, perhaps even in unity, will then, and then only, cease to be the stakes and the pawns of the Russian-American conflict.

It is hard to read the "X" article and come to any conclusion about when negotiation with the Soviet Union would make sense, if ever. Read literally, the article seems to say that there could be no useful diplomacy until the mellowing process was well advanced. We know that Kennan had misgivings about the division of Germany, German rearmament, and the deployment of NATO armies beyond the temporary "modest shield" behind which Western Europe would recover its economic and political stability. He was appalled by the global pretensions of the Truman Doctrine. But no one could guess it from the cold print that was so effectively used to support all of these policies.

Lippmann attacked Kennan for not keeping his eye on "the material cause and reason of the conflict," which was the future of Germany and the military balance in Europe. The columnist appears more pragmatic and hardheaded than the suddenly famous diplomat. If Kennan was right that communism was already a weakening ideology and that the economic foundations of Soviet power were shaky, then the only reason that this underdeveloped country should have been considered a serious political rival was the presence of the Red Army in the middle of Europe. Given the uniquely dominant role of the United States in the world economy and its unique strength as the only big power not crippled by the war, not to mention the attraction its democratic system held for the entire war-shattered world—even Ho Chi Minh was celebrating Washington and Jefferson in 1945—why did the Truman administration not set as its overriding policy objective the redeployment and demobilization of Stalin's land forces and the avoidance of a nuclear arms race? For it was only in the military sphere that the Soviet Union had the chance to be a serious rival to the United States, and as Lippmann points out, a deal with the Soviet Union to withdraw and demobilize their forces in Europe would be largely self-verifying. Such an agreement would provide little employment "for the dialecticians, the ideologists, the sophists, and the causists" who were then building political careers on the murky text of the Yalta accords. Soviet disengagement "is not a matter which can be hidden behind an iron curtain. It is a matter of plain and quite obvious fact."

Lippmann makes a strong case. A German settlement and withdrawal of the armies would "divide the Red Army from the Red International." It would avoid the "continual and complicated intervention" of the United States in the affairs of its allies and would spare the effort and expense of "recruiting, subsidizing, and supporting a heterogeneous array of satellites, clients, dependents, and puppets . . . around the perimeter of the Soviet Union." (Lippmann correctly saw these imperial roles as sources of weakness, not strength, and certainly not as the badge of preeminent or long-lasting power.)

Why did the United States not put Lippmann's strategy to the test? Why did the Truman administration launch its containment strategy by concentrating on the fringes of Europe—Turkey and Greece—rather than on its center? Why did it move so quickly to conclude that military pressure rather than diplomacy was the key to containing Russian power?

In 1947 the United States had a monopoly on nuclear weapons, produced about half the world's goods on its soil, and had most of the world's gold reserves in Fort Knox. The Soviet Union was still in ruins, and Stalin had already begun to destroy the "magical attraction" of communism for people around the world. All over Western Europe, Communists were out of government, although Stalinist parties were still very strong in France and Italy. Stalin was actually taking a conservative approach to revolution, counseling caution to the comrades in Greece, France, and China. In retrospect, it seems inexplicable that the United States at the height of its military and economic hegemony should wish to delay the grand settlement that Lippmann proposed until, in Dean Acheson's words, it had built "situations of strength." Given the conviction that the Soviet Union would acquire nuclear weapons and that, as later suggested in NSC-68, Stalin would use them against the United States whenever he deemed it advantageous to do so, why was nuclear disarmament not the centerpiece of U.S. policy? Why would the United States have a greater edge over the Soviet Union after ten or fifteen years of containment than it already enjoyed in 1947?

Four Ideas

I would suggest as an explanation four powerful political ideas that gripped the Truman administration; each reinforced the

283

other, causing the architects of U.S. Cold War policy to reject the course that Lippmann proposed without even giving it serious consideration. The first was the notion that the atomic bomb was a "winning weapon" under the cover of which the United States could successfully challenge Soviet power at the periphery of the Eurasian land mass. The geopolitical faith that the balance of power would be decided by the control of raw materials, sea lanes, bases, and internal political developments outside of Europe caused the Truman administration to put greater emphasis on military pressure and less on diplomacy. Two years after Japan's surrender in the wake of the atomic attack, it seemed reasonable to expect a more favorable outcome in Europe once the world was organized against Stalin and once the United States had clearly demonstrated, contrary to Roosevelt's comments to Stalin during the war, that the newly proclaimed leader of the Free World was in no hurry to withdraw its forces from the Continent.

The second idea that guided American policymakers was that Stalin was a reincarnation of Hitler, a man of boundless appetite, a barbarian whose word was worthless, and an ideologue as removed from the world of conventional politics as *Der Führer*. You could not do business with Stalin, and even to make the attempt would weaken political support for containment, giving the Soviet dictator an opportunity to divide the coalition against him and to confuse the American people.

The third and perhaps most important strain in American official thinking that pushed Truman's advisers toward a military rather than a diplomatic strategy for dealing with the Soviet Union was concern about Germany. The fear that a Germany that was not locked in an American embrace might conclude a new Rapallo agreement with the Soviet Union and that together the two land powers would attract Japan to a revived totalitarian alliance to challenge American hegemony was the driving force for the policy of partition on which NATO was founded. Within the Truman administration the distrust of Germany two years after the war was too strong to permit a deal with the Soviets based on the "neutralization" of Germany. Worse than the Red Army on the Elbe was the prospect of a power vacuum in Germany. A long-term U.S. military presence on German soil would serve as the glue for the economic integration of an Atlantic community in which the leading role of the United States would be assured for years to come. The military alliance would exert a profound influence on the domestic politics of every Western European country, ensuring that their governments would remain pro-American and centrist.

The fourth and final strain was a deep concern about the volatility of U.S. public opinion. The American people were de-

Why the Cold War Endured

Ronald Steel, professor of international relations at the University of Southern California, argues in a Spring 1992 article in Diplomatic History *that the United States used the Cold War to increase its global influence. He asserts that the United States might have problems adjusting to the end of the conflict.*

What one must ask about the Cold War is not why it ended so soon but why it lasted so long. There were a number of reasons for its longevity: the preference of the Europeans and the Japanese to grow rich rather than to resume the game of power politics; the eagerness of both the United States and the Soviet Union to inherit those roles; the transformation of the Soviet-American geopolitical quarrel into an ideological one that respected no frontiers; and the utility of the conflict in establishing Soviet or American hegemony within their respective areas. . . .

The Cold War had, in fact, developed into an eminently workable international system. It was predictable, economically manageable, politically useful, and militarily unthreatening. This was so because the Soviets, too, had developed a vested interest in its preservation. The Americans kept the Germans in check, and the Europeans kept the Americans in check. The Cold War allowed the Japanese to gain extraordinary economic power as America expended its resources on potlatch objectives, and it gave the Soviets, despite their primitive economy and retrograde social structure, the attributes of a Great Power. For all practical purposes it permitted the Americans to control the foreign policies of their major allies (and potential challengers): the Europeans and the Japanese. And it gave the Chinese a privileged position as the "good" Communists who would antagonize the Russians on their Asian flanks. Despite its considerable costs, the Cold War thus provided something desirable for all of the major participants. No nation had a compelling interest in ending it. From an American perspective it had a particular appeal. The Soviets were unquestionably the weaker power and posed no serious threat to American interests. As one astute critic has written: "The purpose of the Cold War was not victory but the maintainance of a controlled contest.". . .

With the end of the Cold War, the United States will be forced to adjust to a competition where its familiar instruments are inapplicable and where its allies and dependencies are increasingly rivals. It is not merely the end of the Cold War, but a dramatic reshifting of the world power balance. For the American economy, distorted by a half century of reliance on military spending, for American political elites, who had come to believe that they were "born to lead," and for an American public, deprived of an enemy to justify its sacrifices, the experience will be a wrenching and possibly threatening one.

manding demobilization and the armed forces were melting away. In 1946, one third of American exports were being financed through various programs of economic assistance. But conservatives, divining the public mood, were gearing up to block the "giveaway programs" on which the administration's economic and political strategies depended. Impassioned oratory about unpaid World War I war debts echoed through the chamber of the House of Representatives. According to a Gallup poll, a majority of Americans favored high tariffs. The Council of Economic Advisers worried that "a drastic reduction in public outlays plus the rapid demobilization of our armed forces, would lead to heavy unemployment and business dislocation for a substantial period of time." Acheson and Secretary of Defense George C. Marshall had run into trouble with Congress when they tried to present a nuanced view of the situation in Europe, and a consensus swiftly developed in the administration that scaring the hell out of the American people, in [Senator Arthur] Vandenberg's famous phrase, was essential for combating the isolationist mood. The containment strategy required that Americans believe that Stalin represented a threat to their own security. To sell Marshall Plan aid the only way it could be sold, as an instrument of containment, it was important to close off avenues of hope that the problems of Europe could be settled through negotiation with Stalin. "I think it is a mistake," Dean Acheson told the Senate Foreign Relations Committee, "to believe that you can, at any time, sit down with the Russians and solve questions."

The Costs of Containment

Lippmann showed no interest in challenging Kennan on his judgments about Russia's vulnerabilities, much less on the facts the Soviet expert used as the basis for his judgments. His rejoinder rests rather on his assessment of American vulnerabilities that would be likely to develop in a long Cold War. Why, asked Lippmann, do we think that it is ordained that the Soviet Union must break its leg "while the United States grows a pair of wings to speed it on its way?" In his own way Lippmann was as prescient about what would happen to the United States as Kennan was about the fate of the Soviet Union. He was wrong about American staying power through nine administrations, but forty-three years later his columns do serve as an unheeded reminder of the extraordinary costs of containment.

Lippmann sounded like the George Kennan of the 1970s when he zeroed in on the rhapsodical coda of the "X" article. Kennan professed "a certain gratitude to a Providence which, by providing the American people with this implacable challenge [Soviet power and Stalinist ideology], has made their entire security as a nation dependent on their pulling themselves together and accepting the responsibilities of moral and political leadership that history plainly intended them to bear." Lippmann did not question the assertion that it was America's destiny to lead, but he did challenge both the definition of leadership and the strategy for exercising leadership. He was clearer about why he did not like the strategy. Would it not take "a blank check on the Treasury"? How could the American constitutional system be maintained if containment of communism became the national purpose? How would the president know when he was to intervene? Or was the idea to intervene everywhere? Either the president would be too little and too late with his application of "counterforce" or he would have to bypass the Constitution. "A policy of shifts and maneuvers may be suited to the Soviet system of government, which, as Mr. X tells us, is animated by patient persistence. It is not suited to the American system of government."

Lippmann argues that a "free and undirected economy like our own" cannot "be used by the diplomatic planners to wage a diplomatic war against a planned economy." Forty-three years later it is tempting to say that Lippmann was wrong on this score. The "arsenal of democracy," with the world's largest GNP and the world's most formidable military force, has its problems after forty years of unrelenting military budgets, but no one at this point would exchange these difficulties for the problems in the former Soviet Union. Yet the challenge of containment caused profound changes in the American system that Lippmann feared, correctly, would be destructive. The pressures of the military competition, which was assumed in the highest reaches of the Truman administration to be the likely outcome of their policies, forced the "free and undirected economy" to develop its own planned sector; the Pentagon and the huge network of weapons procurement and maintenance facilities it fed is a market system in name only. The impact of four decades of permanent mobilization on the U.S. economy is the subject of considerable contention, but it is obvious that this mobilization transformed the nature of American capitalism—and certainly not in a direction advocated by free-market ideologues. My own view is that despite the periodic stimulus provided by cycles of military spending, military Keynesianism has been a disaster, contributing to budget deficits, loss of competitive position, and the siphoning of investment funds from both public infrastructure—schools, bridges, and the like—as well as from needed industrial and technological development. The spending priorities adopted in the pursuit of containment have had a great deal to do with the decline in American economic power. Lippmann did not exactly predict this, but he raised the issue. Kennan did not. . . .

U.S. Exhaustion

After almost fifty years the Cold War struggle has destroyed the Soviet Union. In the hands of Russian, Belorussian, Ukrainian, and Kazakhstani leaders are thousands of nuclear warheads that can destroy this country, and who will gain control of them in the months ahead is by no means certain. The collapse of Soviet power and the failure of Socialist institutions open up long-term possibilities of democratic transformation. But the prospects for the immediate future may be more political upheavals and economic distress. All of this is adding to the world's immense capital needs at a moment when the United States, debt ridden and more dependent on foreign capital than at any time in this century, can do almost nothing to meet them. The costs of the prolonged political-military struggle that Lippmann called the Cold War can be counted not only in the neglect and deterioration of domestic institutions but also in the loss of American capacity to exercise constructive influence abroad. The world's only global military superpower lacks the material resources to maintain a competitive industrial base, the infrastructure on which a strong economy depends, or even the necessities, much less the amenities, of a good society.

How ironical it is that as Leningrad has been renamed St. Petersburg and as the seventy-five-year obsession with the Soviet Union comes to an end, the United States is now obsessed with talk of its own decline. In 1991, it once again reasserted its strength and staying power by fixing on another underdeveloped country against which it waged a crushing but indecisive war. The United States has paid dearly for its Cold War victory and for the satisfaction of creating the foundations of the Cold War order. But the consequence—as Lippmann rightly predicted and as the last forty-three years have shown—has been political and moral exhaustion.

Chronology

1917	*November* Bolshevik Revolution occurs in Russia; Lenin assumes power.
1918	*July* President Wilson intervenes militarily in the Russian Civil War.
1933	President Franklin Roosevelt extends formal diplomatic recognition to the Soviet Union. The United States is the last major Western power to do so.
1939	*August* Nazi Germany and the Soviet Union sign a nonaggression pact. The treaty enables the Soviet Union over the next months to occupy eastern Poland and the Baltic states of Lithuania, Latvia, and Estonia.
1941	*June* Hitler invades the Soviet Union, making the Soviet Union an informal ally with the Western powers.
1941	*December 7* Japan attacks Pearl Harbor; the United States is at war with Japan and Germany. The "strange alliance" of the United States, the Soviet Union, and Great Britain is a reality.
1943	*November* The Big Three—Churchill, Stalin, and Roosevelt— meet for the first time to begin to discuss the shape of the postwar world.
1945	*February* The Big Three meet for the second and last time. Stalin pledges to enter the war against Japan. The Declaration on Liberated Europe, promising free elections in postwar Europe, is signed.
1945	*August 6 and 9* The United States drops atomic bombs on Japan, bringing an abrupt end to the war in the Pacific.
1945	*October* Secretary of State James Byrnes and Soviet foreign minister V.M. Molotov meet to begin discussions on the fate of postwar Europe.
1946	*March* Winston Churchill delivers his "Iron Curtain" speech at Westminster College in Fulton, Missouri.
	April Soviets reject $1 billion loan from the United States. Moscow also refuses to join the World Bank and the International Monetary Fund.
	June Congress establishes the Atomic Energy Commission under the Atomic Energy Act of 1946, which prohibited the exchange of atomic information.

289

September Commerce secretary Henry Wallace attacks the Truman administration's anti-Soviet foreign policy in a speech in Madison Square Garden.

October Soviet-American negotiations over World War II peace settlement stall.

1947 *March* In a speech to Congress, President Truman announces U.S. intention to support British anticommunism efforts in the Greek Civil War. The result is the Truman Doctrine, a statement of American support for antitotalitarianism everywhere.

June Secretary of State George Marshall announces the Marshall Plan for economic aid to Europe.

July The doctrine of containment is spelled out in an article in *Foreign Affairs Quarterly* by George Kennan. The Cold War is on in earnest.

1948 *February* Communists take over Czechoslovakia.

June Soviets cut off Western powers' access to Berlin. The West responds by airlifting food and supplies into blockaded area.

1949 *July* U.S. Senate ratifies the North Atlantic Treaty Organization, binding the United States to the defense of Western Europe.

September Chiang Kai-shek is driven from power in China. Mao Zedong and the Communists come to power.

Soviets explode their first atomic bomb.

1950 *February* Senator Joseph McCarthy initiates his anticommunist crusade.

June North Korea attacks South Korea. United Nations authorizes deployment of soldiers, including troops from the U.S., to assist South Korea.

NSC-68 is ready for implementation. A creation of the National Security Council, this document spells out the American military stance toward the Soviet Union.

1951 *September* ANZUS Treaty is ratified, binding the United States, Australia, and New Zealand in a pact of mutual military support.

1953 *July* Settlement in the Korean War is finally reached.

1954 CIA engineers overthrow of regimes unfriendly to the United States in Guatemala and Iran.

The Southeast Asian Treaty Organization is ratified, unifying Australia, Great Britain, France, New Zealand, Thailand, the Philippines, Pakistan, and the United States in an agreement to support each other against aggression.

July   The Geneva Accords partition North and South Vietnam.

1955   *January*   Soviet leadership announces that its possession of the hydrogen bomb makes "peaceful coexistence necessary and possible."

The Baghdad Pact, a mutual defense treaty, is signed by Turkey, Pakistan, Iran, Iraq, and Britain. The United States participates informally and later signs bilateral agreements with several of the participants.

May   Warsaw Pact is formed. A mutual defense organization, it is the Communist bloc's equivalent of NATO.

July   Eisenhower and Khrushchev meet for the first time, in Geneva, Switzerland.

1956   *February*   Khrushchev details the "crimes" of Stalin at the Twentieth Party Congress.

October-November   Simultaneous crises in Hungary and the Suez Canal preoccupy the great powers. Moscow crushes anticommunist rebellion in Hungary; Washington refuses to support British, French, and Israeli efforts to regain the Suez Canal.

1957   *October*   Soviets successfully launch *Sputnik*, the world's first artificial satellite.

1958   The growing split between the Soviet Union and Mao's China becomes apparent as Moscow voices disagreement with Mao's "Great Leap Forward" program.

July   U.S. Marines are dispatched to Lebanon; the Eisenhower Doctrine to block Soviet expansion in the Middle East is declared.

November   Khrushchev demands that the United States withdraw its troops from West Berlin and declare it a "free city."

1959   *January*   Communist revolutionary leader Fidel Castro comes to power in Cuba, ousting U.S.-supported dictator Fulgencio Batista.

September   Khrushchev visits the United States.

1960   *May*   Khrushchev announces that the Soviets have shot down an American spy plane known as the U-2; Eisenhower denies it was a spy plane; Khrushchev reveals the captured American pilot; the Paris summit conference is ruined.

November   After a campaign calling for an intensified American commitment to fighting the Cold War, John F. Kennedy is elected president.

1961   *January*   President Eisenhower's farewell address warns against the dangers of the "military-industrial complex" in the United States.

March   Kennedy proposes the Alliance for Progress to extend economic aid to Latin America.

April   A joint Cuban-American effort to overthrow Castro founders in the Bay of Pigs.

June   Kennedy and Khrushchev meet for the first time, in Vienna, Austria. The Soviet leader calls for support for "wars of national liberation" and demands Western withdrawal from Berlin within six months.

July   Kennedy calls for a 25 percent increase in U.S. military spending.

August   The Berlin Wall is erected.

1962   The Kennedy administration intensifies its military commitment to South Vietnam.

October   The Cuban missile crisis unfolds and is defused.

1963   *June*   President Kennedy calls for the relaxation of tensions and a goal of making the "world safe for diversity."

July   The Nuclear Test Ban Treaty is ratified by the U.S. Senate.

November   President Diem of South Vietnam is assassinated.

President Kennedy is assassinated.

1964   *August*   In the Gulf of Tonkin incident, President Johnson orders reprisals against possibly imaginary Vietnamese attackers; the Gulf of Tonkin Resolution passes Congress almost unanimously, officially giving the president discretion to order such defensive measures.

1965   *April*   U.S. Marines are dispatched to the Dominican Republic in the name of anticommunism.

July   President Johnson announces that 150,000 American troops will be sent to Vietnam.

1967   *June*   President Johnson and Soviet premier Kosygin meet at Glassboro, New Jersey.

July   The American troop commitment to South Vietnam reaches 400,000.

1968   *January*   North Korea seizes the U.S.S. *Pueblo*.

February   The Tet Offensive reveals the continuing strength of the North Vietnamese army and the increasing American opposition to the war.

March   President Johnson announces his decision not to seek reelection.

August   Soviet troops move to crush the "Prague spring" in Czechoslovakia.

1969	President Richard Nixon begins the process of "vietnamizing" the war in Vietnam.
1970	*January* In his "State of the World" address, President Nixon unfurls the Nixon Doctrine, designed to have American allies assume some of the military and financial burdens of the containment of communism.
	April Declaring that the United States will not be a "pitiful, helpless giant," President Nixon announces that American troops will be sent into Cambodia to root out North Vietnamese forces.
1971	National security advisor Henry Kissinger explores ways of establishing American contacts with China as a way of further isolating the Soviet Union.
1972	*February* President Nixon visits China.
	July Nixon and Brezhnev sign SALT I, a treaty freezing the number of nuclear missiles possessed by each superpower.
	November President Nixon defeats George McGovern and his call for America to "come home" from Vietnam.
1973	*January* A ceasefire is agreed upon by the United States and North Vietnam; American troops are withdrawn.
	Congress passes the War Powers Act, mandating that "in every possible instance" the president must consult with Congress before sending American troops into a war.
	September The Cold War shifts southward as the United States helps engineer the overthrow of the leftist regime of Chilean president Salvador Allende.
	October Egypt and Syria launch a surprise attack against Israel. Egypt's President Sadat asks for Soviet support.
1974	Angola achieves independence from Portugal. Soviets fly Cuban troops to Angola in a move Kissinger describes as a dangerous escalation of the Cold War.
	July Congress passes the Jackson-Vanik amendment, tying Soviet-American trade to Soviet willingness to permit Jewish dissidents to leave the USSR.
	August Nixon resigns the presidency in the wake of the Watergate scandal.
1975	*April* South Vietnam falls to North Vietnam.
	December The Helsinki Accord is signed. Thirty-five countries, including the United States and the Soviet Union, accept the Eastern European boundaries as permanent. Soviets agree to adopt a more liberal human rights policy.

1977	President Carter openly urges dissidents in the Soviet Union to demand greater freedom.
1978	*September* President Carter scores a coup against the Soviets by successfully mediating the Egyptian-Israeli Camp David Accords, which assure Israel's withdrawal from the strategically important Sinai Peninsula.
1979	*January* The United States extends formal diplomatic relations to China.
	July Presidents Carter and Brezhnev agree to SALT II, which limits each country to twenty-four hundred nuclear arms launchers.
	November The shah of Iran is overthrown; American hostages are seized in Iran.
	December Soviets move militarily to reassert control over Afghanistan.
1981	President Reagan rebuffs Soviet requests to hold arms control talks; the United States begins military buildup to match Soviet military expansion during the 1970s; Cold War rhetoric escalates with Reagan's reference to the Soviet Union as an "evil empire."
	November President Reagan signs the secret National Security Decision Directive 17 authorizing the CIA to train and equip the contra rebels in their war with the Sandinistas in Nicaragua.
1983	President Reagan proposes the Strategic Defense Initiative, which is designed to shoot down enemy nuclear missiles before they reach their targets.
	August Soviets shoot down civilian Korean airliner they claim violated Soviet air space.
	October Terrorist explosion kills 239 U.S. soldiers in their barracks in Lebanon.
	U.S. troops are sent to Grenada to eliminate a regime friendly to Moscow and Castro.
1984	*March* President Reagan visits China and seems to signal a change in U.S. foreign policy by referring to "this so-called Communist China" and agreeing to sell sophisticated weapons to the Chinese.
1985	President Reagan declares the Reagan Doctrine, calling upon the United States to defend "freedom and democracy . . . on every continent."
	The Reagan administration sells arms to Iran and extends clandestine support to the contras in Nicaragua through the profits from the arms sales.
	Mikhail Gorbachev comes to power in the Soviet Union.

1986	Gorbachev begins to withdraw economic support from Soviet satellite states, including Cuba.
	February Gorbachev calls for massive reform of the Soviet system.
	October Reagan and Gorbachev meet at Reykjavik, Iceland, and shock the world by agreeing to remove all intermediate-range nuclear missiles from Europe.
	November The outline of the Iran-contra affair, in which the United States sold arms to Iran, one of its adversaries, is revealed to the American people.
1987	*October* Reagan and Gorbachev meet in Washington to sign a treaty eliminating medium- and short-range nuclear missiles.
1988	*December* Gorbachev renounces the Brezhnev Doctrine, thereby permitting greater freedom to the states of Eastern Europe.
1989	*January* Gorbachev announces final Soviet military withdrawal from Afghanistan.
	June Democracy movement in China is crushed by the Communist regime.
	After free elections, Lech Walesa and Solidarity come to power in Poland.
	September A new regime in Hungary permits East Germans to escape through Hungary to West Germany.
	November The Berlin Wall is reduced to rubble and souvenirs.
	December Communist regimes fall in Czechoslovakia, Bulgaria, and Rumania. Gorbachev formally renounces the use of force, thereby recognizing the end of the Soviet empire.
	Bush and Gorbachev meet in Malta; Bush proposes treaties on nuclear and conventional arms reductions.
1990	The world begins to realize that the Cold War is over.
	March Lithuania declares independence from the Soviet Union.
	May "Two plus four" talks, featuring the foreign ministers of East and West Germany and the World War II allies, the United States, the Soviet Union, Great Britain, and France, pave the way for the reunification of Germany. East and West Germany sign a treaty August 31. Germany is reunited October 3.
	Gorbachev and Bush meet in Washington for a four-day summit beginning May 30. The two countries sign more than a dozen bilateral agreements, including a framework for reducing nuclear weapons, a

ban on chemical weapons, and agreements normalizing trade.

May 29 Boris Yeltsin is elected president of the Russian republic.

November Gorbachev meets with German chancellor Kohl; the two countries sign a nonaggression pact and an accord governing Soviet troop withdrawal from eastern Germany. Germany and Poland later agree to guarantee the permanence of their current borders.

1991

January The Persian Gulf War, in which the United States and the Soviet Union are allied against Iraq, is the first post-Cold War war.

March United States withdraws the last of its intermediate-range nuclear missiles from Europe, completing the terms of the 1987 treaty.

April The Warsaw Pact disbands.

August Coup against Gorbachev fails, signaling the death of communism in the Soviet Union, as well as the end of the Soviet Union.

September 27 Bush announces U.S. elimination of twenty-four thousand nuclear warheads and ends twenty-four-hour alert status of U.S. strategic bombers.

December The republics of the Soviet Union ally together as the new "Commonwealth of Independent States." Gorbachev resigns. The government of Russia, led by Yeltsin, takes over most of the former Soviet government's functions.

Annotated Bibliography

Dean Acheson, *Present at the Creation: My Years in the State Department.* New York: W.W. Norton and Co., Inc., 1969. The memoir of the secretary of state who served under President Truman from 1949 to 1953. Acheson was an important figure in the early history of the Cold War.

Graham Allison, *Essence of Decision: Explaining the Cuban Missile Crisis.* Boston: Little, Brown, and Co., 1971. Remains the definitive history of the crisis. Its emphasis is on the role of bureaucracy in foreign policy making.

Gar Alperovitz, *Atomic Diplomacy.* New York: Vintage Books, 1965. A study of the decision to drop atomic bombs on Hiroshima and Nagasaki. The author is highly critical of the Truman administration for what he considers to have been an unnecessary action.

Stephen E. Ambrose, *Eisenhower: The President.* New York: Simon & Schuster, 1984. Biography of the Republican president who helped to institutionalize the Cold War by maintaining the Cold War apparatus created by Democratic president Truman.

Stephen E. Ambrose, *Ike's Spies: Eisenhower and the Espionage Establishment.* Garden City, NY: Doubleday, 1981. A history of the relationship between Eisenhower and the CIA, which he employed extensively in his prosecution of the Cold War.

Thomas A. Bailey, *America Faces Russia.* Ithaca, NY: Cornell University Press, 1950. A general history of Russian-American relations from the late eighteenth century through the early Cold War period.

George Ball, *The Past Has Another Pattern.* New York: W.W. Norton and Co., Inc., 1982. A memoir written by a leading Democrat and ally of Adlai Stevenson. Ball was also a member of the Johnson State Department and an early "dove" on the war in Vietnam.

Michael Beschloss, *Crisis Years.* New York: Edward Burlingame Books, 1991. A history of the relationship between John Kennedy and Nikita Khrushchev. Surveys many of the missed opportunities to bring the Cold War to an early end.

Michael Beschloss, *Mayday: Eisenhower, Khrushchev, and the U-2 Affair.* New York: Harper and Row, 1986. A scholarly, yet riveting history of the incident that helped end the "Spirit of Camp David" and the Paris Summit of 1960.

Charles Bohlen, *Witness to History.* New York: W.W. Norton and Co., Inc., 1973. Memoir of one of the leading Soviet experts. Bohlen was present at the Yalta Conference and served as ambassador to the Soviet Union during the Eisenhower years.

Henry Brandon, *The Retreat of American Power*. Garden City, NY: Doubleday, 1973. A portrait of the first years of the Nixon presidency written from the perspective of a British journalist.

Paul Browder, *The Origins of Soviet-American Diplomacy*. Princeton, NJ: Princeton University Press, 1953. A history of the pre-World War II and pre-Cold War relationship between these two countries.

Noam Chomsky, *Towards a New Cold War*. New York: Pantheon Books, 1982. Collection of essays by noted radical professor dealing with American foreign policy in the 1970s and early 1980s. Attacks U.S. intervention in Third World countries.

Diane Clemens, *Yalta*. New York: Oxford University Press, 1970. A study of the second and final wartime conference involving Churchill, Roosevelt, and Stalin. Conservatives have held Roosevelt responsible for giving away Poland at Yalta. Clemens is not convinced.

Robert Dallek, *Franklin D. Roosevelt and American Foreign Policy, 1932-1945*. New York: Oxford University Press, 1979. A general history of FDR's foreign policy. The final chapters shed light on the origins of the Cold War.

Lynn E. Davis, *The Cold War Begins*. Princeton, NJ: Princeton University Press, 1974. A history of Soviet-American relations in regard to Central and Eastern Europe in the years immediately following World War II.

John Deane, *The Strange Alliance*. New York: Viking Press, 1947. Memoir of one of the American generals who dealt with the Soviet Union during World War II. Chronicles the American efforts at wartime cooperation.

Hugh De Santis, *The Diplomacy of Silence*. Chicago: University of Chicago Press, 1980. A history of the development of Soviet experts within the U.S. State Department. Details their role in the years after the United States's formal diplomatic recognition of the USSR in 1933, through the end of World War II and the onset of the Cold War.

Robert Divine, *Blowing in the Wind*. New York: Oxford University Press, 1978. A highly readable study of the nuclear test ban debate.

Robert Divine, *Eisenhower and the Cold War*. New York: Oxford University Press, 1981. A brief but excellent study of the Eisenhower years and American foreign policy.

Robert Donovan, *Conflict and Crisis: The Presidency of Harry S Truman, 1945-48*. New York: W.W. Norton and Co., Inc., 1977. A history of the first Truman term by a journalist turned historian. It dwells largely, but not exclusively, on foreign policy and treats Truman in a generally favorable light.

Robert Donovan, *Tumultuous Years*. New York: W.W. Norton and Co., Inc., 1983. Covers the second half of the Truman presidency. This volume is especially good on the Korean War.

Dwight Eisenhower, *Mandate for Change*. Garden City, NY: Doubleday, 1963. The president's memoir of his first term in office. The title belies the reality, which was not so much a period of change as of continuity, especially insofar as the Cold War was concerned.

Dwight Eisenhower, *Waging Peace*. Garden City, NY: Doubleday, 1965. The second volume of the Eisenhower memoirs. It focuses on his efforts to establish a working relationship with Khrushchev in the aftermath of the 1955 summit conference and on the failure of those efforts in the light of the U-2 incident.

Thomas H. Etzold and John Lewis Gaddis, eds., *Containment: Documents on American Policy and Strategy, 1945-1950*. New York: Columbia University Press, 1978. A collection of documents, many of them recently declassified, from various U.S. government and military institutions that were integral in developing and clarifying U.S. foreign policy in the first years of the Cold War. Includes the full text of NSC 68, the important 1950 study by the National Security Council.

Herbert Feis, *Churchill, Roosevelt, Stalin*. Princeton, NJ: Princeton University Press, 1957. A highly detailed account of wartime diplomacy by a former official of the Roosevelt administration who seeks to explain rather than apportion blame.

Herbert Feis, *From Trust to Terror*. New York: W.W. Norton and Co., Inc., 1970. A study of the early Cold War, this volume essentially defends Truman's diplomacy.

Peter Filene, *Americans and the Soviet Experiment, 1917-1933*. Cambridge, MA: Harvard University Press, 1967. An examination of the efforts of numerous Americans to establish contact with the new Soviet Union in the years between the Bolshevik Revolution and the American decision to extend diplomatic recognition to the Soviet Union.

D.F. Fleming, *The Cold War and Its Origins, 1917-1960*. Garden City, NY: Doubleday, 1961. An early revisionist history, this two volume work anticipates much of the New Left criticism of U.S. foreign policy.

Richard Freeland, *The Truman Doctrine and the Origins of McCarthyism: Foreign Policy, Domestic Politics, and Internal Security, 1946-1948*. New York: Alfred A. Knopf, Inc., 1972. A history of the relationship between Truman's version of anticommunism and that espoused by Senator Joseph McCarthy. Freeland argues that McCarthy and McCarthyism were direct by-products of Truman's own anticommunism and his decision to create an internal security apparatus.

John Lewis Gaddis, *Russia, the Soviet Union, and the United States: An Interpretive History*. New York: Wiley, 1978. A general survey for the general reader, it begins with the American Revolution and extends through the Ford years.

John Lewis Gaddis, *Strategies of Containment: A Critical Appraisal of Postwar American National Security Policy*. New York: Oxford University Press, 1982. A series of essays concerning the intellectual underpinnings of national security policy.

John Lewis Gaddis, *The United States and the Origins of the Cold War, 1941-1947*. New York: Columbia University Press, 1972. An early example of a Cold War history that presumes that the roots of the Cold War lie buried in the history of the wartime partnership between the two countries.

Lloyd Gardner, *Architects of Illusion*. Chicago: Quadrangle Books, 1970. A series of essays on the key individuals in the Truman administration who were instrumental in deciding to prosecute the Cold War. The book is written from the perspective of a New Left historian.

Alexander Haig, *Caveat*. New York: Macmillan, 1984. A bitter memoir of the Reagan years written by the president's first secretary of state.

Louis Halle, *The Cold War as History*. New York: Harper and Row, 1967. An iconoclastic history of the Cold War written by a self-styled foreign policy realist and former foreign service officer.

Thomas Hammond, ed., *Witnesses to the Origins of the Cold War*. Seattle: University of Washington Press, 1982. A series of essays on the views of U.S. officials in regard to Eastern Europe.

W. Averell Harriman and Elie Able, *Special Envoy to Churchill and Stalin, 1941-1945*. New York: Random House, 1975. A memoir by the American ambassador to the Soviet Union. Harriman is especially important because he initially believed in cooperation with the Soviets but changed his mind because of Soviet intransigence in Central Europe.

Gregg Herken, *The Winning Weapon: The Atomic Bomb in the Cold War*. New York: Alfred A. Knopf, Inc., 1980. A history of the decision to build the atomic bomb, as well as a history of the role of the bomb in American policy making.

Seymour Hersh, *The Price of Power*. New York: Summit Books, 1983. A devastating critique of Henry Kissinger.

Trumbull Higgins, *The Perfect Failure*. New York: W.W. Norton and Co., Inc., 1987. A history of the Cuban missile crisis.

Roger Hilsman, *To Move a Nation: The Politics of Foreign Policy in the Administration of John F. Kennedy*. Garden City, NY: Doubleday, 1967. Part memoir and part history, this book is less a history of the "politics" of foreign policy than it is a history of foreign policy making at the height of the Cold War.

Michael Hogan, *The Marshall Plan*. Cambridge: Cambridge University Press, 1987. The definitive history of the American decision to extend economic aid to postwar Europe—and of the Soviet decision not to participate in the plan.

William G. Hyland, *The Cold War Is Over*. New York: Random House, 1990. The editor of *Foreign Affairs*, a former CIA Soviet analyst and National Security Council staff member under Henry Kissinger, gives a concise orthodox history of the Cold War, which he traces from Soviet-Nazi alliances in 1939. Most of the book focuses on the Truman, Eisenhower, and Nixon administrations.

Walter Isaacson and Evan Thomas, *The Wise Men*. New York: Simon & Schuster, 1986. History as written by two journalists. A very readable and effective series of portraits of those men (including Dean Acheson, Charles Bohlen, George Kennan, Averell Harriman, Robert Lovett, and John McCloy) who encouraged President Truman to block Soviet expansion in 1947 and who urged President Johnson to de-escalate the war in Vietnam in 1968.

Joseph Jones, *The Fifteen Weeks*. New York: Harcourt, Brace, and World, Inc., 1955. A first hand account of the late winter and early spring of

1947 when the American government wrestled with the problem of the Soviet Union and decided to implement the Truman Doctrine and the Marshall Plan among other Cold War initiatives.

Mary Kaldor, *The Imaginary War: Understanding the East-West Conflict.* Cambridge, MA: Basil Blackwell, 1991. Writing from a European perspective, Kaldor argues that the Soviet Union was exhausted after World War II and posed no great threat to Europe and that the Cold War could have been avoided.

George F. Kennan, *American Diplomacy, 1900-1950.* Chicago: University of Chicago Press, 1951. A series of essays that were originally lectures given at the University of Chicago. The author is the architect of the containment doctrine, and the volume includes the original "Mr. X" essay of *Foreign Affairs* that provided the intellectual underpinning for the policy of containment.

George F. Kennan, *Memoirs, 1925-1950.* Boston: Little, Brown, and Co., 1967. The memoirs of the foreign service officer who made his reputation with the containment doctrine. This volume traces his training as a Soviet expert, his prewar and wartime service in Moscow, his rationale for the containment doctrine, and his criticism of that doctrine as it was implemented.

George F. Kennan, *Memoirs, 1950-1963.* Boston: Little, Brown, and Co., 1972. The continuation of the above volume, it records Kennan's disaffection with the Eisenhower administration, his call for a neutral Germany, his search for an end to the Cold War, and his return to government service as ambassador to Yugoslavia under President Kennedy.

Nikita Khrushchev, *Khrushchev Remembers.* Boston: Little, Brown, and Co., 1970. An important source for the Soviet perspective, especially now that its authenticity has been established.

Gabriel Kolko, *Confronting the Third World.* New York: Pantheon Books, 1988. A history of the impact of the Cold War on American foreign policy as it applies to the Third World battleground between the superpowers.

Walter LaFeber, *America, Russia, and the Cold War, 1945-1990.* New York: McGraw-Hill, Inc., 1991. The best single volume survey of the entirety of the Cold War.

Gordon N. Levin, *Woodrow Wilson and World Politics.* New York: Oxford University Press, 1968. The topic seems to predate the onset of the Cold War, but the author finds the roots of the Cold War in the negative response of the Wilson administration to the Bolshevik Revolution.

Walter Lippmann, *The Cold War: A Study in U.S. Foreign Policy.* New York: Harper, 1947. A brief but thorough critique of the containment doctrine. Questions the ability and willingness of the United States to sustain the policy of containment over any length of time.

John Lukacs, *A New History of the Cold War.* Garden City, NY: Anchor Books, 1966. Written by a Hungarian-American historian, this history argues that the Cold War was in part the result of misperceptions: Stalin wrongly thought the United States was intent on militarily removing communism from Central Europe, and the United States wrongly thought that Stalin was intent on conquering Western Europe by force.

Robert James Maddox, *The New Left and the Origins of the Cold War.* Princeton, NJ: Princeton University Press, 1973. Offers rather harsh critiques on several revisionist historians of the Cold War, including William Appleman Williams and Gar Alperovitz.

Allen J. Matusow, *Joseph R. McCarthy.* Englewood Cliffs, NJ: Prentice Hall, 1970. An anthology of primary and secondary source documents on McCarthy and his times, including speeches by the controversial senator and articles by his critics.

David Mayers, *George Kennan and the Dilemmas of U.S. Foreign Policy.* New York: Oxford University Press, 1988. A critical biography of the architect of containment.

Leonard Mosley, *Dulles.* New York: Dial Press, 1978. A family portrait of the brothers who simultaneously headed the State Department and the CIA during the 1950s.

John Newhouse, *Cold Dawn: The Story of SALT.* New York: Holt, Rinehart, and Winston, 1973. A highly readable history of a highly technical topic.

Richard Nixon, *RN: The Memoirs of Richard Nixon.* New York: Grosset & Dunlap, 1978. A defense of the man and his embattled presidency. The bulk of this autobiography is devoted to Nixon's strong suit, foreign policy.

Thomas Noer, *Cold War and Black Liberation.* Columbia: University of Missouri Press, 1985. A study of the impact of the Cold War on American foreign policy in Africa.

Don Oberdorfer, *The Turn: From the Cold War to a New Era.* New York: Poseidon Press, 1991. Oberdorfer, a reporter on U.S.-Soviet relations for the *Washington Post*, gives a behind-the-scenes look at superpower diplomacy from 1983 to 1990. He argues that one of the prime motivators leading to the end of the Cold War was Ronald Reagan's deep antipathy toward nuclear weapons.

Thomas Paterson, *Soviet-American Confrontation: Postwar Reconstruction and the Origins of the Cold War.* Baltimore: Johns Hopkins University Press, 1973. An economic history of the early Cold War years. This book argues that the United States sought to use its economic power to force the Soviets into line.

Ronald Radosh, *Prophets on the Right.* New York: Simon & Schuster, 1975. A series of essays on early critics of the Cold War and the American empire from the perspective of the Old Right.

Thomas Reeves, *The Life and Times of Joe McCarthy.* New York: Stein and Day, 1982. The best biography of the Wisconsin senator and anticommunist crusader.

Richard Rhodes, *The Making of the Atomic Bomb.* New York: Simon & Schuster, 1987. Prizewinning history of the politics and technology of the building of the bomb.

Arthur Schlesinger Jr., *A Thousand Days*. Boston: Houghton Mifflin, 1965. Memoir of the Kennedy years by the man assigned by the president to be his court historian.

Arthur Schlesinger Jr., ed., *The Dynamics of World Power: A Documentary History of United States Foreign Policy, 1945-1973.* See especially vol. 2, *Eastern Europe and the Soviet Union*, edited by Walter LaFeber. New York: Chelsea House Publishers, 1973. An extensive collection of American, Soviet, and European documents that tell of the origins and continuation of the Cold War.

Bradley Smith, *The Shadow Warriors*. New York: Basic Books, 1983. A history of the wartime intelligence agency, the OSS, and of the CIA in its infancy.

Gaddis Smith, *Morality, Reason, and Power*. New York: Hill & Wang, 1986. The best single volume on the diplomacy of the Carter years.

John Spanier, *American Foreign Policy Since World War II.* 12th ed. Washington, DC: Congressional Quarterly Inc., 1991. A general overview of U.S. foreign policy after World War II through 1990. It argues that the United States has reason to be proud of its overall record.

Ronald Steel, *Walter Lippmann and the American Century*. Boston: Little, Brown, and Co., 1980. A biography of the columnist and pundit. Lippmann did not make Cold War foreign policy, but he had much to say about it. He is especially important for his criticism of the containment doctrine and of the war in Vietnam.

Arthur Stein, *The Nation at War*. Baltimore: Johns Hopkins University Press, 1980. A fine history of the homefront during the Korean War.

Strobe Talbott, *Deadly Gambits*. New York: Alfred A. Knopf, Inc., 1984. A study of arms negotiations during the early years of the Reagan presidency. Talbott is highly critical of the intransigence of the United States.

Harry S Truman, *Memoirs: Year of Decisions*. Garden City, NY: Doubleday, 1955. The first volume of the president's memoirs, it focuses on his role in the onset of the Cold War. The book is noteworthy for its straightforward prose and the absence of doubts and second thoughts.

Richard Walton, *Cold War and Counterrevolution*. New York: Viking Press, 1972. A highly critical account of the diplomacy of John F. Kennedy.

William A. Williams, *The Tragedy of American Diplomacy*. New York: Dell Publishing, 1962. An extended essay on the whole of American foreign policy by the "dean" of post-World War II New Left historians. In Williams's view, the "tragedy" has been the failure of the United States to be open to revolutions elsewhere, including the Soviet Union, China, and Cuba.

Daniel Yergin, *Shattered Peace: The Origins of the Cold War and the National Security State*. Boston: Houghton Mifflin, 1977. A history of the battles within the Truman administration between those suspicious of Soviet motives and those willing to cooperate with them.

For Discussion

Chapter One

1. How does Henry A. Wallace characterize people who promote a tough policy toward the Soviet Union? Do his accusations about their motives strengthen his general arguments?

2. What concessions to the Soviet Union does Wallace believe the United States should consider in order to attain peaceful relations? Which of these concessions does Clark M. Clifford find unacceptable?

3. Wallace presented his views in a public speech. Clark M. Clifford presented his in a secret memorandum. How might these two different settings account for their differences in style and argument?

4. What evidence is presented in the viewpoint by the U.S. State Department Policy Planning Staff concerning Soviet beliefs on the international control of atomic weapons? Does this evidence contradict or refute the arguments made by Henry L. Stimson two years earlier?

5. How important is communist ideology in explaining Soviet behavior, according to George F. Kennan? According to Walter Lippmann? How do differences in interpreting Soviet actions account for their differing foreign policy prescriptions?

6. What is the ultimate end of Kennan's strategy of Soviet containment? What means does he propose to achieve it? Are Lippmann's arguments against Kennan directed at his ends or his means?

Chapter Two

1. How is the strategy outlined by NSC 68 similar to Kennan's strategy expressed in his "Mr. X" article? How is it different?

2. What is the fundamental goal of the leaders of the Soviet Union, according to the authors of NSC 68? What evidence do they provide to support their view?

3. What emphasis does Joseph P. Kennedy place on the Soviet threat to the United States? What threats to U.S. security does Kennedy believe are important?

4. What rhetorical tactics does Joseph McCarthy use in his speech? Why do you think McCarthy's charges of communist subversion were for a time able to gain him significant popular support?

5. How does Kennedy use the Korean War to bolster his arguments?

6. What justifications does Harry S Truman use to explain U.S. involvement in the Korean War? Could his arguments be used to support the all-out strategy espoused by Douglas MacArthur? Why or why not?

7. Over the course of the Cold War, how relevant do you believe MacArthur's argument was that there is no "substitute for victory" in warfare?

8. What advantages does John Foster Dulles see in a U.S. strategy of greater reliance on threats to use nuclear weapons?

9. On what grounds does Hans J. Morgenthau criticize the speech of Dulles? How fundamental are the disagreements between the two men?

Chapter Three

1. What fundamental changes in U.S. policy toward the Soviet Union does John F. Kennedy recommend? Are his arguments compatible with his raising U.S. military spending from 1950s levels?

2. How does Richard Allen support his belief that the Soviet Union was insincere in its calls for peaceful coexistence? How valid do you believe his arguments are?

3. How do J. William Fulbright and Barry Goldwater differ on the ultimate aims of the United States concerning the Cold War? In retrospect, which do you believe was more realistic in describing U.S. goals?

4. How do Walt W. Rostow and D.F. Fleming disagree on the the primary causes of instability and violence in the Third World? How do they differ on the proper role of the United States in the Third World?

5. Do you believe the policies outlined by Rostow accurately describe U.S. goals and actions in Vietnam? Does the Vietnam experience support or refute Rostow's ideas?

6. How does Lyndon Johnson justify U.S. policy in Vietnam? How similar or different are his arguments from those of Harry Truman concerning the Korean War?

7. Do Young Hum Kim's arguments solely attack U.S. policy in Vietnam, or do they question the premises of the entire Cold War? Which arguments show this?

Chapter Four

1. What are the principles of détente listed by Henry A. Kissinger? How different are they from the ideas of "peaceful coexistence" expressed by John F. Kennedy?

2. In what respects has détente failed, according to G. Warren Nutter? Why does he believe the United States is endangered by Kissinger's foreign policy?

3. Why does Henry M. Jackson argue that he is a supporter of genuine détente between the superpowers?

4. What does David Riesman believe should be the top priority of U.S.

foreign policy? How does this priority affect his arguments on human rights?

5. What premises underlie U.S. foreign policy, according to Ronald Reagan? According to Sidney Lens?

6. Robert Scheer argues that the Soviet Union had undergone basic changes that meant the end of the Cold War. What changes does he describe? Why, according to Scheer, has America been reluctant to change its attitude toward the Cold War?

7. Charles Krauthammer argues that yet more changes are needed before the Cold War is over. Of the changes he states are necessary, which have since occurred? Do you think he would argue now that the Cold War is over? Why or why not?

Chapter Five

1. John Lewis Gaddis asserts that the way the Cold War ended revealed its true nature as a fundamentally moral conflict between democracy and communism. Do you agree? Why or why not?

2. Richard J. Barnet emphasizes what the Cold War cost the United States. Does he believe the costs were worth it? Do you? Why or why not?

General Questions

1. Do you believe an alternative to the Cold War was possible in the 1940s? Did the Cold War have to last as long as it did?

2. The viewpoint by Barnet reviews the Cold War in light of the writings of Kennan and Lippmann, both of which were featured in chapter one. In rereading the two viewpoints and Barnet's article, which predictions of Kennan were accurate? Which were not? Which predictions of Lippmann came true?

3. Would you describe the end of the Cold War as a victory for the United States? For the world? Why or why not?

Index

308

219, 222, 234
  in Asia, 113-114
    in Korea, 106-108
    in Vietnam, 178-180
  is false, 169-171
  must respect world opinion, 157-158
  won Cold War, 270-274
Fulbright, J. William, 151, 154, 218, 220, 221

Gaddis, John Lewis, 78, 267
Garthoff, Raymond L., 273
Geneva accords (1954), 189, 198
Germany, 246, 283
  Berlin
    1971 agreement on, 202, 208
    superpower conflict over, 34, 89, 120
    U.S. support for, 140
  human rights in, 222, 223
  superpowers' impact on, 28, 124
  Teheran conference and, 29
  U.S. concerns about after World War II, 284
  West's military, 89
Gervasi, Tom, 244
Goldwater, Barry, 150
Gorbachev, Mikhail, 253
  arms control policies, 251-253, 258-259
  internal reforms, 249, 257-258
  policies ended Cold War, 248-254, 273
    con, 255-263
Graebner, Norman, 94
Great Britain
  atomic bomb development and, 42, 45
  military of, 88-89
  nuclear weapons of, 244
  U.S. alliance with, 69, 70
Greece, 69, 89, 283
  U.S. aid to, 58, 120
Grenada, 239, 245
Gross National Product, 83, 221, 287
Guatemala, 160, 171
guerrilla warfare, 155, 160-163
  history of, 166-167
  Soviet interference in, 161-167
  U.S. efforts to deter, 166, 174-175
    corporate interests in, 169
  U.S. support for, 171
Guevara, Ché, 166, 167

Hagan, Roger, 169-170, 171
Heilbroner, Robert, 170, 172
Hiss, Alger, 94
  McCarthy's accusations against, 96-97
history, 271
Ho Chi Minh, 177, 282
Hoffman, Stanley, 211
Hoover, Herbert, 89
human rights
  in Soviet Union
    détente worsens, 215
    improvement in
      U.S. should pressure for, 217-224
        con, 225-232
      would end Cold War, 260-261
  limits of U.S. policy on, 205
hydrogen bomb, 121

imperialism, 155, 164
  American, 174, 187

Soviet writings on, 137, 145, 146
India, 37, 140
Indo-China. See Vietnam
INF (Intermediate-Range Nuclear
    Forces), 241, 249, 256, 259
intercontinental ballistic missiles,
    201-202, 236, 241, 243
International Atomic Development
    Authority, 48
international community
  should oppose guerrilla war, 166
  Third World's emergence in, 159-160
  U.S. policy to promote, 80, 81
  U.S. should listen to, 157-158
Iran, 165, 185, 246
  CIA in, 160, 171
isolationism, 84-85, 87

Jackson, Henry M., 217, 230, 245
Jackson-Vanik amendment, 217-218
Japan, 28, 37, 246
  atomic bombing of, 41, 42, 44, 228
  Cold War benefits for, 285
Johnson, Lyndon B., 181
  invasion of Santo Domingo and, 171
  on Vietnam, 171, 172, 177

Kennan, George F., 77, 78, 282, 286, 287
  call for end to Cold War, 250
  "long telegram" of, 53, 281
  Mr. "X" article, 51, 63, 278, 279, 281,
    286-287
Kennedy, John F., 133, 139, 206, 269
  inaugural address, 165
  Third World policy, 160
  Vietnam policy 160, 161, 177
Kennedy, Joseph P., 87
Kerry, John, 190
Khrushchev, Nikita S., 139, 141, 148
  during Cuban missile crisis, 133
  Nuclear Test Ban Treaty signing, 147
  peaceful coexistence policy of,
    142-143, 144, 145
  support for Third World revolutions, 161
Kim, Young Hum, 184
King, Martin Luther, Jr., 186
Kissinger, Henry A., 195, 212
  criticism of, 207, 208, 218, 220, 221
Korea, 37, 165, 222
Korean War, 87, 88, 116
  Chinese revolution and, 105-106
  firing of General MacArthur during, 111
  is a mistake, 89, 90, 92
  lack of victory in, 114, 118, 119, 151
  peaceful settlement of, 110-111, 124
  U.S. strategy in, 120
    is flawed, 112-118, 189
    is sound, 105-111
    should attack China, 117
      con, 110
Krauthammer, Charles, 255
Kremlin, 55-56

Laos, 155, 161, 189
Latin America, 155
  Cuba's threat to, 161
  revolutions in, 129, 157, 161, 176
  Soviet involvement in, 233

U.S. aid to, 165
U.S. corporate dominance of, 169, 175
Lens, Sidney, 242
Lindsay, Franklin A., 163
Lippmann, Walter, 62, 277-278, 279, 281-284, 286-288
Lodge, Henry Cabot, 174
loyalty oath, 99, 100
Lubell, Samuel, 152

MacArthur, Douglas, 112, 151
  conflict with Truman, 106, 111, 112
McCarthy, Joseph, 93, 97
  criticism of, 100, 101, 102, 103
  discrediting of, 100
  public reaction to, 99
McNamara, Robert, 190, 243, 252
Mann, Thomas, 60, 223
Mao Zedong (Mao Tse-Tung), 106, 166, 167
Marshall, George C., 63, 107, 286
Marshall Plan, 88, 185, 219, 270
Marxism-Leninism
  description of, 52-53, 271-272
  impact on Soviets, 27, 71
  see also communism; socialism, Soviet
Mathews, William R., 156
media, 93, 95, 100, 281
Mexico, 140
Middle East, 87, 140, 161, 185
  superpower conflicts in, 200, 206, 214
military-industrial complex, 270
  corporations' role in, 169
  Eisenhower's warning about, 135, 175, 254
  Soviet, 230, 252
modernization, 161-162, 165, 167
Moore, Barrington, 175
Morgenthau, Hans J., 125
Mumford, Lewis, 127

nationalism, 211
  Soviet, 53, 232
  Third World, 176, 188
  Vietnamese, 188
national liberation struggles. See revolutions
Nicaragua, 238-239, 249
Niebuhr, Reinhold, 34
Nitze, Paul, 77
Nixon, Richard, 257
  Doctrine, 253-254
  summit with Brezhnev, 197, 199
North Atlantic Treaty Organization (NATO), 185, 202, 239, 259, 270, 284
North Vietnam. See Vietnam (Indo-China)
nuclear blackmail, 237, 259, 280
nuclear freeze, 234, 235, 240, 243, 247
Nuclear Test Ban Treaty, 134, 141, 147, 229
nuclear testing, 152, 153, 229
nuclear weapons
  after collapse of Soviet Union, 288
  changes in U.S., 243
  conflict with human rights policy, 226, 228, 232
  make peace essential, 26, 134-135, 156, 196
  negotiations on, 140, 197, 200-201, 206
    arms buildup encourages, 236, 238
    Gorbachev's initiatives on, 251-253, 258-259

have helped Soviets, 214
proliferation of, 246-247
role in Cold War, 275-276
superiority in
  futility of seeking, 200-201
    con, 210
  Soviet, 211-212, 236
    con, 243-247
  U.S. threats to use, 245-246
  see also atomic bomb
Nutter, G. Warren, 207
Nye, Joseph S., Jr., 227

oil, 28, 87, 237, 239

Panama, 170
Payne, James L., 222
peace
  desire for after World War II, 26, 28
  is possible, 136
  must be foreign policy priority, 31, 134
    dangers of, 208
  nuclear weapons make essential, 26, 134-135, 156, 196
  Soviet definition of, 148-149
  see also peaceful coexistence
Peace Corps, 160, 219
peaceful coexistence, 196
  Soviet advocacy of, 142-143
    designed to overthrow capitalism, 143-145
  U.S. and Soviets should seek, 133-141
    con, 142-149
Philippines, 37, 113, 160
Podhoretz, Norman, 237
propaganda, 37, 149

Reagan, Ronald, 233, 248, 253
  exaggerated Soviet threat, 243-247
Red Army, 71-72, 272-273, 284
revolutions, 78, 129, 146, 148, 157
  Third World communist
    U.S. should oppose, 159-167, 222
    con, 157, 168-176, 188
Riesman, David, 225
Roosevelt, Franklin D., 29
Rosenberg, Julius and Ethel, 95
Rostow, Eugene V., 214
Rostow, Walt W., 159, 174
Rusk, Dean, 187
Russia
  expansion of, 71-72
  invasions of, 27
  see also Soviet Union

Sakharov, Andrei, 218, 219, 220, 223, 232
SALT (Strategic Arms Limitation Talks), 197, 200, 221
  during Carter presidency, 229, 230
  is benefecial, 201-202
  is harmful, 208, 214
  land-based missiles and, 201-202
Scheer, Robert, 248
Schlesinger, Arthur, Jr., 269
socialism, Soviet
  belief in class struggle, 147
  belief in struggle against capitalism, 54
  efforts to spread, 55, 146

South Vietnam. *See* Vietnam (Indo-China)
Soviet Union
  arms control policies, 251-253, 258-259
  at UN sessions, 37, 47, 106
  atomic bomb
    efforts to acquire, 42, 47-49, 93
    use of, 80
  collapse of, 288
  communism in
    will destroy itself, 60, 278-279, 280
      con, 64
  diplomatic policy of, 56, 57
  domination of Eastern Europe
    Berlin, 34
    U.S. should ignore, 28, 90, 91, 176
      con, 58, 72, 73
  economy of
    as war-based, 82
    development of, 59
    problems in, 199, 213-214, 220-221, 258
    reforms in, 257-258
    U.S. should not aid, 214-215, 257
  expansionism of, 78-79, 80, 94-95, 140
    cessation of would end Cold War,
      261-262
    in Central America, 238-239
    in Korea, 107-108
    peaceful coexistence and, 145-146
    U.S. should thwart, 35, 51-61,
      77-86, 85, 159-167
      con, 62-73, 87-92, 168-176, 188
  Fifteenth Party Congress (1927), 145
  forced labor in, 59
  freedom of press, 224, 229, 261
  government of
    as aggressive, 33, 53, 78-79, 80
    lack of popular support for, 59
    totalitarian policies of, 53, 54, 56, 57, 59
  hostility toward U.S., 55, 79, 83-84, 106, 137
  human rights in, 205, 217-232, 256, 260-261
  ideology of, 52-53, 262-263, 269
  Jews in, 219, 230, 251
  military power of, 79-80, 198, 221
    buildup in, 235-236, 238, 239, 243, 258
    Red Army, 71-72
    used to intimidate West, 82, 84
  peaceful coexistence policy of, 143-149
  perestroika in, 250-253, 256, 280
  propaganda of, 37, 38, 149
  threatens U.S., 233-241
    con, 242-247
  Twentieth Party Congress (1956), 144, 145
  U.S. relations with
    decline in, 26
    détente, 195-206
      con, 207-216
    during Reagan presidency, 248-249
    encouraging peace, 25-31, 136, 137, 156
      con, 32-40, 148
    lack of trust in, 81, 247
    seeking total victory, 150-153
      con, 154-158
    use of hot line, 140
  U.S. threatens, 245, 280
  World War II's impact on, 137
Spanier, John, 159-160
spying, 96, 229
Stalin, Joseph, 27, 29, 142, 144-145, 284

START (Strategic Arms Reduction
  Talks), 241
*Statement of the 81 Communist and
  Workers Parties*, 145
Stimson, Henry L., 41
Stone, I.F., 101
Strategic Defense Initiative (SDI), 248,
  253, 259
submarines, nuclear, 236, 240, 241, 243, 244

Taiwan (Formosa), 106, 112, 115-116, 117, 165
technology
  impact of on Third World, 161-162
  military, 173, 215
  nuclear, 200, 215
  U.S.-Soviet cooperation in, 197, 203,
    210, 214-215
Teheran Conference, 29
Third World
  communist revolutions in
    do not threaten U.S., 170
    U.S. should oppose, 159-167, 222
      con, 157, 168-176, 188
  debt, 175
  modernization's impact on, 161-162, 167
  Soviet involvement in, 162-164, 211, 214
  U.S. corporate interests in, 169, 175
  U.S. policy toward, 163
    history of, 160
    is imperialistic, 174
    promotes development, 182
    promotes impoverishment, 175
Tonkin Gulf Resolution, 178
totalitarianism, 281
  growth of, 94-95
  McCarthyism promoted, 103, 104
  U.S. must oppose, 58, 262
  see also democracy; freedom
trade, 37
  corporate interests in, 169, 223
  does not promote peace, 209-210
  U.S.-Soviet, 39, 197, 215, 221-222
    Jackson-Vanik amendment and, 218
    link to human rights, 219
tribalism, 229, 232
Truman, Harrys, 27
  Doctrine of, 33, 58, 63, 73, 171, 185,
    272, 282, 283
  Korean War and, 105, 114
  McCarthyism and, 97, 99
  on relations with Soviets, 44, 58, 270, 274
  Third World and, 160
Turkey, 69
  U.S. aid to, 58, 120, 283
  U.S. installations in, 245
Tydings Committee, The, 99
Tydings, Millard, 99, 100

United Nations, 45
  Atomic Energy Commission, 47
  is ineffective, 90
  Korean War activity, 106, 109, 110, 111
  on human rights, 218-219
  purpose of, 58
  should have military power, 31
  Soviet behavior at, 37, 106
  Third World development
    programs, 182

311